CONTENTS

AN ROINN COMHSHAOIL, OIDHREACHTA AGUS RIALTAIS ÁITIÚIL
DEPARTMENT OF THE ENVIRONMENT, HERITAGE
AND LOCAL GOVERNMENT

architectural heritage protection

GUIDELINES FOR PLANNING AUTHORITIES

EXPLANATION OF ABBREVIATIONS USED IN THE TEXT

2000 Act	Planning and Development Act 2000 (No.30 of 2000)
2001 Regulations	Planning and Development Regulations 2001 (S.I. No. 600 of 2001)
ACA	Architectural Conservation Area
ASPC	Area of Special Planning Control
EIS	Environmental Impact Statement
ICOMOS	International Council on Monuments and Sites
NIAH	National Inventory of Architectural Heritage
RMP	Record of Monuments and Places
RPS	Record of Protected Structures
TGD	Technical Guidance Document to the Building Regulations
UNESCO	United Nations Educational, Scientific and Cultural Organisation
uPVC	Unplasticised polyvinyl chloride

FOREWORD

Regeneration of our old buildings and their continued re-use is in all our interests. It ensures that the present generation can experience and enjoy the physical expression of past generations. It is the essence of sustainable development. The process of regeneration in itself requires the maintenance of traditional building techniques and skills. It places an emphasis on quality of work and maintains jobs in an area largely untouched by modern mechanisation. All of this is good for our sense of well-being in this more hurried age.

I welcome the publication of the *Architectural Heritage Protection Guidelines for Planning Authorities*. These guidelines are a practical guide for planning authorities and for all others who must comply with Part IV of the Planning and Development Act 2000 on the protection of the architectural heritage.

These provisions charge both planning authorities and owners with new responsibilities to protect our architectural heritage and are reflected in the new records of protected structures adopted by planning authorities throughout the State. Such responsibilities need support and I am pleased to say that a comprehensive package of measures has been introduced by Government in recent years. The National Inventory of Architectural Heritage was established to provide both expert and independent data to planning authorities on buildings of value. A new grant scheme, operated by the planning authorities, was introduced for the conservation of protected structures, and conservation officers have been employed to assist the work of the planning authorities.

Building on these foundations, the guidelines will further support the effort of protecting our architectural heritage and are an expression of the Government's commitment to nurturing our built heritage.

I thank all who have made submissions and who have contributed in any way to the preparation of the guidelines for their support and interest.

I would like especially to remember the late Rachel MacRory, architectural historian of Heritage Policy Division, who worked tirelessly towards achieving legislative protection for the architectural heritage and assisted in the preparation of these guidelines until her untimely death in 2002. These guidelines will stand testament to her commitment to Ireland's built heritage.

Dick Roche, T.D.,
Minister for the Environment, Heritage and Local Government
December 2004

Legislative and Administrative Provisions

PART 1

Introduction

1.1 Why Protect Our Architectural Heritage?

1.1.1 Our architectural heritage is a unique resource, an irreplaceable expression of the richness and diversity of our past. Structures and places can, over time, acquire character and special interest through their intrinsic quality, continued existence and familiarity. The built heritage consists not only of great artistic achievements, but also of the everyday works of craftsmen. In a changing world, these structures have a cultural significance which we may recognise for the first time only when individual structures are lost or threatened. As we enjoy this inheritance, we should ensure it is conserved in order to pass it on to our successors.

1.1.2 Sympathetic maintenance, adaptation and re-use can allow the architectural heritage to yield aesthetic, environmental and economic benefits even where the original use may no longer be viable. The creative challenge is to find appropriate ways to satisfy the requirements of a structure to be safe, durable and useful on the one hand, and to retain its character and special interest on the other.

1.1.3 The conservation-minded approach entails changing assumptions about existing buildings and thinking carefully about how they can be used or redeveloped so as to conserve and highlight their qualities. At as early a stage as possible in the process of designing for change, emphasis should be put on identifying and holding on to the inherent character of the structure and its physical and aesthetic strengths. Old buildings can perform as well as, and sometimes better than, new ones in terms of the durability and flexibility of their materials or their adaptability in use. The most appropriate interventions tend to be low key and can be financially economical. Specialised conservation techniques to prolong the existence of structures often rely on empathy with the original constructional materials and methods.

1.1.4 Structures can be read as historic evidence just like written documents, and can aid the understanding of past conditions and of how society changes. Social history is revealed by structures such as market houses, hump-backed canal bridges, stables, servants' staircases in eighteenth-century houses, public water-pumps and even by details such as bootscrapers outside front doors. There are personal histories and events of the distant past that leave their mark on places, whether these be mansions, grand schemes of town planning, bullet holes or masons' marks. The evidence presented by a surviving structure should be carefully examined for clues to the understanding of the buildings themselves.

Past social conditions are often powerfully illustrated by structures that have survived from former times

1.1.5 The endless variety of the existing built environment is available to us for inspiration and precedent. Decisions made as to the siting and construction of buildings are often the result of practical applied knowledge, and represent the skill and insight of their creators. Historic villages, towns and cities can be living urban environments of great quality to the advantage of their users. Where they exist, we should conserve them.

1.1.6 Cultural tourism is increasing and playing a significant part in the tourist economy. The conservation of our built environment contributes to the attractiveness of our country as a place that we can enjoy and invite others to visit. Many people are employed in the heritage sector in Ireland. The promotion of local history for tourism purposes is a significant part of the economy and should be closely bound up with a genuine appreciation of the historic environment that is the backdrop for all visitors, national and foreign alike.

Heritage is a resource and many heritage sites contribute to the local economy as tourist destinations

1.2 New Legal and Policy Framework to Protect the Architectural Heritage

1.2.1 International charters and conventions[1] have informed and influenced government policy and legislation for protecting the architectural heritage. These documents were formulated mainly in the late twentieth century and arise from a sustained attempt to articulate, at international level, principles that would inform decisions about how the cultural value of the built environment is to be treated. Implicit in these principles is a wider set of values and priorities relating to social, cultural and economic life. The various charters require that all interventions respect the physical, historic and aesthetic character and integrity of cultural property.

1.2.2 UNESCO's *Convention Concerning the Protection of the World Cultural and Natural Heritage* was drawn up in 1972 and ratified by Ireland in 1991. This convention notes that the cultural and natural heritage is increasingly threatened with destruction. Each state party to the convention recognises that the duty of ensuring identification, protection, conservation, presentation and transmission to future generations of this heritage belongs primarily to that state. The *Convention for the Protection of the Architectural Heritage of Europe*, drawn up by the Council of Europe and signed at Granada in 1985, was ratified by Ireland in 1997. Commonly known as the Granada Convention, it provides the basis for our national commitment to the protection of the architectural heritage. The convention is a means of proclaiming conservation principles, including a definition of what is meant by architectural heritage such as monuments, groups of buildings and sites. It seeks to define a European standard of protection for architectural heritage and to create legal obligations that the signatories undertake to implement. It stresses the importance of 'handing down to future generations a system of cultural references'. It relies for its effectiveness on its signatory countries implementing their own national protective regimes.

1.2.3 It is in the context of international initiatives such as the Granada Convention, as well as increasing awareness nationally, that Ireland has legislated for the increased protection of the architectural heritage. This wider acknowledgement of the need to conserve the built heritage recognises the social and economic benefits of conserving this part of our common inheritance and also the place of conservation in policies of sustainable development.

1.2.4 The state is also directly responsible for the care and maintenance of a large proportion of our architectural heritage, built by government departments, offices or agencies, or inherited by them at the founding of the state. The government's policy on architecture[2] seeks to reconcile the many, sometimes conflicting, responsibilities in relation to architectural heritage in its own building stock, and, where possible, to enhance the preservation of the architectural heritage in its care. The government has set out a number of actions in this regard in its policy, to ensure that state authorities are aware of the historic building stock within their ownership and have information and guidance on formulating a conservation strategy.

1 *See bibliography for reference details*

2 *Action on Architecture,* Section 2.2.5

Public authorities, in the discharge of their functions, erected many fine buildings that are treasured today for their architectural and historic qualities

The provision to protect structures of technical, social or scientific interest can encompass a great range of historic structures

1.2.5   The government has taken significant steps towards the conservation of the architectural heritage through the introduction of comprehensive and systematic legislative provisions included in the planning code, of which these guidelines form part. These new legislative measures are supported by an architectural heritage advisory service at national level; the establishment, on a statutory basis, of the National Inventory of Architectural Heritage (NIAH); a scheme of grants for protected structures; and support for the employment of conservation officers by local authorities.

1.3   Part IV Planning and Development Act 2000

1.3.1   The conservation principles of care and protection of the architectural heritage were first introduced under earlier planning legislation which facilitated the listing of significant buildings and the formulation of policies and objectives relating to such structures. These legislative provisions were superseded by the introduction of the Local Government (Planning and Development) Act 1999 and then by Part IV of the Planning and Development Act 2000. The main features of the 2000 Act are:

a)   planning authorities have a clear obligation to create a record of protected structures (RPS) which includes all structures or parts of structures in their functional areas which, in their opinion, are of special architectural, historical, archaeological, artistic, cultural, scientific, social or technical interest. This record forms part of a planning authority's development plan;[3]

b)   planning authorities are also obliged to preserve the character of places and townscapes which are of special architectural, historic, archaeological, artistic, cultural, scientific, social or technical interest or that contribute to the appreciation of protected structures, by designating them architectural conservation areas (ACAs) in their development plan;[4]

Terraces, groups or complexes of structures can be protected in an architectural conservation area where necessary to preserve their character

c)   development plans must include objectives for the protection of such structures and the preservation of the character of such areas to ensure proper and sustainable planning and development;

d)   new responsibilities are given to the owners and occupiers of protected structures to maintain them and planning authorities have additional powers to ensure that buildings are not endangered either directly or through neglect.[5] Financial assistance, in the form of conservation grants, is available from planning authorities to assist in this process;

As well as assisting individual owners, planning authority conservation grants can help foster endangered craft skills such as thatching

e) the owner or occupier of a protected structure may seek a declaration from the relevant planning authority to determine the works to the structure that would materially affect its character and therefore require planning permission, and those works which may be carried out as exempted development;[6]

f) where a structure is protected, the protection includes the structure, its interior and the land within its curtilage and other structures within that curtilage (including their interiors) and all fixtures and features which form part of the interior or exterior of all these structures. All works which would materially affect the character of a protected structure, or a proposed protected structure, will require planning permission.[7]

1.4   Other Relevant Legislation

1.4.1   A number of other Acts, plans and national guidelines, in addition to Part IV of the Planning and Development Act 2000, should be considered when including structures in the RPS and carrying out forward planning or development control duties. Primary among them are the National Monuments Acts 1930 - 2004. These Acts and other relevant powers or orders applicable to the protection of the built heritage are listed in the bibliography below.

1.4.2   The scope of the National Monuments Acts includes monuments of architectural, historical or archaeological interest, allowing overlap with the 2000 Act which protects structures of special architectural, historical, archaeological, artistic, cultural, scientific, social or technical interest.

Many structures are of both architectural and archaeological interest and suitable for protection under the Planning Acts in addition to the National Monuments Acts

1.5   Purpose of these Guidelines

1.5.1   These guidelines are issued under Section 28 and Section 52 of the Planning and Development Act 2000. Under Section 52 (1), the Minister is obliged to issue guidelines to planning authorities concerning development objectives:

a) for protecting structures, or parts of structures, which are of special architectural, historical, archaeological, artistic, cultural, scientific, social, or technical interest, and

b) for preserving the character of architectural conservation areas.

1.5.2   Guidelines issued under Section 28 of the Act require planning authorities (including An Bord Pleanála) to have regard to them in the performance of their functions. Planning authorities are also required under Section 28 to make copies of these guidelines available for inspection by members of the public.

6 See Chapter 4   7 See Chapter 6

1.5.3 Part 1 of these guidelines includes the criteria to be applied when selecting proposed protected structures for inclusion in the RPS. It also offers guidance to planning authorities on issuing a declaration on a protected structure and on determining planning applications in relation to a protected structure, a proposed protected structure or the exterior of a building within an ACA.

1.5.4 Part 2 contains supplementary detailed guidance to support planning authorities in their role to protect the architectural heritage when a protected structure, a proposed protected structure or the exterior of a building within an ACA is the subject of development proposals and when a declaration is sought in relation to a protected structure.

1.5.5 While these guidelines are primarily addressed to planning authorities, it is intended that they will also be of assistance to owners and occupiers of protected structures, of proposed protected structures or buildings within ACAs and to those proposing to carry out works which would impact on such structures.

1.5.6 Under the Act, protected structures which are regularly in use as places of public worship are subject to special requirements.[8] Chapter 5 below deals specifically with:

 a) the issue of declarations, in respect of protected structures which are regularly used as places of public worship;
 b) the consideration by planning authorities of applications for development affecting the interior of such protected structures which are regularly used as places of public worship, and
 c) consultation with appropriate persons or bodies for the purpose of ascertaining liturgical requirements where a declaration is sought in respect of a protected structure that is regularly used as a place of public worship.

1.6 **Administration of Architectural Heritage Protection**

1.6.1 The protection of the architectural heritage is administered at both local and national level. At local level, responsibility for protection under the 2000 Act rests with the planning authorities while, at national level, the Minister for Environment,

Heritage and Local Government has an involvement in the formulation and implementation of policy. Other bodies such as An Bord Pleanála and the relevant prescribed bodies also have roles to play.

1.6.2 The protection of structures under the National Monuments Acts is administered at national level.

1.7 **Planning Authorities**

1.7.1 Planning authorities are empowered to protect the architectural heritage, in the interest of the proper planning and sustainable development within their respective functional areas, and to prevent its deterioration, loss or damage. This will be reflected in the adoption of suitable policies for protecting the architectural heritage in their development plans and giving practical effect to them through their development control decisions, generally by liaison between planning officers and conservation officers.

1.7.2 The duties of a local authority apply across all its functions, for example as a planning authority, a building control authority, a fire authority and so on, to act positively to protect the architectural heritage when exercising their functions.

1.8 **Minister for the Environment, Heritage and Local Government**

1.8.1 The Minister's functions in relation to the protection of the architectural heritage include:

 a) acting as a prescribed body under the Regulations for the purposes of Part IV of the Act;[9]
 b) responsibility for drawing up the statutory legislative and policy framework for planning, including these guidelines, in relation to the protection of the architectural heritage;
 c) provision of grants to planning authorities including reimbursement for assistance provided in respect of works to protected structures;
 d) provision of support for a network of conservation officers at local authority level;
 e) compilation of the NIAH, a survey of structures of special architectural heritage interest in the state, which will provide information to planning authorities supporting the compilation of the RPS;
 f) provision of an architectural heritage advisory

unit within the Heritage and Planning Division of the Department. The advisory service is principally available to planning authorities. Where owners or developers raise issues in relation to individual structures, they are referred in the first instance to the planning and conservation officers of the relevant planning authority;

g) issuing of recommendations concerning the inclusion of particular structures in the RPS;[10]

h) ensuring the protection of the built heritage under the provisions of the National Monument Acts;

i) making submissions or observations on certain development by or on behalf of state authorities.[11]

1.9   Prescribed Bodies for the Purposes of Part IV of the Act

1.9.1   The prescribed bodies in relation to the protection of the architectural heritage are set out in the Planning and Development Regulations 2001.[12] They include the Minister for the Environment, Heritage and Local Government, the Heritage Council, the Arts Council, Bord Fáilte and An Taisce.

1.9.2   The prescribed bodies are sent notification of planning applications where it appears to a planning authority that the development:

a) would involve the carrying out of works to a protected structure or a proposed protected structure;

b) would involve the carrying out of works to the exterior of a structure within an ACA or an area specified as an ACA in a draft development plan or a proposed variation of a development plan, or

c) might detract from the appearance of any of the above structures.

1.9.3   The prescribed bodies must also be sent notification of statutory steps to review, draft, vary and make development plans[13] and of proposals to make additions to or deletions from the RPS.[14] The planning authority processes the observations of the prescribed bodies in the same way as all other submissions in relation to an application.

1.9.4   Under Section 30 of the Act, the Minister may not exercise any power or control in relation to any particular case with which a planning authority or An Bord Pleanála is or may be concerned. However, this does not apply to those functions transferred to him from the Minister for Community, Rural and Gaeltacht Affairs (originally transferred from the Minister for Arts, Heritage; Gaeltacht and the Islands) by the Minister for the Environment and Local Government (Performance of Certain Functions) Act 2002. These include his functions as a prescribed body under Part IV of the Act.

10 Section 53 (1), 2000 Act

11 Section 181, 2000 Act and Part 9, 2001 Regulations

12 Article 28 (1), 2001 Regulations

13 Section 11, 12 and 13, 2000 Act

14 Section 55 (1) (b), 2000 Act

The Development Plan
Record of Protected Structures

CHAPTER 2

2.1 The Record of Protected Structures

2.1.1 Each development plan must include policy objectives to protect structures or parts of structures of special interest and to preserve the character of architectural conservation areas within its functional area.[1] The primary means of achieving the former objective is for the planning authority to compile and maintain a record of protected structures for its functional area to be included in the development plan. A planning authority is obliged to include in the RPS every structure which, in its opinion, is of special architectural, historical, archaeological, artistic, cultural, scientific, social or technical interest. This responsibility will involve the planning authority in reviewing its RPS from time to time (normally during the review of the development plan) with a view to making additions or deletions.

2.1.2 Protecting the architectural heritage is an important function of the planning authority. Care should be taken when compiling the RPS that all reasonable research has taken place and that all structures included merit protection. The superficial condition of a structure should not rule out its inclusion in the RPS. The eligibility of any structure may be reassessed at a later time if further relevant information becomes available.

2.2 Protected Structures and Proposed Protected Structures

Protected structures

2.2.1 A 'protected structure' is defined as any structure or specified part of a structure, which is included in the RPS.

2.2.2 A structure is defined by the Act as 'any building, structure, excavation, or other thing constructed or made on, in or under any land, or any part of a structure'. In relation to a protected structure or proposed protected structure, the meaning of the term 'structure' is expanded to include:

a) the interior of the structure;
b) the land lying within the curtilage of the structure;
c) any other structures lying within that curtilage and their interiors, and
d) all fixtures and features which form part of the interior or exterior of the above structures.[2]

Structures located within the curtilage of a protected structure are also protected along with their interiors, fixtures and features

2.2.3 Where indicated in the RPS, protection may also include any specified feature within the attendant grounds of the structure which would not otherwise be included.[3]

Protection can extend to features within the attendant grounds of a protected structure provided they are specified in the RPS. Alternatively they can have a separate listing in their own right

2.2.4 There are no categories or grades of protected structures under the Act. A structure is either a protected structure or it is not. Details of the nature and extent of protection for each individual structure can be ascertained by issuing a declaration under Section 57 of the Act.

Proposed protected structures

2.2.5   A 'proposed protected structure' is a structure whose owner or occupier has received notification of the intention of the planning authority to include it in the RPS. Most of the protective mechanisms under the Act apply equally to protected structures and proposed protected structures. However, an owner or occupier of a proposed protected structure cannot apply for a declaration under Section 57. A planning authority cannot serve a notice to require works to be carried out in relation to the endangerment of a proposed protected structure, nor can a notice requiring restoration of character be served in relation to a proposed protected structure. A planning authority cannot acquire a proposed protected structure under Section 71.

2.2.6   Once a planning authority notifies an owner or occupier of the proposal to add a particular structure to the RPS, protection applies to that proposed protected structure during the consultation period, pending the final decision of the planning authority.

2.3 Compiling the Record of Protected Structures

2.3.1   A planning authority may add or delete a structure from its RPS by the following procedures as appropriate:

a)   in accordance with a review or variation of its development plan as set out in Section 12 of the Act or

b)   at any other time by following different prescribed procedures laid out under Section 55.

2.3.2   The making of an addition to, or deletion from, the RPS is a function that is a matter for the elected representatives.[4]

2.3.3   Most planning authorities will have an RPS that came into existence on 1 January 2000 in accordance with the provisions of the Local Government (Planning and Development) Act 1999. All structures 'listed' for either preservation or protection in a development plan at that date became 'protected structures'. The task of deciding which further structures should be included in the RPS may be done on a case-by-case basis in three stages:

a)   identification;

b)   assessment and

c)   notification.

2.4 Stage 1: Identification

There are a number of means by which a planning authority can identify structures of special interest within its functional area.

Planning authority 'lists'

2.4.1   Under earlier legislation, planning authorities will generally have already compiled, through their development plans, a list of structures which they wished to 'preserve' or 'consider for preservation'. While some structures may have been altered since they were listed, it is recommended that all of those on the existing lists, particularly those only listed for 'protection' (rather than 'preservation'), be reassessed.

National Inventory of Architectural Heritage

2.4.2   The National Inventory of Architectural Heritage (NIAH) is a unit within the Department of Environment, Heritage and Local Government engaged in compiling an evaluated record of the architectural heritage of Ireland. Where an NIAH survey of a particular area has been published, relevant planning authorities will be provided with information on structures within the area of that survey. The planning authority can assess the content of, and the evaluations in, an NIAH survey with a view to the inclusion of structures in the RPS according to the criteria outlined in these guidelines.

Ministerial recommendations

2.4.3   The Minister may make recommendations to a planning authority under Section 53 (1) of the Act concerning the inclusion in the RPS of a structure, specific parts of any structure or specific features within the attendant ground of a structure. A planning authority must have regard to any recommendation made to it by the Minister. Should a planning authority, following consideration, decide not to comply with a ministerial recommendation, it is obliged to inform him in writing of the reason for this decision.[5]

2.4.4   The Minister may make recommendations regarding individual structures at any time. In addition, where an NIAH survey has been carried out, those

4 *Section 54 (2), 2000 Act*   5 *Section 53 (3), 2000 Act*

structures which have been attributed a rating value of international, national or regional importance in the inventory will be recommended by the Minister to the planning authority for inclusion.

Inventories carried out by planning authorities

2.4.5 Where an NIAH survey has not been undertaken or completed, and officials or consultants with the requisite skills are available, planning authorities are advised to generate their own inventory data. It is recommended that planning authorities, when carrying out or commissioning their own inventory, follow the recording and evaluation procedures developed by the NIAH. In some cases, it may be possible to carry out such surveys in partnership with the NIAH so that the results of the survey can be formally added to the national inventory.

The Record of Monuments and Places

2.4.6 The Archaeological Survey of Ireland (a unit within the Department of Environment, Heritage and Local Government) has carried out a document-based survey of sites of archaeological potential. This information has been used as the basis for inclusion in the Record of Monuments and Places (RMP), established under the National Monuments (Amendment) Act 1994, which gives statutory protection to those sites.[6]

2.4.7 Generally, it is only appropriate to give protection through the RPS to RMP sites which also constitute part of the architectural heritage. For example, this could include upstanding remains such as buildings, standing walls, vaults, enclosed spaces and the like, which may be subject to re-use. Earthworks, for example, would be unlikely to be re-used. Similarly RMP sites described as 'site of', where there are no visible remains above ground, would not generally be appropriate for inclusion in the RPS nor would an archaeological artefact (such as a graveslab), as these do not come under the definition of a 'structure' within the meaning of the Act.

Upstanding structures protected under the National Monuments Acts can be considered for inclusion in the RPS such as this building which contains a substantial amount of mediaeval fabric

2.4.8 Once a recorded monument satisfies any of the criteria of special interest for inclusion in the RPS, the planning authority should use the protective mechanisms offered by planning legislation. While there is an overlap, inclusion in the RPS usefully supplements and expands the protection afforded under the National Monuments Acts. Pre-1700 churches in use, especially, should be protected under planning legislation, as these are excluded from the provisions of the National Monuments Acts.

Other sources

2.4.9 Available research sources will vary from one area to another. Potential protected structures may be identified by using one or more of the following sources:

a) earlier architectural surveys including An Foras Forbartha reports;

b) a range of repositories listed in Appendix A below;

c) historic maps which show the topography of an area and how it evolved;

d) textbooks and academic theses in the areas of architecture, history, historical geography, history of art or social history;

e) books and other publications such as historic guidebooks, local histories, pamphlets or street directories;

f) consultation with special interest or local interest groups;

g) public consultation.

2.5 Stage 2: Assessment

Using Part 2 of these guidelines

2.5.1 A planning authority must decide whether a structure is worthy of inclusion in the RPS by identifying the characteristics of special interest which would merit its inclusion. Part 2 of these guidelines indicates features which may contribute to the character and special interest of a structure, under the heading 'Identifying special features for protection'. The criteria given below should be applied when selecting proposed protected structures for inclusion in the RPS. Illustrative examples are also provided. Although there is no statutory requirement to do so, it is recommended that reference to the relevant category, or categories, of special interest be included in the file of the RPS.

---

[6] *Section 12 (1), National Monuments (Amendment) Act 1994*

Protecting part of a structure

2.5.2   Although it is possible to give protection to part only of a structure, the initial assessment should include the whole of the structure including the interior and rear of the structure, the land within its curtilage and any structures in the curtilage before it is established that only a specified part of the structure is worthy of protection. Where only a part of a structure is currently listed for protection, consideration should be given to extending protection to the entire structure. For example, where the protected structure is a plaque, a shopfront or a façade, the entire structure of which the element is part may also be of interest and worthy of protection. The protection of a façade alone should generally only be considered where there is no surviving interior of any interest, for example where the building has previously been gutted and the façade is the only remaining feature of the original historic building. Generally a façade relates integrally to its building, which may retain interior detail of note including, for example, the original spatial plan, shop-fittings or decorative elements such as chimneypieces, staircases, window shutters or cornices. Elements of the external envelope and/or within the curtilage may also be of intrinsic interest and worthy of protection; these might include the roof, the rear elevation, outbuildings or other site features.

In some cases only part of a structure should be protected as with this church gable wall behind which lies a modern structure

Assessing structures of local interest

2.5.3   It is the responsibility of the planning authorities to make their own assessment of the most appropriate way to protect structures that have not been inspected by the NIAH or those given a rating of 'local importance' by the inventory. In light of the authority's own assessment of the special interest of a structure, it may decide whether it is more appropriate to protect the structure by inclusion in the RPS or within an ACA. Protection by inclusion within an ACA may be more appropriate where a group of structures is of value because of its contribution to the streetscape or other area and where the interiors and curtilages do not merit the level of protection afforded by the RPS.

Categories of special interest

2.5.4   The Act requires that a protected structure be of special interest under one or more of the following categories.[7]

a) Architectural;
b) Historical;
c) Archaeological;
d) Artistic;
e) Cultural;
f) Scientific;
g) Technical;
h) Social.

2.5.5   These categories are not mutually exclusive, for example, a structure may be of historical, as well as architectural, interest. The RPS should represent the diversity of the architectural heritage within a planning authority's functional area and include structures with various special interests. The strength of an RPS depends on the clarity of the assessment procedures, which should be impartial and objective.

2.5.6   The purpose of protection – the control and management of future changes to a structure – should be borne in mind when evaluating those special interest categories which may not relate directly to the physical fabric, such as historical, social and cultural interests. This would occur where, for example, a building is of interest because of its connection with a historic figure although the structure may have been largely altered since that figure lived there.

7 Section 51 (1), 2000 Act

Architectural interest

2.5.7 The characteristics of architectural interest may be attributed to a structure or part of a structure with such qualities as the following:

a) a generally agreed exemplar of good quality architectural design;

b) the work of a known and distinguished architect, engineer, designer or craftsman;

c) an exemplar of a building type, plan-form, style or styles of any period but also the harmonious interrelationship of differing styles within one structure;

d) a structure which makes a positive contribution to its setting, such as a streetscape or a group of structures in an urban area, or the landscape in a rural area;

e) a structure with an interior that is well designed, rich in decoration, complex or spatially pleasing.

Innovative design of any period can be of special architectural interest, whether the architect is renowned or anonymous. Also of special architectural interest can be the harmonious arrangement of architectural styles of different periods

Historical interest

2.5.8 The notion of historical interest underpins a general belief that it is worthwhile to preserve and conserve structures, sites and information from past centuries. The level of importance of the historical connection and its relationship to the existing fabric of the structure should be assessed. The historical interest relating to a structure or parts of a structure may be identified in various ways.

a) A structure may have historical interest as the location of an important event that occurred in, or is associated with it, or by its association with a historic personality. Some events or associations may be so important that the place retains its significance regardless of subsequent alteration. Where an otherwise unremarkable structure has historical associations, it may be more appropriate to commemorate the association with a wall-mounted plaque. Where the decision is difficult, it is helpful to discover whether other buildings connected with the personality or event still exist (and if they are protected) and to make an assessment that takes account of the value of such a group.

b) A structure may have influenced, or been influenced by, an historic figure. Important people may have lived in the structure or have been otherwise associated with it – for example its patron, designer or builder. Places in which evidence of an association with a person survive, in situ, or in which the settings are substantially intact, are of greater significance than those which are much changed or in which much evidence does not survive.

c) Historical interest can be attributed where light is thrown on the character of a past age by virtue of the structure's design, plan, original use, materials or location.

d) A structure may be a memorial to a past event;

e) A structure itself may be an example of the effects of change over time. The design and fabric of the structure may contain evidence of its former use or symbolic meaning. This may be the case with former gaols or churches that have since changed and, in so doing, illustrate a historic development.

f) Some fixtures and features may survive, for example in consistory courts and courts of law, that are important evidence of former liturgical or legal practice and may have special historical interest for that reason.

g) Some unusual structures may have historical or socio-historical interest, for example, early electricity substations, 'Emergency' era military pillboxes or sentry-boxes. Although not yet of popular heritage significance, such structures can nonetheless have special historical and social interest.

h) Special historical interest may exist because of the rarity of a structure. Either few structures of an identifiable type were built at a particular time, or few have survived. In either case, the extant structure may be one of the few representative examples of its time that still exists in the national, regional or local area. The rarity of surviving examples of a building type can ensure that special historical interest accrues to them. A planning authority should give careful consideration to protecting any examples of rare structures in its area, bearing in mind the degree to which past interventions may have altered their character.

Some structures may be linked with a specific historic event or period in time such as the Treaty Stone (top) and the Emergency era pillbox (bottom), while the special interest of others may lie in the accumulation of historical evidence contained within their built fabric (middle)

Archaeological interest

2.5.9   Special archaeological interest is essentially defined by the degree to which material remains can contribute to our understanding of any period or set of social conditions in the past (usually, but not always, the study of past societies). The characteristic of archaeological interest in the context of the RPS must be related to a structure. Structures of special archaeological interest may also be protected under the National Monuments Acts.

2.5.10   Structures can have the characteristics of both archaeological and architectural interest as these are not mutually exclusive. For example, the party walls or basements of houses of later appearance may contain mediaeval fabric and reveal information of archaeological interest. The standing walls of a sixteenth-century towerhouse will have both characteristics of interest. Fragments of early fabric, including carved or worked stone, may have been re-used in later buildings giving these structures archaeological significance as the current context of historically significant material. A complex of industrial buildings may have archaeological interest because of its potential to reveal artefacts and information about the evolution of industry that may be useful to archaeologists, historians and the public.

A structure of special archaeological interest will contribute to an understanding of the past whether through the information it can provide on past industrial processes (top), or its built form, having a corbelled upper floor (middle) or its reuse of fragments from an earlier building (bottom)

Artistic interest

2.5.11 Special artistic interest may be attributed to a structure itself, or to a part of a structure, for its craftsmanship, design or decoration. Examples could include:

a) examples of good craftsmanship;

b) decoratively carved statuary or sculpture that is part of an architectural composition;

c) decoratively-carved timber or ceramic-tiled shopfronts;

d) ornate plasterwork ceilings;

e) decorative wrought-iron gates;

f) religious art in a place of public worship such as the Stations of the Cross or stained-glass windows;

g) fixtures and fittings such as carved fireplaces, staircases or light-fittings;

h) funerary monuments within a graveyard;

i) the relationship of materials to each other and to the totality of the building in which they are situated, if these have been designed as an ensemble.

2.5.12 For an artistic work to be given protection under the Act, its degree of annexation to the structure should be taken into account. If the work of art is effectively fixed to the structure, it can be considered a part of the structure and therefore protected.

Elements of artistic interest can make a significant contribution to the character of a structure whether created by a renowned artist such as Harry Clarke (top) or by lesser known or anonymous craftsmen of any era (middle and bottom)

Cultural interest

2.5.13   The characteristic of cultural interest permeates the architectural heritage and can, in the broadest terms, include aesthetic, historical, scientific, economic or social values of past and present generations. Special cultural interest apply to:

a)   those structures to which the Granada Convention refers as 'more modest works of the past that have acquired cultural significance with the passing of time';

b)   structures that have literary or cinematic associations, particularly those that have a strong recognition value;

c)   other structures that illustrate the development of society, such as early schoolhouses, library buildings, swimming baths or printworks. If these associations are not related to specific aspects of the physical fabric of a structure, consideration could be given to noting them by a tourism plaque or other such device.

Carnegie libraries (top) are physical reminders of the development of culture and learning in society, while buildings such as the Tyrone Guthrie Centre (bottom) foster present-day creative artists. These buildings may be deserving of protection for their special cultural interest in addition to any other special interest they may have

Scientific interest

2.5.14   The scientific interest, or research value, of a structure will depend on the importance of the data involved and on its rarity and/or quality. Its scientific interest should also be assessed as to how well it represents the area of research in question and the degree to which the structure may contribute further objective information. For example:

a)   the results of scientific research may be seen in the execution of the structure;

b)   the materials used in the structure may have the potential to contribute to scientific research, for example extinct pollen or plant species preserved in the base layers of ancient thatch roofs;

c)   the structure may be associated with scientific research that has left its mark on the place, such as early Ordnance Survey benchmarks carved into stonework.

The use of a structure such as the Great Telescope at Birr Castle (top) can contribute to its special scientific interest. So too can physical evidence of scientific research on the built fabric such as Ordnance Survey benchmarks (middle) or the archaeo-botanical evidence to be gleaned from historic underlayers of thatch or other organic materials (bottom)

Technical interest

2.5.15 Special technical interest in a structure relates to the art of the structural engineer in devising solutions to problems of spanning space and creating weatherproof enclosures. It may be found in structures which are important examples of virtuoso, innovative or unusual engineering design or use of materials. A structure may be of special technical interest for one or more of the following reasons:

a) it displays structural or engineering innovation evidenced in its design or construction techniques such as the use of cast- or wrought-iron prefabrication or an early use of concrete;

b) it is the work of a known and distinguished engineer;

c) it is an exemplar of engineering design practice of its time. For example, a bridge may be a masonry arch, an iron suspension or a concrete span;

d) it displays technically unusual or innovative construction or cladding materials, such as early examples of glazed curtain walling, prefabricated concrete plank cladding or Coade stone;

e) contains innovative mechanical fixtures, machinery or plant or industrial heritage artefacts that describe the character of production processes. The specifically industrial aspect of some sites like mill buildings, mill-ponds, tailings or derelict mines can often have a technical heritage value;

f) purely special technical interest can be ascribed to the innovative engineering qualities of a structure, as distinct from the building's appropriateness for use, or its appearance or form.

Special technical interest can be associated with civil engineering achievements such as the construction of bridges, canals and aqueducts and also with the early or innovative use of materials such as concrete or steel

Social interest

2.5.16 The characteristic of special social interest embraces those qualities for which a structure, a complex or an area has become a focus of spiritual, political, symbolic or other sentiment to any group of people. A community may have an attachment to a place because it is an essential reference point for that community's identity, whether as a meeting place or a place of tradition, ritual or ceremony. The configuration, disposition or layout of a space or group of structures, where they facilitate behaviour that would otherwise be difficult or impossible, may be of social interest. This category of special interest may sometimes not be directly related to the physical fabric of a particular structure or structures and may survive physical alteration. Care should be taken to recognise the pattern or internal relations of the parts of the structure that constitute its special interest, in order to ensure that they be conserved.

Special social interest may be attributed to buildings such as almshouses which provide evidence of the social structure of past communities (top). This special interest may also exist in buildings such as Ardnacrusha generating station (middle) which marked the commencement of rural electrification, fundamentally altering the lives of many. Structures which provided a focal point for a community's religious or spiritual activity such as holy wells (bottom) may also be of special social interest

2.5.17 The fixtures and features that testify to community involvement in the creation of a structure, or have a spatial form or layout indicating community involvement in the use of a structure, could include such elements as memorials, statues or stained-glass panels.

2.5.18 A structure may display vernacular traditions of construction and may be set in a group or area which illustrates the social organisation of the inhabitants. Most obviously this would include thatched cottages. In vernacular buildings, elements of the plan-form (for example, direct-entry, lobby-entry, doors opposite one another, bed outshots etc), as well as the roofing material of otherwise ordinary structures may be distinctive and have special social interest.

2.5.19 Types of decoration may have artistic as well as social interest, such as shell houses or the local manifestation of exuberant or astylar stucco decoration where it is particular to a town or region.

2.5.20 A social interest could also be attributed to structures illustrating the social philosophy of a past age, as in the case of philanthropic housing developments. Structures which illustrate a particular lifestyle or social condition, for example holy wells, are to be found in many parts of the country. Care must be taken to ensure that there is sufficient physical fabric to such places for them to be defined as 'structures'.

2.6 Stage 3: Notification

Procedures for notification

2.6.1 Valid notification of all owners and occupiers under the Act is necessary for a structure to become a proposed protected structure.[8] The Act has two separate procedures by which a planning authority notifies owners and occupiers of proposed additions to, or deletions from, the RPS.

a) The notification procedure under Section 12 (3) is used for alterations proposed as part of the making, or reviewing, of a development plan;

b) The notification procedure described in Section 55 can be used at any other time.

8 Section 2, 2000 Act

Content of the notice

2.6.2 Under each of the above procedures, notice of the proposal to include a structure in the RPS must be served on each person who is the owner and occupier. The notice must include the particulars of the proposal such as information identifying the structure and its location and stating why it is proposed to include the structure in the RPS.

2.6.3 The notice must state where and when particulars of the proposed addition or deletion may be inspected and the time period for making submissions with regard to the proposal. This time period is ten weeks under Section 12 (3) (b) and six weeks under Section 55 (2) (a). The notice must state if the structure has been recommended for inclusion by the Minister.

Serving the notice

2.6.4 The planning authority must make reasonable efforts to ascertain the identity of the owners and occupiers of a proposed protected structure. Where the owner cannot be identified, and no occupier is available to receive the notice, it is acceptable to affix a notice in a conspicuous place on or near the land or premises. For the avoidance of any doubt, the planning authority should keep a dated photograph[9] of the notice fixed to the structure for future reference, together with a record of who affixed it, in the event the service of the notice is challenged.

2.6.5 It is possible that a part of the curtilage, or a specified feature within the attendant grounds of the structure, may not in fact be in the ownership or control of the notified party. In such cases both the owner and occupier of the principal structure and the owner and occupier of the specified feature must be notified separately.

2.6.6 The planning authority should take the opportunity at this stage of informing owners and occupiers clearly and simply of their rights and obligations under the legislation. A copy of the leaflet *PL12 - A Guide to Architectural Heritage*[10] could be included with the notification and may be helpful.

The attendant grounds of a protected structure may contain structures and other features of interest such as follies which should be identified and included in the protection. Sometimes these may be in different ownership to the main building and their owners will require separate notification

Public display of proposed additions and deletions

2.6.7 In addition to the obligation to notify the owners and occupiers of each individual structure, there is a requirement for a public notice. This should take the form of a notice published in at least one newspaper circulating within the planning authority's functional area. This notice should contain the same information as the notice to owners and occupiers.

---

[9] The image taken should be of a form which would be acceptable as evidence to support enforcement action or prosecution, such as a conventional photograph on film or a digital photograph on formatted disc

[10] Available from the Department's offices, Custom House, Dublin 1

Consideration of submissions

2.6.8 The planning authority must consider all submissions and observations before making its decision as to whether the proposed addition or deletion should be made. Where the proposed addition has been recommended by the Minister, the planning authority is obliged to forward to the Minister for his observations copies of all submissions and observations received. The Minister's subsequent observations, if any, must be taken into consideration in the planning authority's decision.

2.6.9 Where submissions or observations are received following the procedures outlined in Section 12 (2) and (3), that is, during a making or the review of a development plan, the manager will compile the submissions or comments into his/her report, including, if available, the advice of the conservation officer, for the members' consideration in advance of adoption of the plan.[11]

Notification of the decision

2.6.10 The planning authority must then make its decision as to whether or not to make the proposed addition or deletion. Under Section 12 (6) the decision will be made when the development plan is formally adopted. Under Section 55 (4), the decision must be made within twelve weeks of the end of the public consultation period.

2.6.11 The planning authority must then notify the owners and occupiers of the protected structure of its decision. This must be done as soon as may be under Section 12 (13) or within two weeks under Section 55 (5).

Transfer of ownership of a protected structure

2.6.12 The RPS carries through from one development plan to the next. Once notification has been carried out, there is no requirement to re-notify owners or occupiers when a new development plan is being made, unless deletion is proposed.

2.6.13 All future occupiers or purchasers of a protected structure or proposed protected structure are subject to the same duty of care as applied to the owner or occupier originally notified of the inclusion of the structure in the RPS. A planning authority is not required to re-notify future owners or occupiers of the protected status or proposed protected status of a structure.

2.6.14 It should be noted that Section 56 of the Act states that, where a structure is included in the RPS, its inclusion may be registered under the Registration of Title Act 1964, in the appropriate register maintained under that Act, as a burden affecting registered land within the meaning of that Act.

Transitional arrangements under the 1999 Act

2.6.15 The transitional arrangements following commencement of the Local Government (Planning and Development) Act 1999 created a temporary exception to the notification procedures. Under Section 38 of that Act, any reference to the protection or preservation of a structure, or part of a structure, in a development plan current on 1 January 2000, including under the heading 'Consideration for preservation', 'List 1' or 'List 2' and even 'Streetscape' automatically made it a protected structure within the meaning of the 1999 Act. Owners and occupiers of these structures were notified of the changed status of these structures and given an opportunity to comment in advance of a decision being made to include the structure formally within the RPS. If the transitional arrangements were not availed of, a planning authority should use the provisions under Section 55 of the 2000 Act.

2.7 Deleting Structures from the Record of Protected Structures

2.7.1 Structures are deleted from the RPS by similar procedures to those laid down for making additions. Deletions will take place where the planning authority considers that the protection of a structure, or part of a structure, is no longer warranted. This will generally take place only when the structure has entirely lost its special interest value through major accident or where new information has come to light which proves that the special interest value was mistakenly attributed. Deletion from the RPS may also come about where it has been decided that a more appropriate method of protecting a particular structure would be by including it within an ACA. However, in such cases, the planning authority should be confident that the interior of the building is not of special interest before deleting it from the RPS.

[11] *Section 12 (4), 2000 Act*

2.8 The Form of the Record of Protected Structures

2.8.1 The Minister has prescribed the form of the RPS under Article 51 of the Planning and Development Regulations 2001.

2.8.2 The RPS should be clear and comprehensible. All protected structures within the functional area of a planning authority should be referred to in a single numbered list, ordered alphabetically by postal address, with each structure given a reference number unique in that planning authority area. For the sake of clarity there should be no organisational subdivision of the RPS into separate lists, for example of industrial heritage, houses, bridges, or for different geographical areas, or by perceived importance like 'national', 'regional' or 'local' (even if these are indicated by the NIAH), as this could lead to misunderstandings. Such categorisations or typologies, may, of course, be referred to, but should not be used to organise the list.

2.8.3 Table I below shows how the information in an RPS could be laid out. This format will facilitate those:

a) familiar with the county but who only know the names of towns;
b) with access to detailed 6 inches:1 mile scale (or equivalent) Ordnance Survey maps;
c) with access to 'Discovery' series 1:50,000 scale Ordnance Survey maps which have the National Grid lines superimposed, and
d) checking the protection status of a particular building at a given address.

Identifying number
2.8.4 Each individual structure, including the constituent buildings of a terrace or a village group, should be given a separate entry in the RPS and numbered with a unique identifying number for the RPS of that planning authority.

Address
2.8.5 In rural areas, the townland is generally the most important component of an address. If a townland name is not unique in the county area then either the electoral ward or name of the nearest postal town should be given. Where two or more structures in the same townland are to be protected, the structure's name or summary identification should be used to augment the townland name (for example, 'Brian Boru's well') and should clearly identify each. However, this must be used in conjunction with other locational information, such as a mapped location for the building, Describing a building as, for example 'Murphy's farmhouse', may lead to confusion should ownership of the building subsequently change.

2.8.6 In urban areas, some or all of the following should be used to identify structures:

a) town name;
b) townland or district name, if appropriate. Where available, postal district numbers should be used;
c) street name;
d) number on the street;
e) name of building.

2.8.7 Table I indicates possible approaches to setting out information on locating a structure, which will be useful in different circumstances. In the case of a village, there may be no street names and the townland divisions are useful. By placing the townland after the town name in RPS, all the buildings in the town appear in sequence. In the case of a town where the whole town lies within a single townland, the town name again has the primary classification function, followed in this case by the street name, and by the house number, where available. Where a town contains several townlands, as well as street names, it will usually be more convenient to give prominence to the street name rather than the townland name. Townland names and town names can be intermingled in the RPS so long as this does not create ambiguity.

2.8.8 A structure may be located on a street corner or on a street that has two alternative names. Where a structure's location is known by two names, or straddles two townlands (as is frequently the case with bridges), the structure may be included in the list under both names but retaining a single reference number.

Description
2.8.9 This column should give a brief common-sense description of the function of the structure to be protected, such as 'bridge', 'thatched house', 'country house', 'demesne features' or 'business premises'. If part only of a structure is to be protected, the specific part should be identified, for example, 'gateway only'.

Location Map

2.8.10 A map (or maps) of suitable scale to show the location of an individual structure should be prepared and kept together as a set. The clearest way this can be done is by relating a point on the structure to the National Grid. The location of the structure should also be marked on as large a scale map as practicable. However, accurate postal addresses will allow most users of the RPS to access the information. The map location for each individual protected structure should be indexed to the RPS list. The number of the appropriate Ordnance Survey map on which the structure is represented should be stated within the RPS.

National Grid co-ordinates

2.8.11 Supplying the National Grid co-ordinates for the location of the structure is the least ambiguous way of locating a protected structure. These can be read from the superimposed grid printed on the 1:50,000 scale 'Discovery' series map or from scales in the margins of 1:1,000 scale maps. Particular care should be taken to quote the correct grid reference number. A ten-digit grid reference is acceptable for buildings in rural areas. In urban areas, it will be necessary to quote twelve-digit numbers. Some planning authorities will have GIS systems that can give the grid reference for particular locations automatically.

Notes and specified features in the attendant grounds

2.8.12 This column may be used to clarify the identity of the structure. If necessary, this could be by reference to a former use of the structure – for example, 'furniture factory' under the 'Description' column might be clarified in the 'Notes' column as 'Former Royal School'. Identifying the religious denomination could help differentiate two churches in the same locality dedicated to the same saint.

2.8.13 This column may also be used to specify any features in the attendant grounds of a protected structure which contribute to its character. For example, reference to 'all demesne features' could be used, if appropriate, to extend protection to those structures with a historical relationship with a country house.

2.8.14 If it would assist to describe the overall character of the protected structure, this column may be used qualitatively to summarise its setting, for example 'character enhanced by isolated cliff-top location' or 'located in a mature woodland setting'.

Cross-referencing inventory reference numbers

2.8.15 Where a NIAH survey has been carried out, each structure recorded will have been assigned a unique registration number. Where it would not cause confusion, the NIAH registration number may be indexed to the RPS.

2.8.16 If the structure has been included in the Record of Monuments and Places (RMP) under the National Monuments Acts, this should be indicated in the RPS, by reference to the RMP twelve-digit letter and number code. This will serve to alert the owner of the structure, as well as the planning authority, to its additional statutory protection.

2.9 Planning Authority's Protected Structures Files

2.9.1 When setting up a database for the RPS, the planning authority may consider providing extra fields to the internal file. These could include:

a) the categories of special interest attributed to the structure;

b) the names of all notified owners and occupiers of the protected structure, and the date when this information was ascertained;

c) a tick-box indicating whether or not the extent of the curtilage has been determined;

d) when protection was first extended to the structure, if this is known;

e) whether the planning authority has a photographic record of the structure;

f) whether the planning authority has historical or bibliographic documentation of the structure on file;

g) whether the structure is also the subject of protection under the National Monuments Acts;

h) whether a conservation grant has been given for the structure and details thereof;

i) whether other archives are known to hold information on the structure;

j) whether a declaration has been issued;

k) whether any endangerment notices have been issued and details thereof;

l) reference numbers of planning applications relating to the site;

m) any other relevant information.

2.10 Availability of the Record of Protected Structures

2.10.1 The RPS forms part of the development plan. However, as structures can be added to, or deleted from, the RPS at any time, the planning authority must maintain a continually updated copy of the record. This may be kept with the planning register at the public counter of the planning offices as a hard copy, in electronic form on a website, or both. The primary function of the RPS should be the unambiguous identification of the structures concerned. Individual records of each protected structure should be kept at the planning authority's offices.

2.10.2 When collecting information from the owners or occupiers of structures, officers of the planning authority should clarify that it will be held on an understanding of confidentiality, subject to the requirements of the Freedom of Information Acts 1997 - 2003 and other legal requirements. Care should be taken, especially in relation to internal fixtures, in the disclosure of this information as it may be personal or because the release of such information might result in unwarranted loss to the owner or occupier of a protected structure.

2.10.3 The RPS files may therefore be in two parts – one that is publicly accessible and one that is confidential in so far as it relates to the private aspects of the property. Individual files on each protected structure should be handled in a way that respects the owner's confidentiality and the security needs of the structure and should be kept in a safe store at the offices of the planning authority. The file should be fully accessible to the owner or occupier of the structure who has given his/her assent for the collection of the information.

2.10.4 The public file should contain the basic identifying information as summarised above. The private file should contain copies of any descriptions, declarations, photographs, correspondence and maps.

2.11 **Sample File Sheets for the Record of Protected Structures**

2.11.1 **Sample file sheet for the RPS No.1**

Planning authority:	Donegal Co. Council
Unique identity number:	40900101
Address:	Malin Tower, Ardmalin townland, near Malin Town, Inishowen Peninsula
Description:	Signal Tower
Ordnance Survey Map:	6": 1 Mile scale, Sheet DG 001
National Grid co-ordinates:	E023975 N459550
Special interest:	Architectural, historical, scientific
Site features:	Includes adjacent c.1940 concrete-built look-out post

Map indicating location of structure:

2.11.2 **Sample file sheet for the RPS No.2**

Planning authority: Tralee Town Council, Co. Kerry

Unique identity number: 101

Address: Courthouse, Ashe Street

Description: Courthouse

Ordnance Survey Map: 1:1,000 scale, 5587 - 5

National Grid co-ordinates: E083760 N114441

Special interest: Architectural, historical, artistic

Site features: None

Map indicating location of structure:

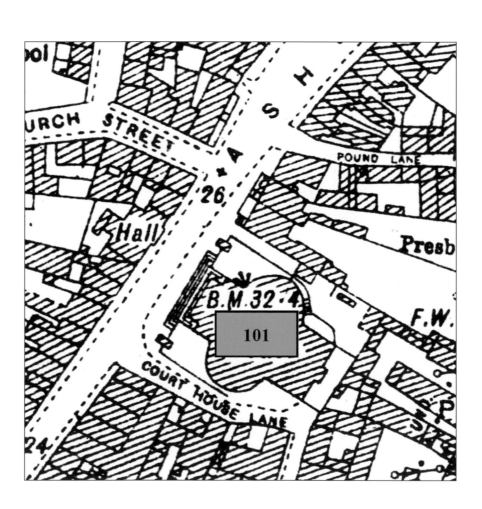

Table I Sample Format for the Record of Protected Structures

Ref. no.	Building Address	Townland	Town	Description	O.S. 6" map ref.	National Grid Reference	Notes (including features of attendant grounds)
1	Ballymahon Courthouse	Ballymahon	Ballymahon	Courthouse	27	21557.25715	
2	Brianstown House	Brianstown	Longford	Country house	13	20845.27711	
3	Carrigglas Manor	Carrickglass Demesne	Longford	Country house	14	21661.27747	Including outbuildings, gateways and gate lodges
4	Castlecor House	Castlecore	Ballymahon	Country house	26	21371.25714	
5	Castleforbes	Castleforbes Demesne	Newtown Forbes	Country house	8	20977.28032	Formerly a convent
6	Castlewilder	Castlewilder	Colehill	Country house	23	22395.26116	
7	Cloncallow House	Clooncallow	Ballymahon	Demesne feature	27	21752.25615	Entrance gates
8	Coolamber Manor	Cloonshannagh	Edgeworthstown	Country house	15	23524.27320.	Agricultural college
9	Colehill House	Colehill	Colehill	Country house	23	22189.26050.	
10	Cornollen House	Cornollen	Longford	Country house	13	20840.27581	
11	Doory House	Doory	Ballymahon	Demesne feature	23	21670.26194	Entrance gates
12	Doory House	Doory	Ballymahon	Demesne feature	23	21861.26029	Entrance gates
13	Foxhall Church (in ruins)	Foxhall	Legan or Lenamore	Church	24	22545.26439	Including graveyard
14	Corn Mill	Grillagh	Killashee	Mill	18	20681.26931	
15	Ledwithstown House	Ledwithstown	Ballymahon	Country house	22	21087.25945	
16	Lismore House	Lismore	Newtown Forbes	Country house	13	21125.27717	
17	McGuinness	Lyanmore	Ardagh	House	19	22000.26800	
18	Mosstown	Mosstown	Keenagh	Demesne feature	22	21163.26382	Dovecote
19	Newcastle House	Newcastle	Ballymahon	Country house	27	21851.25695	Formerly a convent
20	Rathcline Castle	Rathcline	Lanesboro	C17th house	17	20004.26687	
21	St Mary's R.C. Church	Smithfield	Legan or Lenamore	Church	24	22445.26361	Including graveyard
22	Cathedral of St Mel (in ruins)		Ardagh, Ardagh Demesne	Church	19	22039.26862	
23	St Patrick's Church (C of I)		Ardagh, Ardagh Demesne	Church	19	22033.26863	
24	McGroarty's		Ardagh, Ardagh Demesne	House	19	22000.26800	
25	McGonagle's		Ardagh, Banghill	House	19	22000.26800	
26	McGinley's		Ardagh, Banghill	House	19	22000.26800	
27	McGarrigle's		Ardagh, Banghill	House	19	22000.26800	

Table II An Outline of Record of Protected Structures Procedures

1. Identify possible additions to the RPS

Possible sources include:

> Previous development plans
> NIAH survey, if available
> Ministerial recommendations, if any
> Planning authority's own inventories
> Appropriate structures protected under the National Monuments Acts
> Local surveys, local knowledge or submissions from interested parties
> Documentary sources

See 2.4

2. Assess potential additions

> Evaluate the special interest(s) of the structure
> Establish the format of the record

See 2.5

See 2.8
& Table I

3. Use appropriate procedure (Note: similar procedures are used for making both additions to, and deletions from, the RPS)

> Section 12 when making the development plan
> Section 55 at any time during the life of the development plan

See 2.6

3a. Section 12

> Notify owners and occupiers and invite submissions
> Send notice to the Minister, the other prescribed bodies and those bodies specified in S.12(1)(a)
> Advertise preparation of draft in the press
> Display draft plan which includes proposed additions to, and/or deletions from, the RPS
> Receive comments, prepare Manager's Report and present to council members
> Members accept or amend the plan which includes the proposed RPS
> Advertise and display amendments if material alterations are to be made
> Members make final decision
> Notify owners and occupiers of decision as soon as possible
> Inform Minister, in writing, of any decision not to comply with a recommendation made under S.53 of the Act

3b. Section 55

> Notify owners and occupiers and invite submissions
> Send notice to the Minister and other prescribed bodies
> Advertise proposals in the press
> Consider any observations or comments received
> If structure was recommended by Minister, forward submissions to him/her for observations
> Have regard to any observations from the Minister
> Members make decision on proposed addition or deletion
> Inform owners and occupiers of decision within two weeks
> Inform Minister, in writing, of any decision not to comply with a recommendation made under S.53 of the Act

The Development Plan
Architectural Conservation Areas

CHAPTER 3

3.1 Introduction

3.1.1 An architectural conservation area (ACA) is a place, area, group of structures or townscape, taking account of building lines and heights, that is of special architectural, historical, archaeological, artistic, cultural, scientific, social or technical interest or that contributes to the appreciation of a protected structure, and whose character it is an objective of a development plan to preserve.[1] An area of special planning control (ASPC) is all, or part, of an ACA which a planning authority considers of special importance to, or as respects, the civic life or the architectural, historical, cultural or social character of a city or town in which it is situated.[2] A planning authority recognises, by making provision in the development plan for the protection of these areas, that in many cases, the protection of the architectural heritage is best achieved by controlling and guiding change on a wider scale than the individual structure, in order to retain the overall architectural or historic character of an area.

3.1.2 ACA policies should be supported by, and be consistent with, other policies of the development plan especially those relating to development control. An objective to preserve the character of an ACA, once approved by the elected members of a council, carries through from development plan to development plan and remains an objective of the planning authority unless subsequently modified by the members.

3.1.3 The legislation relating to ACAs and ASPCs is contained in Chapter II of Part IV of the Planning and Development Act 2000.

3.2 Identifying Areas for Protection

3.2.1 Although many planning authorities may have designated non-statutory conservation areas prior to the commencement of the 2000 Act, the Act provides that all development plans must now include objectives for preserving the character of ACAs, if there are places, areas, groups of structures or townscape of special interest or which contribute to the appreciation of protected structures, situated within a planning authority's functional area.

3.2.2 The character and special interest of many localities within the functional area of a planning authority will suggest themselves as candidate ACAs. These should be carefully assessed. Many planning authorities are already engaged in fruitful participatory processes with community groups and interested parties to devise planning policies for towns, villages and urban areas across the country.

3.2.3 ACA legislation may be used to protect the following:

a) groups of structures of distinctiveness or visual richness or historical importance;

Historic town or village cores are often appropriate to designation as ACAs

---

1 Section 81, 2000 Act   2 Section 84 (1), 2000 Act

b) the setting and exterior appearance of structures that are of special interest, but the interiors of which do not merit protection;

c) the setting of a protected structure where this is more extensive than its curtilage;

d) designed landscapes where these contain groups of structures as in, for example, urban parks, the former demesnes of country houses and groupings of archaeological or industrial remains;

e) groups of structures which form dispersed but unified entities but which are not within the attendant grounds of a single dominant protected structure.

3.2.4 The physical expression of the significance of an area may consist of building lines and heights, patterns of materials, construction systems, or architectural elements that are repeated within the area and give it a sense of harmony, such as the use of timber sash windows in an eighteenth-century streetscape. Alternatively, an area can be an exemplar of a widely dispersed pattern of structures or spaces on a national or international scale, in which case the significance and the basis for its protection is based on the wider ensemble of which it may be a component.

The survival of distinctive materials and local detailing can add to the character of an ACA including joinery patterns, paving materials and boundary railing styles

3.2.5 The boundaries of a candidate ACA should make physical, visual and planning-control sense. It may be necessary to refer back to the core characteristics of the area in order to establish the most appropriate boundary lines. The choice of boundary may be influenced by considering the importance of the various views into and out of the area, but it is not necessary to include all territory encompassed by such views. The character of the edges of the area may gradually degenerate in some parts due to dereliction. Whether or not degraded parts should be included may be resolved by reference to the historical research to see if these areas once formed a coherent part of the overall place.

The boundaries of an ACA should make physical and practical planning sense and may need to be defined with the help of historical research especially in urban areas

3.2.6 In preparing a draft development plan, a planning authority should evaluate all potential ACAs. These candidate areas should be inspected, and their distinctiveness, significance and special interest evaluated and documented. In some cases, in addition to the planning authority's technical staff, it may be necessary to seek the advice of conservation consultants with a variety of skills, for example, architects, ecologists, landscape designers, engineers, archaeologists or architectural historians.

3.2.7 Historical research may be carried out where this is necessary to justify the designation of an ACA or to clarify specific preservation objectives. This might include documentary or archival research and the study of maps and old photographs. In recent years there has been an increase in the publication of local historical studies. Research of primary sources, however, should be undertaken with clearly defined aims in mind, as there is much material available.

3.2.8 The Minister may assist in the identification of these areas when publishing National Inventory of Architectural Heritage (NIAH) surveys or when commenting on draft development plans. Where they have been published, the NIAH town surveys may be used to identify groups of structures that merit protection, in particular groups of buildings given 'local importance' or higher ratings because of their 'streetscape or setting' value.

3.2.9 A planning authority should, when reviewing its development plan, take the opportunity to review structures currently in the Record of Protected Structures and determine whether an ACA designation would be a more appropriate form of protection. The exterior appearance of structures can make a contribution to the character of an area. However it may be inappropriate to protect the interiors of some structures, which would happen if they were included in the RPS. On the other hand, an individual structure within a proposed ACA may itself be of special importance. The planning authority should then consider whether it merits inclusion in the RPS, in addition to being included within a designated ACA.

3.2.10 It is at the discretion of the planning authority to make the policies to protect these areas appropriate to the particular circumstances. Small areas containing only a few properties might require ACA policies in lieu of inclusion in the RPS. Detailed policies may also be appropriate to provide protection to the setting of a protected structure where there are properties outside its curtilage which have a particularly strong relationship with it. Larger, or more architecturally disparate, areas can be given more general forms of protection. These could include general policies aimed at protecting the integrity of original or traditional styles of windows, doors or roofing materials prevalent in the area, together with more specific policies for sub-areas. Where resources are scarce, policies can be developed, applied and implemented in phases, including ensuring that the character of the whole area is treated as an ensemble from the outset. It should be noted that there are obvious drawbacks to this approach.

3.3 Identifying the Character of the Area

Categories of Special Interest

3.3.1 The categories of special interest in relation to individual structures have been set out in Chapter 2 above. Many of the recommendations and criteria in that chapter regarding the protection of individual structures will also be of relevance to ACAs.

Architectural interest

3.3.2 Many buildings were consciously designed to contribute visually to the character of their setting, beyond the boundaries of the curtilage on which they were built. They respond to the street, road or landscape in which they are situated. Later rebuildings on a mediaeval curving street, visible perhaps in faceted façades and narrow plots, relate to the communal history of settlement in a town. Subtle repetitive patterns of chimneys, window or door-openings on a street, where traditional construction methods used a shared palette of materials, can give the area character and a sense of scale and harmony. The volume or massing, plot size, boundary alignments and street frontage alignment of the built environment can be part of the heritage of an urban area.

Although one or more outstanding buildings may form the nucleus of an ACA, the design and layout of all structures within the area will be important to establishing its special architectural interest

3.3.3   Urban design schemes initiated in the past by civic authorities or landlords, aimed to present a more fashionable or coherent appearance to towns or villages, often to stimulate economic growth. Often a street grid was laid out in advance of development. Occasionally leases stipulated building heights and other details, although construction may have taken at least a generation to complete. The result may be an architecturally impressive townscape in one or more styles or a picturesque 'designed' village, such as Dunmore East, Co. Waterford. Demesnes were also laid out or 'improved' with vistas, follies, eye-catchers and water features in the styles of the day. The nineteenth-century urban cemeteries benefited from a designed approach, as each was laid out and landscaped with an eye to its visual impression, with avenues, stands of yews and vistas terminated by landmark chapels or monuments.

Local authorities and private land owners often instigated urban improvement schemes such as the creation of streets, town parks or garden suburbs which can be of special architectural interest

Historical interest

3.3.4   The plan of plots, boundaries and streets in towns and cities contain a record of past urban life, frequently inscribed in structures that have endured through time. The historic urban townscape is vital to the setting of prominent civic structures such as courthouses, cathedrals, museums or railway stations. The survival above ground of urban defences (town and city walls), in whatever condition, can be one of the most important defining characteristics of a historic place. Urban design elements such as nodal or radial street patterns, squares, market places and surviving mediaeval burgage plots also contribute to the historical character of a town.

The historic urban plan form can be an important defining characteristic of a place. In both these examples, buildings have been built upon, or incorporate parts of, mediaeval town defences thus preserving the line of the earlier structures within the modern day street pattern

3.3.5   In a rural area the lack of change can constitute the historical interest of a place, as it may clearly show its particular character unmediated by subsequent alterations. Here too the historical layout and relationship of structures to each other may be of equal importance to the intrinsic architectural or social character of each, or may be vital to an appreciation of a protected structure which is central to the area. A large-scale purpose-built complex of structures, such as the ruins of Crinkill Barracks outside Birr, Co. Offaly, can be of socio-historical interest.

In rural areas, former settlements or groups of buildings can survive substantially intact thus adding to the special historical interest of the area

Archaeological interest

3.3.6 The retention of archaeological deposits in situ, with targeted excavation and conservation projects, is recognised as an important strategy for securing more knowledge about the past. In urban areas, this consideration may inform a conservation strategy for the standing structures above. An ACA may coincide with a zone of archaeological potential or an archaeological area. In these cases, care should be taken to ensure that the conservation policies adopted successfully mediate between the different pressures and requirements of both the above-ground and below-ground structures. It often transpires that structures which have been substantially rebuilt above ground retain their mediaeval basements, as for example in the historic centre of Kilkenny. The recognition of such fabric, especially within an area which retains its burgage plots or defensive structures, may be vital to gaining an understanding of the archaeological character of the area.

An ACA may be designated for its special archaeological interest where upstanding archaeological remains survive and such an area may therefore overlap or coincide with statutory protection under the National Monuments Acts

Artistic interest

3.3.7 The consistent use of crafted materials, such as paving or walling in local styles or materials, can contribute to the special artistic interest of an area, for example the use of Moher 'slate' roofs in Ennistymon. Styles of decoration such as moulded terracotta embellishments can be very characteristic of late nineteenth-century terraces.

Conscious artistic input can bring special interest to otherwise ordinary structural elements such as slate-hanging, brickwork, chimneystacks or shopfronts within an area

3.3.8 Public sculpture, utilities or memorials, as well as being works of art in their own right, can be the artistic focus of a public space which has been formally designed to present them. A formally laid out landscape or townscape could also be of artistic interest. This may include the radial streets or avenues on the baroque model which set up vistas of important structures within an area such as in the layout of the village of Portlaw, Co. Waterford.

The formal garden at Heywood, Co. Laois is a work of art by an outstanding architect, Edwin Lutyens. Many well-designed memorials, gardens and public spaces are of artistic interest whether or not their designer is known

Cultural interest

3.3.9 Public spaces may facilitate particular forms of behaviour. These include the spaces formed to facilitate markets, fairs, outdoor theatre or communal celebrations. Areas of towns and cities may, over time, have become a focus for culture, where adjacent parks, libraries, colleges and museums prompt a convergence of informal as well as formal cultural activities within and around the buildings and spaces, as at Trinity College Dublin.

Cultural activities based in or around architecturally significant buildings or spaces such market squares can contribute to the special interest of an area

Scientific interest

3.3.10 Geophysical or astronomical alignments in a landscape may be the intentional work of past designers. The curtilage or attendant grounds of a structure within an ACA may comprise living elements that form a habitat or an ecosystem that creates a spatial enclosure and a habitable or pleasing environment, as at Garinish Island, Co. Cork. Botanical gardens, whether in private or public ownership, are also examples of places where structures and landscaping form habitats for exotic plant species.

The special scientific interest of an area may arise from the presence of important natural habitats or geographical features (top), from its connection with scientific research or as the location of a collection of scientific interest such as a botanical garden (bottom)

Technical interest

3.3.11 An industrial-heritage landscape related to mine-working, chemical extraction or milling can be of special technical interest. The industrial landscape of the Bridge End of Ramelton, Co. Donegal was host to a linen-works, flour-mill and iodine plant and could be said to be of technical interest for that reason.

The special technical interest of an area may derive from its association with industrial heritage areas or landscapes such as harbours, ports, railways and canals

3.3.12 At Portlaw, Co. Waterford, a town designed around the production of cotton, the landscape of the vicinity of the industrial site was moulded by its processes. There are weirs, mill-races, a tailings pond and a canal. In contrast, the industrial heritage of Monivea, Co. Galway is now evident mainly from the wide village green, which was created as a flax-drying green in the late eighteenth century, laid out on axis with the castle entrance.

These mill buildings at Slane Bridge are of outstanding importance as an example of an early purpose-built industrial complex dating from the start of the Industrial Revolution

Social interest

3.3.13 Special social interest may be found in town parks and communal greens laid out with trees, benches and water fountains, and often sited especially to improve the surroundings of urban dwellers. A 'new town' suburb, such as New Tipperary, may be of social interest due to its origins for housing workers of a particular industry or as a slum resettlement programme. Rural 'clachan' settlements may be of social interest. These settlements are usually characterised by irregularly juxtaposed dwellings and outbuildings, often without formal streets or alleys between, and with an integral link to the land historically farmed in rundale strips.

Special social interest in an area may be attributed to sites of religious significance and places of pilgrimage such as holy wells or holy trees (top). Public spaces of social interest may be centred around surviving historic features such as horse troughs (bottom)

3.4   Setting and Architectural Conservation Areas

3.4.1   The influence of the setting of groups of structures on the character of the group or the wider area should be considered when identifying this character. The topography of an area, natural features such as woodlands and aesthetically important vistas to and from the area, can all be aspects of the setting.

The setting of an area, together with views in and out of it, can contribute greatly to its overall character and should always be considered when assessing its importance

3.4.2   The contribution of setting to the character of the architectural heritage should not be underestimated. A building in a rural setting may have a different, but equally noteworthy, relationship with its surroundings from that of a building in an urban place. The location of a structure may have been designed to relate to a particular landscape feature, as, for example, in the way that Powerscourt House relates to the Sugarloaf Mountain. Follies, eye-catchers, gazebos and towers were all usually positioned and designed to enhance their setting or the designed landscape in which they are situated. The attendant grounds around a country house were often moulded into a coherent landscaped entity in accordance with current aesthetic and economic ideas.

3.4.3   In addition, or as an alternative to protecting such groups of structures as an ACA, the planning authority could consider employing other types of protection such as including objectives in the development plan to preserve a view or prospect. This would be recommended where it is necessary to preserve a long-distance designed vista between structures or features such as at the Conolly Folly at Maynooth, which was designed to be visible from Castletown House although located several kilometres apart.

Protecting views to and from important structures within an ACA should be considered when drawing up objectives for the area

3.5   Public Consultation

3.5.1   There is no requirement under the Act to notify individual owners or occupiers of lands in an ACA of the designation of the area. However, the success of the planning authority's objectives to preserve the character of these areas will often depend to a large extent on public knowledge and broad acceptance of those objectives. The planning authority should consider involving interested parties in drawing up these objectives and should publicise any special requirements or policies it intends to implement in order for development control policies to be effective. Such an approach is particularly important as the owners and occupiers of property in an ACA are not entitled to a declaration under Section 57 of the Act (unless, of course, the structure is a protected structure in addition to being located within the ACA).

3.5.2   It is recommended that a planning authority consult with the owners and occupiers on the proposed designation at an early stage, and consider
(i) holding public meetings and workshops,
(ii) publishing newspaper notices of its intentions, and
(iii) distributing leaflets to all properties in the area.

Such leaflets could communicate the assessment of the significance of the area mentioned above, including:

a) why the area has been selected as an ACA;
b) what is its history and special features;
c) an explanation of the statutory protection proposed;
d) what measures may be taken to protect the character, such as expanding the new limitations to exempted development;
e) how individual property owners and occupiers can help protect its character by diligent and timely maintenance;
f) examples of good conservation practice locally;
g) any financial assistance the planning authority may be able to offer;
h) where advice and further information is available.

3.5.3　Almost inevitably the public consultation process will not engage all of those with a stake in the future of the place (not all owners will reside within the area). If it appears that a structure of some importance within the area is vacant, and perhaps deteriorating, it may be worthwhile making reasonable efforts to find the owner and inform him or her of the proposed designation.

3.5.4　The planning authority may take account of initiatives to identify ACAs made both by owners and occupiers of an area themselves and by third parties, such as community groups and the prescribed bodies.

3.6　Architectural Conservation Areas and the Development Plan

The development plan

3.6.1　The designation of an ACA takes place as part of the making or the review of a development plan or as a variation to an existing development plan. The extent, special interest and a description of the character of an ACA should be identified in the relevant development plan. If all or part of the area is covered by a local area plan, it should also be set out in the appropriate county, town, borough or city development plan. This should be in the form of a map delineating the area and a concise description of its features of interest and the architectural patterns and details to be found in the area. It should contain a statement of the objective to preserve its character.

3.6.2　The formulation of ACA policies can be incorporated into a development plan by means of variations of the plan. Where a report is prepared in relation to the inclusion of an ACA in the draft or varied plan, it should aim to include the following information:

a) a statement of the objectives and policies of the planning authority in relation to the preservation of the character of the area;
b) a map showing the relevant boundaries of the area;
c) a written description of the character of the area and its main places or spaces, to include a description of the special architectural, historical, archaeological, artistic, cultural, scientific, social or technical interest of the area, as appropriate, which gave rise to its selection;
d) an annotated photographic record of the general character of the area, including streetscapes and landscapes, where this would assist to describe the area;
e) a comprehensive annotated photographic record of the exteriors of all structures in the area visible from areas to which the public have access;
f) if appropriate, a written description of the materials and construction techniques of the structures and surfaces which contribute to the character of the area, augmented by illustrations where appropriate, and
g) the additional development control policies relevant to the area, including any other statutory designations or policy objectives

3.6.3　Where possible, an inventory of the exterior of the structures, and of features of the area should be carried out when it is being defined, as it is a useful tool for the management of an ACA. Where it is not possible to compile an inventory at that time, it should be an objective of the planning authority to undertake one at a later time.

Written description

3.6.4　The written description of the character of the ACA referred to above may address some or all of the following as appropriate:

a) the location of the area, including its relation to its surroundings, noting any important views or vistas and topographical features which help to define it;
b) the history of the area, when it was developed

or laid out and by whom, whether it was formed as a single project or was developed over time;

c) the form and arrangement of public and open space, street pattern and property divisions including streets or squares, described in terms of the architectural style, homogeneity of the building type (if appropriate), the physical form of the space, its dimensions and interconnection to other spaces, and its relationship to privately owned property. For example, there may be networks of public steps and laneways accessed under carriage arches;

d) reference to distinctive streetscapes and views that are of special interest, including landmarks such as strategically sited buildings, monuments or memorials, architectural or design features including any terraces or groups of buildings forming subsidiary elements or spaces, or infrastructural elements such as railways or canals that are significant either historically or visually;

e) the range and intensity of its current socio-economic functions, mentioning how the economic functions contribute to, or detract from, its character;

f) the condition of the existing fabric and the degree to which the age or type of the materials of a structure contributes to the character of the area;

g) a schedule of the protected structures and recorded monuments located in the area and their contribution to its character;

h) trees, watercourses and open space, in both public and private ownership and their contribution to its character;

i) street furniture and fixtures in public spaces and historic features that survive, and their date;

j) the predominant surface materials of the ground plane, such as paving or kerbstones, and the main construction or cladding materials of the structures that enclose significant spaces;

k) features that detract from the character of the area, where the integrity of the area has been compromised by demolition of historic fabric or by development inappropriate to its character;

l) non-physical characteristics of the public spaces, such as the association of the area with a particular economic, social or cultural activity, relative freedom from (or vulnerability to) vehicular traffic, absence of noise, human scale, uniqueness.

3.6.5   Consideration should be given in the description not only to the façades and frontages of buildings facing the major thoroughfares, but also to the roofscape, side streets and lanes, and the rear appearance of buildings, including characteristics of their plots such as mews buildings, which may also contribute to the character of the area.

Illustrations

3.6.6   Visual material can often describe the general characteristics of an area more succinctly than a written description. Maps, photographs, diagrams and drawings can be used in conjunction with the written statement. Maps should show the boundaries of the ACA and sub-areas within it that are subject to specific detailed policy objectives. Significant features and structures and zoning provisions may also be indicated through illustrations. Photographs can be used to identify typical elements and the general quality of streetscapes or settings. Systematic photography of structures that contribute to the character of the area can most definitively describe the visual aspects of character and set out baseline information about the actual condition of structures at the time when protection commences. Photographs of significant views into and out of the area should be included where relevant.

3.6.7   The boundaries of the area should be clearly marked on the most up-to-date map available. In urban areas, this should be at a scale of 1:1,000 or 1:2,500 as appropriate. The information should be checked on the ground and take cognisance of well-recognised existing geographical boundaries. It is generally preferable for the boundary of an ACA to coincide with the rear boundary of properties in urban areas. The buildings, boundary walls and space enclosed by the street or road would then be included in the area.

Interaction with other forms of statutory protection

3.6.8   Other forms of protection of the environment that affect the ACA should be noted in the written description. These include protection under the National Monuments Acts of zones of archaeological potential and the location of sites included in the Record of Monuments and Places. Protection of the natural heritage may include Special Areas of Conservation, Natural Heritage Area designations, landscape conservation areas and tree preservation orders.

Zoning and land use

3.6.9 The social and economic functions that are catered for in the area or in its vicinity may influence its character. The functional zoning and other objectives in the development plan should be examined to check if they would conflict with the objective to protect the character of the area and its surroundings, for example removing any obsolete area designations. If there is potential conflict between the existing fabric whose character is worthy of protection and potential inappropriate use proposals, modifications to the zoning provisions may be necessary. Planning authorities should try to develop zoning objectives which will support the ACA by encouraging the types of economic and social uses that will benefit from being in this location and benefit the area generally. Specific policies, such as financial support for restoration of character, may be devised to anticipate and overcome any problems. The provision of a zoning and land-use policy for the conservation of the character of the area should lead to the protection of this character, and prevent the degradation of its visual amenity or economic value. It might be appropriate to constrict 'open for consideration' uses or expand them to target more directly the social or economic character of the area.

3.7 Development Control in Architectural Conservation Areas

3.7.1 In an ACA, the carrying out of works to the exterior of a structure will be exempted development only if those works would not materially affect the character of the area. This is in addition to the requirement under Section 4 (1) (h) of the Act that for works to be exempted, they must be consistent with the appearance of the structure itself and neighbouring structures. For example, the construction of a small house-extension within an ACA may require planning permission, although it may be exempted development elsewhere.[3] If the particular character of the ACA is described in the development plan, works to a structure that would affect that character can require planning permission.

3.7.2 The inclusion of policies and development control objectives for an ACA in the development plan would familiarise owners and occupiers of buildings, and other interested parties, with the measures the planning authority will use to assess impacts to the particular features that give rise to the special character of the area.

3.7.3 The processes of change – development, dereliction or widespread replacement of original elements or finishes – that may pose a threat to the character of the area should be clearly analysed and documented. Indeed the very elements that characterise the area may make it vulnerable. This may be the case with an industrial town in which the traditional industries have closed or a rural village where the traditional houses are now seen as too small for modern use. From this, future development issues that will affect structures in the area can be more easily identified and its socio-economic needs addressed in a way that would not adversely affect its character. In a particular area where plots to the rear of buildings have been subject to periodic redevelopment and are no longer of special interest, the objectives of the ACA may only apply to the frontage including the ridge line and chimney stacks. Clearly, it is most satisfactory if the necessary objectives are developed in conjunction with the initial stages of developing an ACA. If they are not, it should be done as soon as possible thereafter and inserted as a variation into the development plan. Unless acceptable parameters of development are set as objectives, it may be difficult to ensure that all permitted proposals comply with the character of the area in their nature, extent and details.

3.7.4 Written development objectives could make clear recommendations in relation to some or all of the following as appropriate:

a) views and prospects to be preserved and any consequent restrictions on building lines and heights and other development parameters where the construction of new structures is permitted within the ACA;

b) appropriate standards of maintenance and repair works;

c) criteria for assessing proposals for demolition of structures or parts of structures;

d) criteria for the design and location of advertising hoardings, signage, awnings, canopies, flagpoles, banners, satellite dishes, masts and pylons, floodlighting, cctv cameras and other building attachments;

e) private car parking, for example, policies regarding the conversion of front gardens for use as off-street parking, and design of on-street parking bays;

f) the policy of the planning authority in relation to enforcement and restoration of character in the area;

g) detailed objectives in relation to sub-areas within the ACA;

h) the acceptability of amalgamation of plots, including where there are no externally visible effects;

i) where a burial ground is an ACA, stipulations regarding the form and materials to be used for new memorials;

j) interrelation between this and other forms of protection, for example, tree preservation orders;

k) design guidelines for sub-areas or particular sites including the architectural patterns that should be respected (for example, window/wall ratios, plot divisions, roof design and provision of machinery on roofs);

l) the range of acceptable plot ratios;

m) acceptable materials and finishes for new development (for example, wall surfaces or window-frame material);

n) where new construction may be permitted, especially in rural ACAs, and

o) environmental issues arising from new construction or management of the public realm (such as waste disposal arrangements).

3.7.5   A planning authority may also wish to indicate standards of documentation for planning applications and any additional types of condition which it may consider appropriate to attach to a condition of permission in an ACA. For example, a landscape management plan or character impact statement taking into account the objectives for preservation of the character of the area may be requested as part of an application.

3.8   Features and Structures Detrimental to the Character of the Area

3.8.1   An ACA will not necessarily be of uniform character, nor its built fabric be found, or continue to be, in good condition. Where it is possible to identify them, structures or features that detract from the

character of the area should also be noted. This could include buildings or derelict sites that have a clearly detrimental effect on the character of the area. Other aspects of an area which detract from its character could include excessive traffic or intrusive traffic signage, advertising hoarding, inappropriate replacement windows and the like. The planning authority should consider the appropriate steps open to them to minimise or avoid these. Policies or objectives could be adopted for the replacement of structures or features that are unacceptably intrusive, where their replacement or substantial alteration would improve the character of the area as a whole.

Policies on traffic control and car-parking can affect the character of an ACA

Inappropriate small-scale alterations may gradually make a significant impact on an area and erode its character

3.9   Design Briefs for Sites or Sub-Areas

3.9.1   While the design of new buildings can, and should, be controlled under general planning authority powers, design briefs for appropriate sites can form part of the policy for the preservation of the character of an area. Design briefs may be appropriate for sites or structures that have been identified as needing new economic functions, or which do not contribute to the character of the area and for which partial or complete redevelopment would be acceptable. It is also possible to identify green- or brown-field sites that should, if developed, harmonise with the character of the area and where design guidelines could mould the architectural and urban form. Suggested uses for these sites could be set out. In general, and in order to avoid prescriptive design solutions, these should be in written form and only illustrated with a map to indicate the site or area to which they relate.

3.10 Criteria for Assessing Proposals within an Architectural Conservation Area

Proposals for new development

3.10.1 When it is proposed to erect a new building in an ACA, the design of the structure will be of paramount importance. Generally it is preferable to minimise the visual impact of the proposed structure on its setting. The greater the degree of uniformity in the setting, the greater the presumption in favour of a harmonious design. However, replacement in replica should only be contemplated if necessary, for example, to restore the character of a unified terrace and should be appropriately detailed. Where there is an existing mixture of styles, a high standard of contemporary design that respects the character of the area should be encouraged. The scale of new structures should be appropriate to the general scale of the area and not its biggest buildings. The palette of materials and typical details for façades and other surfaces should generally reinforce the area's character. In certain circumstances, it may be appropriate to require a written assessment of the impact of the proposed structure on the character of the area.

The construction of new buildings of a high quality contemporary design within a historic area can be successfully achieved

Proposals for demolition

3.10.2 Where it is proposed to demolish a structure that contributes to the character of an ACA or to demolish behind a retained façade, the onus should be on the applicant to make the case for demolition. The planning authority should consider the effect both on the character of the area and on any adjacent protected structures. When it is proposed to demolish an undistinguished building in an ACA, the proposed replacement should not be of lesser quality or interest than the existing one and should not adversely affect the character of the area.

3.10.3 The applicant and the planning authority should consider the material effect that that proposed demolition may have on the character of the ACA:

a) Does the structure (or part of the structure) to be demolished contribute to the character of the area?

b) What effect would removal of the structure have on the setting of other structures in the area, the balance of an architectural composition or the setting of any adjacent protected structures?

c) Would the character and special interest of the whole of the structure or of the ACA be diminished by the demolition of a part?

d) Has the extent and potential impact of the proposed demolition been minimised?

e) Are there alternatives to demolition, even where the structure is in poor condition?

f) In the case of accidental damage, could demolition be avoided and the structure saved by carrying out repairs or providing temporary support or shelter to the fabric?

g) Is partial demolition justifiable in the interests of the retention of the remainder of the structure?

h) If the special interest of the structure lies in its largely unaltered state, could permission be given to demolish any part of it without damaging that special interest?

i) Has the incorporation of the structure (or part of the structure) into a new development on the site been given adequate consideration?

j) What are the merits of alternative proposals for the site, taking into consideration the development plan objective to conserve the character of the area?

Proposals for retention

3.10.4   Proposals for retention permission in an ACA should be considered as any other application. Applications for the retention of a development that conflicts with any policies for the area or that would set an undesirable precedent might be made acceptable by imposition of conditions or by requiring the removal and/or replacement of certain elements or details. In such cases the applicant could be asked to submit a visual impact assessment or to revise the proposal in full or with regard to specific details. If it is decided to refuse the retention of significant replacement elements such as windows or doors, it is important that enforcement action be undertaken.

3.11   Management of Architectural Conservation Areas

3.11.1   The planning authority should consider taking an active approach to the conservation and management of ACA, in particular through works carried out by the planning authority itself and by public utilities. Consideration should be given as to how to manage infrastructural developments, street or road openings. The location and form of street furniture such as telephone kiosks, bus stops, street lights, traffic signage, street nameplates, together with any proposed alteration to existing historic furniture, have the potential to impact upon the character of the area, as does the location of power and telephone cables. Paving should be carefully considered, in particular where good examples of stone paving and kerbstones exist in situ. Wider issues such as road-widening, bypasses and other large-scale infrastructural developments adjacent to an ACA may also have an impact on its character or patterns of use.

Care should be taken within an ACA regarding the siting of structures related to public utilities and traffic management

3.11.2   The following actions, to be undertaken by the planning authority itself, could be included in the policy objectives of the development plan that relate to an ACA. The planning authority may:

a)   set out local authority priority projects, including strategic management plans, for the preservation or improvement of streetscape or landscape (as the case may be) in the area;

b)   programme and co-ordinate works to minimise temporary disruption and permanent impact;

c)   identify property in the ACA that may merit acquisition and conservation to maintain the area's character;

d)   set out objectives regarding traffic management and placement of street furniture;

Traffic management projects should aim to present the area to its best advantage whilst providing a service to both inhabitants and visitors

e)   set out objectives regarding licences issued for appliances and service cables, etc. on public roads;

f)   set out objectives regarding pavement and road-surfacing materials that are compatible with the character of the area and support its functional requirements;

g)   set out objectives on the nature and size of commercial and road signage (including, if necessary, limitations on size, location, materials and method of illumination), and signage identifying the ACA, as such at the entry points;

h)   set out the requirements for the conservation of the living components of designed landscapes that form part of the ACA, such as trees and other planting;

i)   set out objectives for the mitigating the visual impact of waste disposal bins which need to be sited near or fronting important structures or spaces;

Consideration should be given to the storage of waste disposal bins as these can have a large visual impact on an area

j) set out policies for the use of notices with respect to dangerous structures or derelict sites issued under the Local Government (Sanitary Services) Act 1964 or the Derelict Sites Act 1990.

3.12 Integration with Other Forms of Protection

3.12.1 Planning authorities could consider the use of other forms of conservation designation in parallel to an ACA. For example, a rural ACA could be supplemented through the development plan by objectives to preserve the character of the landscape, including views and prospects, or in a demesne, woodland or designed landscape. The use of tree preservation orders may be considered.

3.12.2 Other forms of legislation may be applicable. All or part of the area could be protected under the National Monuments Acts. It may also happen that the area or part of it is protected under the Wildlife Acts. Where several designations exist or are proposed for the one area, care should be taken to ensure coherence between all conservation objectives.

3.12.3 Where there are multiple dimensions to the heritage, the planning authority could consider including a conservation plan or conservation statement in the development plan which would encompass all the heritage values present in the area that should be conserved. A conservation plan explains the significance of the site, identifies threats, both direct and indirect, to the heritage and sets out policies for retaining the significance in any new use, management regime or alteration of the site. It should be carried out at the assessment stage of a management plan, as it takes the future protection of the special interest of the site as its starting point. A conservation statement is a short statement of what is on the site, why it is important, what issues need to be addressed to conserve the various heritage features, and what needs to be done as a result.

3.13 Areas of Special Planning Control

Designation

3.13.1 The Act provides powers to planning authorities not only to conserve the character of certain areas but also, in urban areas of special importance, to enhance that character; that is, to restore it and to require owners and occupiers to conform to a planning scheme.[4] The area must be all or part of an ACA of special importance to the civic life of the city or town or to the architectural, historical, cultural or social character of the town or city in which it is situated. The designation of an area of special planning control may only be applied in cities or larger towns, that is, in county boroughs, boroughs, urban districts or towns having town commissioners that have a population in excess of 2,000.[5]

Areas of architectural heritage significance may coincide or overlap with those of natural heritage importance. In the case of this demesne, the trees of the estate are subject to a tree preservation order

4 Section 84, 2000 Act   5 Section 84(6), 2000 Act

As designation of an ASPC has the potential to impose considerable burdens on the owners and occupiers of buildings in the area and allows for compensation to those persons, the designation of an ASPC would generally only be suitable in very particular circumstances.

Objectives

3.13.2   It is envisaged that the planning authority would take a proactive approach toward conservation and enhancement within an Area of Special Planning Control. The scheme may include objectives to promote civic amenity and design, to upgrade the area or buildings within it, to maintain and repair buildings and develop sites. A number of possible objectives are listed under Section 84 (2) of the Act. As well as promoting one or more new uses, existing uses within the area can be controlled or the scheme can indicate that the continuance of an existing use would be inappropriate in the area. More detailed control of works can be part of the scheme for the area; for example, control of the use or quality of building materials.

Notification to owners and occupiers

3.13.3   As the legislation envisages that the designation of an ASPC would have a substantial impact on the owners of property within it, they must be individually notified and consulted on the proposal. The contents of this notice are prescribed under Section 85 (3) (b). Owners and occupiers can seek a declaration under Section 87 (3) which would specify the impact of the designation on them and the measures that they will have to take to comply with the scheme. Where the restoration objective being formulated by the planning authority affects only a small number of owners or occupiers, and it is not appropriate to designate an ASPC, it may be appropriate to negotiate directly with those owners and occupiers on conserving or restoring their properties.

Notification to prescribed bodies and the public

3.13.4   Section 85 of the Act requires a planning authority which has passed a resolution to designate an ASPC to notify that fact in writing to the Minister, the Heritage Council, An Taisce, the Arts Council, Bord Fáilte and the appropriate chamber of commerce.[6] The planning authority must also notify An Bord Pleanála.[7] The notification must be accompanied by copies of the scheme.

3.13.5   A notice of the preparation of the scheme must be published in one or more newspapers circulating within the city or town concerned, indicating where and when details of the scheme can be examined and inviting submissions or observations.

Review of schemes for areas of special planning control

3.13.6   A planning authority is obliged to review its scheme for an ASPC as circumstances require but not later than six years after its first approval or its latest review. The scheme can then be amended or revoked and the decision published in a newspaper notice.

6 *Article 55, 2001 Regulations*   7 *Section 85 (2) (a), 2000 Act*

Table III An Outline of Designation Procedures for Architectural Conservation Areas

1. Identify potential ACAs within the planning authority area

Possible sources include

> Research using old and current maps, photographs and/or documentary sources
> NIAH surveys, if available
> Planning authority's own surveys
> Local surveys or local historical studies
> Submissions from interested parties

See 3.2

2. Evaluate the special interest of the potential ACA

> Inspect the extent of the area
> Establish the boundaries of the area to coincide, where possible, with existing physical and/or visual boundaries
> Identify the character of the area
> Note buildings of particular significance to the character of the area
> Note also important streetscapes, vistas, planting and the like
> Note the influence of setting on the area, including views in and out of it
> Identify those parts of the area that detract from its character and special interest

See 3.2 - 3.4

3. Establish policies and objectives for the area

> Undertake a photographic survey of the area
> If appropriate, carry out an architectural inventory of the structures and features within the area
> Write a description and appraisal of the area explaining its character and special interest
> Write policies and objectives for preserving the character of the area
> Review the status of protected structures within the area
> Ensure the objectives of the ACA do not conflict with other objectives such as zoning or with other statutory designations

See 3.5 and 3.6

4. Designate the ACA using the procedures of

> Section 12 when making the development plan
> Section 13 as a variation of the development plan

5. Procedures

> Send notice to the Minister, the other prescribed bodies and those bodies specified in the Act
> Advertise preparation of draft plan, or draft variation, in the press
> Display draft plan, or draft variation, which includes proposed ACA
> Receive comments, prepare Manager's Report and present to council members
> Members accept or amend the plan, or variation, which includes the proposed ACA
> Advertise and display amendments if material alterations are to be made
> Members make final decision on adopting the development plan, or the variation
> Publicise the final decision of the planning authority, as appropriate
> ACA designation carries through to next development plan unless modified by the members

See S. 12 and S. 13 of the 2000 Act

Declarations

4.1 Purpose and Limits of a Declaration

4.1.1 Where a building is a protected structure or a proposed protected structure, works which are normally exempt from the requirement of planning permission are not exempted development where they would materially affect the character of a protected structure or any element of it which contributes to its special interest. Section 57 of the Planning and Development Act 2000 allows the owner or occupier of a protected structure to make a written request to the planning authority for a declaration as to the type of works the authority considers would or would not materially affect the character of the protected structure. It should be noted that Section 57 does not apply to proposed protected structures nor to buildings within ACAs.

4.1.2 In relation to protected structures and proposed protected structures, the definition of 'works' in the 2000 Act is expanded from 'construction, excavation, demolition, extension, alteration, repair or renewal' to include 'any act or operation involving the application or removal of plaster, paint, wallpaper, tiles or other material to or from the surfaces of the interior or exterior of a structure'.[1] Any or all of these works have the potential to materially affect the character of a protected structure.

The application, and subsequent removal, of paint from terracotta (and soft stones such as sandstone) can cause damage to the material and jeopardise its future conservation

The rendering of the terraced building on the left has altered the character, not only of the individual building, but of a terrace of protected structures

4.1.3 Declarations may be used as a formal advice mechanism for the owner and occupier of a protected structure as issues arise which require clarification and for which an owner or occupier may need the reassurance of formal written notification from their planning authority. Declarations can be issued to permit specific minor works, including enabling works that, in the opinion of the planning authority, would not materially affect the character of the protected structure. However, it is always preferable to inspect, assess and give formal recommendations for the complete structure where this is feasible, to ensure that its full character is taken into account in the declaration. A declaration relating only to a specific part of a structure should clearly state its limited purpose.

4.1.4 A declaration must not exempt works that would have a material effect on the character of a protected structure. A declaration cannot exempt development that would not otherwise be exempt from a requirement for planning permission.

4.1.5 It is not necessary for the applicant to have any specific works in mind when applying for a declaration. Indeed, if the owner or occupier is contemplating major works to a protected structure, pre-planning discussions with the planning authority may be advisable and, depending on the outcome, the submission of a planning application.

4.1.6 Declarations relating to places of public worship are subject to special considerations.[2]

4.1.7 The issue of a declaration is a service that the planning authority provides to the owner or occupier of a protected structure in order to clarify for them their duties and rights. Owners and occupiers of protected structures should be encouraged to avail of this service by highlighting its availability, for example, in the development plan or in locally produced information leaflets. While the owner or occupier of a proposed protected structure may not seek a formal declaration, they may nonetheless be given informal guidance on exempted development issues in relation to their structure.

[1] Section 2 (1), 2000 Act

[2] Section 57 (5), 2000 Act; see also Chapter 5 below

4.2 Role of An Bord Pleanála

4.2.1 Under Section 13 of the Planning and Development (Amendment) Act 2002, any person to whom a declaration has issued under Section 57 (3), or a declaration reviewed under Section 57 (7) of the 2000 Act, may refer the declaration to An Bord Pleanála for review. This referral must be made within four weeks of the date of issue of the declaration. The details of any such declaration issued by the planning authority or of a decision by the Board must be entered on the planning register and the protected structure file kept by the planning authority. In addition, a copy of the declaration or decision must be available for inspection by the public during office hours at the offices of the planning authority.

4.3 Preparation and Evaluation Procedures for Declarations

4.3.1 The following advice relates to a declaration issued under Section 57 of the Planning and Development Act 2000 and should not be confused with the declaration and referral provisions in Section 5 of the same Act.

4.3.2 Where a declaration is sought, the planning authority should have regard to the detailed notes below and in Part 2 of these guidelines in order to relate the special interest of the protected structure to the type of works that would affect it. Where necessary, the planning authority should avail of expert architectural conservation advice in this matter. It is not appropriate to issue a declaration without inspecting the structure.

4.3.3 Applicants should be asked to provide all information they may possess relevant to processing the declaration and to allow full access to the structure, or to that part of it that is in their ownership or occupancy, in order to facilitate and expedite the declaration process.

4.3.4 The inspector should check whether a previous declaration has been issued for the structure or any adjacent protected structures and should also consult the record of the details of any relevant decisions on declarations forwarded to the planning authority by An Bord Pleanála.

4.4 Inspection

4.4.1 The inspection of the protected structure should be made by a suitably qualified person competent to make a qualitative assessment of the potential impact of works on the character and special interest of the protected structure. The inspector should refer as necessary to historic maps, photographs or other documents to inform his or her assessment of the structure. The inspector should delineate the boundary of the property that the declaration is considered to cover, taking into account maps or other documents provided by the applicant. He or she should note if any part of the structure is omitted from the declaration by virtue of being in separate ownership, even where this may be within the curtilage of the protected structure or be a specified feature in the attendant grounds.

4.4.2 The inspector may be the first person to visit the site on behalf of the planning authority and to interact with an owner or occupier regarding the architectural heritage aspects of their property. Where appropriate, the inspector should use the opportunity to point out the character and special interest of the protected structure to the owner or occupier and be prepared to interest them in its proper conservation and maintenance. The inspector should inform the owner or occupier of the benefits of using good professional advice and contractors experienced in conservation when undertaking works to the structure.

4.4.3 The structure, or the relevant part of the structure, should be inspected, internally and externally, including all ancillary structures or features. The structure's composition, construction materials and the features that constitute its character and special interest should be identified and documented. Where possible, this should be carried out to standards of the National Inventory of Architectural Heritage. Where this is not possible, a freestyle summary description of the structure should be prepared as part of the evaluation. The inspector should briefly describe any other nearby structures, not necessarily the subject of the current declaration but which may have been originally associated with it. This will allow for a fuller understanding of the history or development of the site. The description of the structure as inspected is essential to ensure no misunderstanding occurs with regard to its condition at the time, including dilapidations that it is not the purpose of the declaration to remedy. However, the description of the structure is secondary to the categorisation of the works into those that would, and would not, materially affect its character.

The inspection should, wherever possible, be extended to include the structures within the curtilage of the protected structure and their interiors

There may be other structures nearby which have an association with the structure that is the subject of the inspection and will contribute to a fuller understanding of the site, such as earlier houses, castles or industrial remains

4.5 Evaluation

4.5.1 Taking into account its special interest, character and sensitivity to change, the capacity of the structure to be affected by works should be evaluated. Reference could be made to the sample phrases set out in paragraph 4.12 below to identify the types of works that would or would not affect its character.

4.5.2 Relevant information in the following documents should be taken into account:

a) Part 2 of these guidelines;
b) previously issued declarations on the planning register;
c) any relevant information included in the RPS of determinations issued by An Bord Pleanála;

d) *Conservation Guidelines* published by the Department of the Environment and Local Government in 1996.

4.5.3 The senior planner for the area and the conservation officer, where available, should agree the type of works that would or would not be considered exempted development in respect of the particular protected structure. Care should be taken to ensure that the advice given is unambiguous. It should be set out in a format that is clear to read and easy to understand for people unfamiliar with specialist terminology.

4.5.4 The information in the RPS file may not include the precise extent of the curtilage of the protected structure. If possible, the planning authority and owner or occupier should agree at this stage what they consider to be its extent, in order to issue a declaration that refers to the whole of the protected structure including its curtilage. If this is impossible or impractical, the applicant should be asked to supply any information relating to the extent of the property in respect of which the declaration is sought. Without knowing the extent of the property, the declaration can still be completed but should clearly state that the curtilage has not been determined, meaning that the declaration relates only to the principal structure, or part thereof, and to any other named structures but not necessarily to the full curtilage.

4.6 The Declaration Form

4.6.1 Suggested information to be included in a declaration is set out in a sample declaration form at Table IV below. The following information should be included as a minimum:

a) name of applicant for the declaration;
b) applicant's status in relation to the structure;
c) date of request for the declaration;
d) date of inspection by the planning authority's appointed inspector;
e) date of issue of the declaration;
f) unique identity number of the protected structure from the RPS;
g) location of the structure, for example, using National Grid co-ordinates;
h) address of the structure;
i) protection status of the structure under the Planning and Development Act 2000 and under

the National Monuments Acts 1930 – 2004 (if any);

j) a brief description of the protected structure;

k) if the structure has been recorded by the National Inventory of Architectural Heritage, its NIAH registration number;

l) a list of works which would materially affect the character of the structure and as a result require planning permission;

m) a list of works which would not materially affect the character of the structure.

4.6.2 The planning authority is required to keep details of any declaration issued on its planning register. Planners dealing with subsequent planning applications and members of the public should be able to view the declaration at the offices of the planning authority, subject to the privacy restrictions recommended in paragraph 4.7 below.

4.7 Privacy

4.7.1 The complete declaration file will include information relating to the special architectural, historical, archaeological, artistic, cultural, scientific, social or technical interest of the protected structure. However, in the interests of respecting the privacy and security of a building's owners and occupiers, it may be necessary to hold much of the information collected in the course of the declaration inspection in a reserved part of the file on the protected structure. Any photographs or information of a sensitive nature relating to the interior of a building obtained in the course of the inspection should be kept in that reserved part of the declaration file.

4.7.2 Consequently, it is recommended that the file be in two parts: one that is readily available to the public and would include information that is public in nature and another part that is reserved in the interests of respecting the privacy and security of the owner or occupier.

4.7.3 The provisions of the Freedom of Information Acts 1997 - 2003 shall be applicable in any instance.

4.8 Requests to Exempt Urgent Works or Enabling Works

4.8.1 In cases where the planning authority is notified of a need to carry out specific urgent works, the relevant officer should first ascertain if the works are indeed urgent and necessary. If satisfied that they are, the planning authority should inform the owner in writing, identifying the specific works necessary to protect the fabric of the building. If it is felt that they are not urgent and necessary, the planning authority should advise that a declaration be sought or, where relevant, planning permission. The remedies available under the Act for such cases include Section 59 (Notice to require works against endangerment) or Section 60 (Notice to require the restoration of character). One or other, or both, of these Sections of the Act may be invoked if necessary, preferably with the agreement of the owner or occupier so that works can proceed without delay.

Urgent works may be needed to secure the fabric of a building following damage

4.8.2 Where enabling works are required to determine the type or scale of works necessary, and these enabling works are not extensive, excessively invasive and would not result in irreversible damage, the planning authority may consider specifically exempting such works by means of a declaration. However, where the works would materially affect the character of the protected structure, then planning permission will be required.[3]

Opening-up works may be needed to allow a full understanding of the structure prior to making development proposals but these works should not damage its special interest

4.9 Protected Structures in Multiple Occupancy

4.9.1 A protected structure may consist of a single site or building and yet be subdivided into several unrelated occupancies. For example, a building may have been divided into flats, or a former outbuilding may no longer be in the same ownership as the main house. Where one of a number of occupiers requests a declaration and an inspection is arranged, the declaration issued will relate only to the part of the structure for which the request was made. Consideration should be given at that time to encouraging the other occupiers of the structure to seek a declaration for the structure as a whole, as is recommended above. A declaration encompassing the entire protected structure would help ensure that repairs and maintenance are approached in a coherent manner by all occupiers.

4.10 Review of Previously Issued Declarations

4.10.1 It may be necessary from time to time for the planning authority to review a previously issued declaration or to issue a declaration for a complete structure in place of one or more declarations already issued in respect of part or parts of the structure. It may also, for example, be necessary to take cognisance of new information forwarded to it by the owner or occupier, An Bord Pleanála or by members of the public in relation to a protected structure where declarations have previously been issued. In the light of any such information, a planning authority may wish to reconsider works previously deemed to be exempted development or the references to works included in, or indeed omitted from, the previously issued declaration.

4.10.2 If it is appropriate to modify the declaration as to what works would require planning permission, a revised declaration should be issued as soon as is practicable. The review of a declaration will not affect any works carried out in reliance on the declaration prior to review.[4]

4.11 Maintenance

4.11.1 The declaration should indicate works considered to be routine maintenance which can be undertaken without materially affecting the character of the protected structure. In considering routine maintenance in a declaration, care should be taken to require that the works always follow conservation principles and best practice.[5]

4.12 Sample Phrases for Use in Declarations

4.12.1 Some or all of the phrases below could be used in drawing up declarations. The use of a phrase in a declaration should be construed to refer to all the works detailed under that heading unless exceptions are made. The phrases or headings set out below do not refer to mutually exclusive types of works. Therefore, particular care should be given to ensuring that unambiguous advice is given.

4.12.2 This should not be seen as an exhaustive list, and the circumstances of each protected structure may require reference to specific types of works that are not included in this list. The detailed guidance notes in Part 2 of these guidelines under the heading 'Identifying the special features for protection' are designed to assist planning authorities in carrying out inspections for declarations. Depending on the individual circumstances and the special interests of the structure, the following works might require planning permission:

Changes to the exterior appearance of walls, roofs or openings

4.12.3 Works which would materially alter the character of the exterior of a building may include the following:

a) walls: comprehensive (as opposed to localised) repointing; repointing in a style or material other than the existing; removal of render; re-facing in an applied layer of masonry, brick, wood, plaster or paint; mortar repairs of brick or stone; damp-proofing of walls; cleaning of masonry; removal or relocation of decorative plaques; painting of any previously unpainted surface; addition of new masonry to a ruinous structure or removal of existing material;[6]

Repointing which uses methods and materials other than the originals may alter the character of the building as has happened with the example on the left of this photograph

b) roofs: works that would result in damage to, or removal of, original or early surviving chimneys; damage or removal of natural slate roof-covering; replacement of existing structural elements, rainwater goods, coping stones, gable or eaves parapets; addition of fascia boards or boxing in of eaves; removal or reconstruction of features such as bell-cotes, crenellations, finials or any other feature of the roofscape; the fitting or removal of rooflights;[7]

The removal of chimney stacks can damage the appearance of an entire building

c) openings: alterations to structural openings; replacement of doors or windows; repair of windows where replacement of sashes or casements is required; replacement of single glass panes with double-glazed units, reinforced glass or textured glass; renovation, removal or replacement of features such as fanlights, letterboxes, bell-pulls or other door ironmongery; provision or removal of patent reveals or other dressings; painting of any previously unpainted surfaces; permanent removal of paint from fanlights[8].

Uncoordinated programmes of stone cleaning can create aesthetic problems in terraces of similar buildings

The replacement of original features, in this case the fanlight and door, with substitutes made from inappropriate materials should not be considered exempt

Changes to the internal layout

4.12.4 Alterations to the internal layout, including those required for fire safety purposes or to improve access; alterations that would affect the original or early surviving plan form or section; the insertion of fixed partitions; the breaking out of new openings between rooms or spaces; the insertion of new doors or screens; the alteration of floor levels; the insertion of suspended ceilings; alterations to the layout or form of stairwells.[9]

6 See also Chapter 8   *7 See also Chapter 9*   *8 See also Chapter 10*   *9 See also Chapter 11*

The insertion of new partitions may require planning permission

In these examples, interior features of importance have been damaged and any proposed repair will require to be carried out to a high standard in order for the work to be considered exempted development

The careful removal of later alterations of little interest, such as this half floor and steps, may be exempted by a declaration

Changes to the internal surfaces, finishes or linings

4.12.5 Alterations, including those required to meet the requirements of the Building Regulations, that would involve the loss of, removal of or damage to original or old internal joinery items (such as windows and windowcases, staircases, doors and doorcases, skirting-boards, dado rails, panelling or decorative plasterwork); fitting of mounted signage; alterations to or replacement of, floor surfaces; replacement of integral floor coverings or structural elements; works to plasterwork ceilings or masonry or plaster vaulting including any work that has an effect on cornices or other associated details; removal of fireplaces or chimneypieces including mantel shelves, hearthstones or chimneybreasts; alteration or removal of staircases and all associated joinery masonry or plaster elements; alteration or removal of important fixtures or fixed furniture, such as built-in seating, counter-tops, bar gantries or cupboards; the removal of paint or wallpaper.[10]

[10] See also Chapter 11

[11] See also Chapter 11

Installation or repair of internal mechanical services

4.12.6 Insertion of fire detection or security systems, equipment or fixtures; fixing of panelling; installation of lifts or dumb-waiters; rewiring or replumbing.[11]

Poorly-executed and badly-located service installations can have a serious effect on the character and appearance of a protected structure

Extensions

4.12.7 The building of an extension to a premises including one which affects an existing opening or requires the breaking out of a new opening or which conflicts with existing architectural elements.

Changes within the curtilage of the building

4.12.8 The breaking out of new openings in, or rendering or repointing of, existing walls within, or forming the boundary of, the curtilage; the erection of structures for agricultural purposes; the taking down of features such as statuary; the removal of other hard landscaping features such as paving, terracing, railings or fencing.[12]

4.13. Exemptions

4.13.1 It could be indicated in a declaration that, depending on the nature of the works involved and the special interest of the structure, some works to a protected structure might not require planning permission. Some examples are given below.

The alteration or demolition of original boundary walls and railings can rarely be considered exempted development

Redecoration

4.13.2 The application, but not removal, of paint or wallpaper, where plasterwork features or underlying coatings or underlays are not compromised, and the repair of damaged plasterwork in compatible materials to match existing work.

Restoration of character

4.13.3 Replacement of previous inappropriate alterations such as uPVC or aluminium windows with appropriately detailed replacement windows; replacement of fibre-cement roof tiles with natural slate.

12 *See also Chapter 13*

These replacement windows, although in many respects well detailed, have horns on the sashes, which is incorrect for the period of the building

Demolition or alteration of a modern extension

4.13.4 Where this is defined graphically on a drawing or plan or otherwise specified.

Routine maintenance

4.13.5 Regular maintenance to keep a building weathertight; the securing but not the replacement of existing elements of windows and doors; clearance of gutters and downpipes; refixing of loose slates; repainting of previously painted surfaces; repair and maintenance works carried out in accordance with the Department of the Environment and Local Government *Conservation Guidelines*; minor alterations to services (but excluding the installation of major services such as lifts and air-conditioning).

4.14 Sample Declarations

4.14.1 The sample declaration form shown in Table IV may be used as a template when issuing a declaration. Two examples of declarations follow, Tables V and VI, to illustrate how the declaration process can be operated. In the case of the Example A, a sketched drawing is necessary to the facilitate the understanding of the declaration. In each case the declaration gives certainty to the owner and/or occupier of the property as to their responsibilities under the Planning and Development Act 2000.

Example A

4.14.2 The complex example illustrated in Table V requires a map and sketch section to ensure that the declaration can be clearly understood. It shows how the declaration can be used to inform an owner or occupier of the parts of the structure that are sensitive from an architectural heritage point of view, and in which alterations would therefore require planning permission. It also shows the owner or occupier, in a general way, what alterations to the structure can be effected without requiring planning permission under the Act. In this case, the declaration would suggest to the owner or occupier to confine renovations to the parts of his property that do not have architectural heritage value unless he or she applies for planning permission. The drawing will also suggest to an owner or occupier where new development could be located on the property to minimise interference with the architectural heritage.

Example B

4.14.3 The example shown in Table VI indicates how a declaration could treat a building with a fine exterior of high-quality materials but which retains no internal fabric of architectural heritage interest. This gives the occupier a clear idea of how to retain what is valuable about the building, while acknowledging that changes can be carried out internally as exempted development.

Table IV Sample Declaration Form

Declaration

In accordance with Section 57 (2) of the Planning and Development Act 2000

Planning Authority:

This declaration specifies what works would, or would not, in the opinion of the planning authority materially affect the character of the protected structure, or any element thereof, and, as a result, require planning permission. Under the Act, protection extends to the entire structure including its interior and the land lying within its curtilage. It also extends to any other structures lying within the curtilage of the protected structure, to their interiors and to all fixtures and features that form part of the interior or exterior of any of these structures. Where specified in the Record of Protected Structures, protection may also extend to any other feature within the attendant grounds of the protected structure.

Nothing in this declaration exempts works that would not otherwise be exempt from a requirement for planning permission. Changes of use or intensification of the current use may require planning permission. If in doubt, the owner/occupier should consult the planning authority for further advice before commencing any works.

Applicant Name:

Status (i.e. Owner or Occupier):

Date of Request for Declaration: | **Date of Inspection:**

Date of Issue of Declaration: | **Previous Declaration(s):**

Address: | **Location:**

Name of Building: | National Grid co-ordinates: E   N

Address 1: | O.S. Map Type:

Address 2: | Map Sheet:

Address 3: | Site Number:

Protection Status:	Y/N		Details:
Under the Planning and Development Act 2000:			
Record of Protected Structures	Y	N	
Architectural Conservation Area	Y	N	
Under the National Monuments Acts 1930 - 2004:			
Record of Monuments and Places	Y	N	
Zone of Archaeological Potential	Y	N	
Preservation Order or Temporary P.O.	Y	N	

NIAH Registration Number (if applicable):

Brief description of the structure:

Table IV continued...

Works which would materially affect the character of the protected structure and, as a result, require planning permission:

Works which would not materially affect the character of the protected structure:

Special remarks:

Any further documentation attached (annotated maps or plans, photographs, sketches, notes, etc.)? Y/N

Signed by Inspector:

Signed by Planning Authority Officer:

Date:

Date:

Table V Sample Declaration Example A

Declaration

Issued in accordance with Section 57 (2) of the Planning and Development Act 2000

Planning Authority: Ballyfoyle Town Council

This declaration specifies what works would, or would not, in the opinion of the planning authority materially affect the character of the protected structure, or any element thereof, and, as a result, require planning permission. Under the Act, protection extends to the entire structure including its interior and the land lying within its curtilage. It also extends to any other structures lying within the curtilage of the protected structure, to their interiors and to all fixtures and features that form part of the interior or exterior of any of these structures. Where specified in the Record of Protected Structures, protection may also extend to any other feature within the attendant grounds of the protected structure.

Nothing in this declaration exempts works that would not otherwise be exempt from a requirement for planning permission. Changes of use or intensification of the current use may require planning permission. If in doubt, the owner/occupier should consult the planning authority for further advice before commencing any works.

Applicant Name: Dermot Kehoe

Status (i.e. Owner or Occupier): Occupier

Date of Request for Declaration: 20/7/03   **Date of Inspection:** 8/8/03

Date of Issue of Declaration: 11/9/03   **Previous Declaration(s):** None

Address:

Name of Building: Central Hotel

Address 1: 25-27 O'Connell Street

Address 2: Ballyfoyle

Address 3: Co. Donegal

Location:

National Grid co-ordinates: E 123456   N 654321

O.S. Map Type: 1:1000 scale

Map Sheet: 5432-10

Site Number: 876

Protection Status:	Y/N	Details:
Under the Planning and Development Act 2000:		
Record of Protected Structures	Yes	Development Plan 2002; p.32; Ref No. 249
Architectural Conservation Area	Yes	Development Plan 2002; p.45
Under the National Monuments Acts 1930 - 2004:		
Record of Monuments and Places	No	-
Zone of Archaeological Potential	No	-
Preservation Order or Temporary P.O.	No	-

NIAH Registration Number (if applicable): 40800424, 40800425, 40800426, 40800427

Brief description of the structure:

Mid-terrace, eleven-bay, four-storey hotel comprising three former terraced houses constructed c.1830; having two and three-storey extensions to the rear constructed c. 1970; with outhouse and yard beyond mews lane.

Table V Sample Declaration Example A, continued...

Works which would materially affect the character of the protected structure and, as a result, require planning permission:

Area I (coloured blue on attached sketches):	Area II (coloured orange on attached sketches):
i) changes to internal layout;	i) alterations to exterior appearance, and
ii) changes to exterior appearance;	ii) extensions.
iii) changes to internal surfaces, finishes or linings;	Area III (outlined in orange on attached sketches):
iv) installation or repair of services, and	i) removal of cobblestones, and
v) extensions.	ii) demolition of stone boundary walls.
	Area IV (coloured yellow on attached sketches):
	i) extensions, and
	ii) any internal structural re-ordering in the proximity of Areas I and II above.

Works which would not materially affect the character of the protected structure:

Area I (coloured blue on attached sketches):	Area III (outlined in orange on attached sketches):
i) painting and decoration, and	Area IV (coloured yellow on attached sketches):
ii) routine maintenance.	i) changes to external appearance;
Area II (coloured orange on attached sketches):	ii) changes to internal layout;
i) changes to internal layout;	iii) redecoration, and
ii) changes to internal surfaces, finishes or linings;	iv) routine maintenance.
iii) installation or repair of internal services;	
iv) redecoration, and	
v) routine maintenance.	

Special remarks:

Note, this property was recorded by the NIAH in four separate sections which correspond to the four separate areas above.

Any further documentation attached (annotated maps or plans, photographs, sketches, notes, etc.)? Y/N
Yes, annotated sketch plans and sections attached.

Signed by Inspector:	Signed by Planning Authority Officer:
Date:	Date:

Table V Sample Declaration Example A - Map

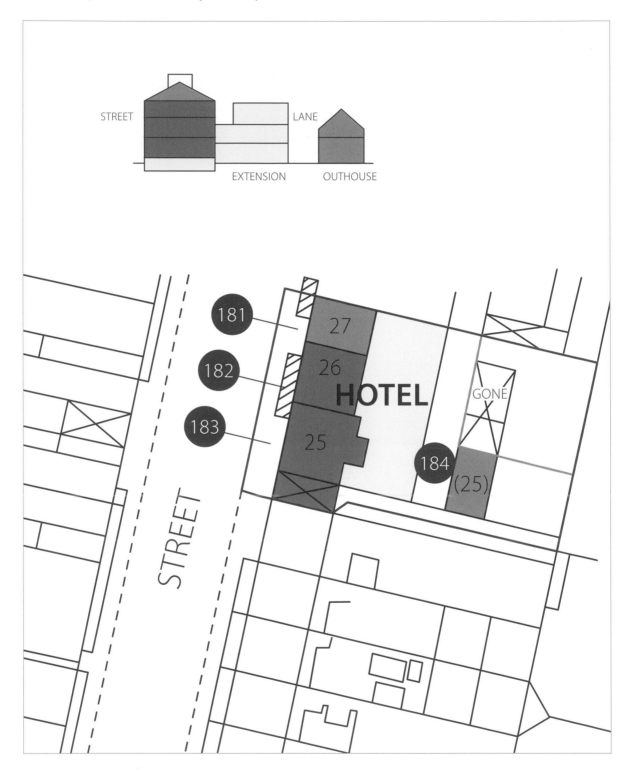

Table VI Sample Declaration Example B

Declaration

Issued in accordance with Section 57 (2) of the Planning and Development Act 2000

Planning Authority: Westmeath County Council

This declaration specifies what works would, or would not, in the opinion of the planning authority materially affect the character of the protected structure, or any element thereof, and, as a result, require planning permission. Under the Act, protection extends to the entire structure including its interior and the land lying within its curtilage. It also extends to any other structures lying within the curtilage of the protected structure, to their interiors and to all fixtures and features that form part of the interior or exterior of any of these structures. Where specified in the Record of Protected Structures, protection may also extend to any other feature within the attendant grounds of the protected structure.

Nothing in this declaration exempts works that would not otherwise be exempt from a requirement for planning permission. Changes of use or intensification of the current use may require planning permission. If in doubt, the owner/occupier should consult the planning authority for further advice before commencing any works.

Applicant Name: Prudential Bank Ltd.

Status (i.e. Owner or Occupier): Owner

Date of Request for Declaration: 10 January 2004   **Date of Inspection:** 15 February 2004

Date of Issue of Declaration: 25 February 2004   **Previous Declaration(s):** Yes, issued 22 May 2001 (see RPS file)

Address:

Name of Building:	Prudential Bank
Address 1:	Main Street
Address 2:	Corballymore
Address 3:	Co. Westmeath

Location:

National Grid co-ordinates:	E 123456 N 654321
O.S. Map Type:	6 inch: 1 mile Ordnance Survey
Map Sheet:	50
Site Number:	004

Protection Status:	Y/N	Details:
Under the Planning and Development Act 2000:		
Record of Protected Structures	Y	Development Plan 2000; p.27; Ref. E004
Architectural Conservation Area	Y	-
Under the National Monuments Acts 1930 - 2004:		
Record of Monuments and Places	N	-
Zone of Archaeological Potential	Y	RMP Ref. WM050-010 'Town'
Preservation Order or Temporary P.O.	N	-

NIAH Registration Number (if applicable): N/A

Brief description of the structure:

Detached four-bay, two-storey over basement, late-Victorian redbrick bank, designed by William Caldbeck and constructed c.1880; having a fine carved stone doorcase and hood mouldings to façade with a shallow balcony at first floor level over the entrance. Interior remodelled c.1975 and outbuildings demolished.

Table VI Sample Declaration Example B, continued:

Works which would materially affect the character of the protected structure and, as a result, require planning permission:

i) changes to external appearance, and

ii) extensions.

Works which would not materially affect the character of the protected structure:

i) internal works, and

v) routine maintenance.

Special remarks:

Building interior comprehensively altered c.1975 with no original internal detailing surviving. At the same time the outbuildings were demolished to make way for car-parking. However, the building retains a fine façade and continues to be an important element of the streetscape of the town.

Any further documentation attached (annotated maps or plans, photographs, sketches, notes, etc.)? Y/N

No

Signed by Inspector:

Signed by Planning Authority Officer:

Date:

Date:

Table VI Sample Declaration Example B - Map

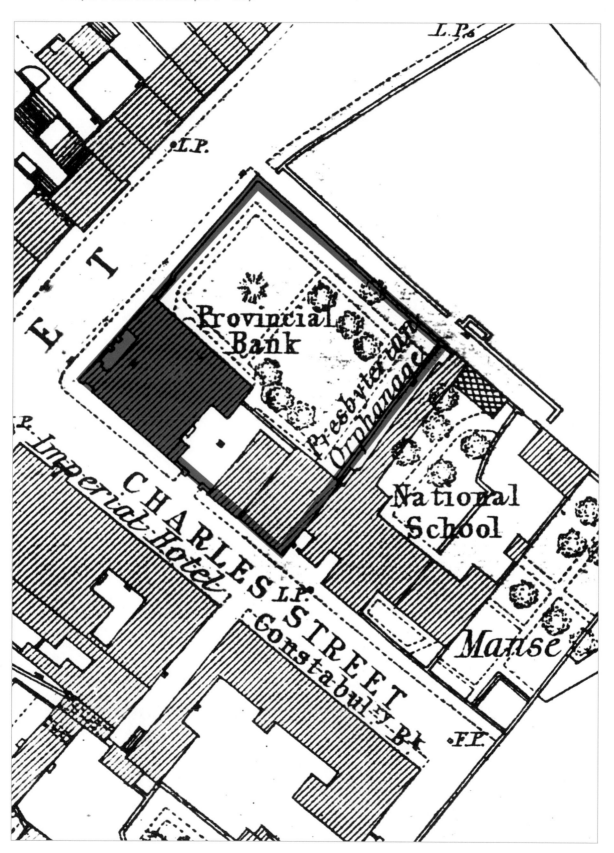

Table VII An Outline of Declaration Procedures

1. When notifying owners and/or occupiers of protected structures:

> Inform them of their right to request a declaration under S.57 of the Act
> Inform them of the implications of development on a protected structure
> Explain the declaration procedure and how it might best suit their purposes
> Inform them of the type and detail of information they should provide when applying for a declaration

See 4.1

2. On receiving a request for a declaration:

> Establish the status of the person making the request (i.e. owner or occupier)
> Confirm that clear information as been submitted as to the extent of the property in that person's ownership or control
> Consult the planning register for any previous declarations issued
> Consult An Bord Pleanála's record of determinations for any relevant precedents
> Consult background material relating to the protected structure such as historic maps, photographs, NIAH survey and other documents

See 4.2 and 4.3

3. When inspecting the structure:

> Organise an inspection of the protected structure by the conservation officer, other competent officer or a consultant with appropriate expertise
> Establish with the applicant the extent of the property to which the declaration will relate
> If the protected structure is in multiple occupancy, consider encouraging the other owners/occupiers to seek a declaration for the structure as a whole*
> If appropriate, engage with the applicant in pointing out the character and special interest of the structure and its proper conservation
> If possible, inspect adjacent structures which may originally have been associated with the protected structure
> Photograph the protected structure, concentrating on those parts of it which contribute to its special interest

See 4.4

*See 4.9

4. When writing the declaration:

> Consult Part 2 of these guidelines
> Consult with the relevant senior planner and conservation officer to agree the type of works that would or would not materially affect the character of the protected structure
> Write a freestyle, summary description of the structure
> Compile a list of works which would materially affect the character of the structure
> Compile a list of works which would not materially affect its character
> Include details of other relevant statutory protection which may apply
> Ensure the relevant content of any previously-issued declarations is included

See 4.5 and 4.6 and sample Declaration Forms

5. On issuing the declaration:

> Issue the declaration as a Manager's Order within 12 weeks of receipt of the request for the declaration
> Attach the declaration to the planning register
> Add to the public file photographs and any other information collected during the declaration process, retaining any sensitive material on a reserved part of the file in the interests of the privacy and security of the applicant

See 4.6 and 4.7

Places of
Public Worship

CHAPTER 5

Good stewardship, through appropriate maintenance and repair, has ensured the survival of thousands of historic places of public worship throughout the country

5.1 Architectural Heritage Protection for Places of Public Worship

5.1.1 Church buildings of various denominations constitute a substantial part of our architectural heritage and cultural patrimony. Places of public worship are often the finest and most prominent buildings in their locality and, because of their particular architectural, historical and social interest, proposals to alter such buildings will require careful consideration by the planning authority.

5.1.2 The heritage significance of church buildings, including their fixtures and features, lies in their central role in the community as places of public worship, usually over many generations. This patrimony is made up of works of architecture, painting and sculpture, as well as fittings and liturgical furnishings; features that have constituted the highest artistic expression of faith. The churches and their communities have, through their stewardship, kept and maintained these structures in good order, often through difficult times, so that they are now part of our architectural heritage. It is recognised that generally this continues to be done effectively and with great care.

¹ The guidance contained in this chapter was first published in a document entitled 'Architectural Heritage Protection for Places of Public Worship - guidelines for planning authorities', published by the Minister in November 2003 following consultation with representatives of the four main churches.

Places of public worship are often repositories of works of art such as painting and sculpture which continue to be added to by each generation as with this newly carved capital in Loughrea Cathedral

In this example, the original decorative paint scheme is being recreated based on detailed evidence

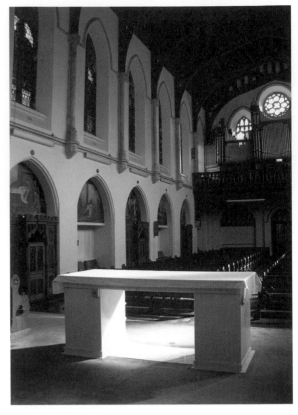

The adaptation of places of public worship may be sought to reflect revisions in liturgical requirements

5.2   Respecting Liturgical Requirements

5.2.1   Church buildings are used for the public worship of their congregations which includes many forms such as traditional services according to established rites, freer forms of a charismatic and evangelical form, experimental, occasional and devotional expressions of worship, teaching and mission. Respecting liturgical requirements includes recognising that churches may wish to adapt places of public worship in the light of contemporary revisions of their worship and mission. Thus church authorities may, in their places of public worship, require flexibility in the provision and arrangement of seating, in the openness of space, for example, for a baptismal font area; for the enlargement of an existing sanctuary or chancel or for the relocation of the altar-table and lectern. A church authority may also seek flexibility in the associated use of buildings and spaces within the curtilage, such as for access to another space or building for processions, children's liturgy and Sunday school.

5.2.2   The essential character of a church, expressed in its fabric and features, arises from its function as a place of public worship. When considering a declaration relating to a protected structure that is regularly used as a place of public worship or an application for planning permission for development to the interior of a protected structure that is regularly used as a place of public worship, the legislation provides that the planning authority shall respect liturgical requirements.

5.2.3   In relation to declarations, this may mean that some works which are necessitated by liturgical requirements and which have a material effect on the character of the structure do not require planning permission. Careful consideration should be given to the scale and potential impact of the works on the specific character of the individual structure. This is a matter of judgement to be made by the individual planning authority following consultation with the relevant church authority (see paragraph 5.3.1 below).

5.2.4 Many factors should be considered by a planning authority before issuing a declaration as to the type of works it considers would or would not materially affect the character of a protected structure that is regularly used as a place of public worship. The basic considerations are the effects, if any, of proposed works on the special interest of the structure, including its interior, and whether proposed alterations are necessitated by the liturgical requirements of worship. Planning authorities should consider whether any substantial structural changes or alterations to the existing plan-form are required for the proposed alterations, for example, the subdivision of important existing spaces, as well as any consequential effects in other parts of the building. Any proposed removal or alteration/destruction of important fixtures and fittings, for example galleries, box pews or fixed seating will require careful consideration. The age, rarity and craftsmanship of the internal fixtures and fittings can contribute to the architectural coherence of the whole building and, even where not original to the building, the internal fixtures and fittings can be an important part of a later remodelling of the interior. Impact on decoration, for example any interesting decorative schemes such as stencilled decoration, tiling or panelling, should be taken into account. It would also be appropriate to consider any proposals to minimise the impact of proposed changes. Any proposals to store or salvage fixtures and fittings proposed for removal should also be assessed carefully.

5.2.5 Where the planning authority determines that proposed works to the interior of a protected structure that is regularly used as a place of public worship require planning permission, it shall respect liturgical requirements in reaching a decision on the application for permission.

5.2.6 In a changing environment, the use that will generally give the greatest protection to a church that is a protected structure is as a church serving the community. Where works are proposed that are not required by the liturgy, but would facilitate a religious use continuing in a place of worship, the planning authority should respect the architectural heritage of the structure. In addition, it should consider whether the proposed works are directed at accommodating other compatible activities within the building or in its curtilage. This may help to ensure its continued viability in community use, primarily as a place of public worship. Such alterations would require a grant of planning permission.

Internal fixtures such as box pews, confessional boxes and altar rails can be significant elements of the character of the place of public worship

5.3   Consultations with Churches and Religious Authorities

5.3.1   In order to ensure that the appropriate balance is struck between the protection of the architectural heritage, and the need for continued use of the protected structure as a place of public worship, early consultation between the planning authority and the relevant church authority is necessary. Through this consultation, the planning authorities will ascertain the liturgical requirements in each case. The religious authorities consulted by the Minister have agreed to establish the following bodies (which, as well as liturgy, will draw on relevant expertise in art/architectural heritage) for consultations:

Roman Catholic Church

5.3.2   The consultations will be on a diocesan basis. Historic Churches Advisory Committees (or equivalent agencies) are to be established on a diocesan or inter-diocesan basis to advise the bishop on the heritage/historical factors in a place of worship for which a declaration is requested or a planning application is made. Each Committee will advise on the necessary documentation, including liturgical requirements, which will be forwarded to the planning authority. It will also be available for consultations with the planning authority. For churches vested in religious orders, the consultations will be with the provincial or regional superior (or in some monastic communities, the abbot or abbess).

Church of Ireland

5.3.3   The Representative Body of the Church of Ireland, subject to the Constitution of the Church of Ireland and pursuant to the powers granted to it to hold properties for the uses of the Church by the Irish Church Act 1869, will establish an Historic Churches Advisory Committee to advise dioceses and parishes on all matters pertaining to either a request for a declaration or a planning application concerning any place of public worship that is a protected structure.

Presbyterian Church in Ireland

5.3.4   The Presbyterian Church in Ireland will establish an Historic Churches Advisory Committee, appointed by the Board of Mission in Ireland, whose postal address is Church House, Fisherwick Place, Belfast, BT1 6DW.

Methodist Church in Ireland

5.3.5   The Methodist Church in Ireland is governed by the Annual Conference. All matters relating to consultations and declarations will be advised through the Conference Office, which will be responsible for appointing relevant persons to act on behalf of the Methodist Church in Ireland, and will regulate the supply of the necessary documentation for planning authorities.

5.4   Consultations with Other Religious Denominations and Communities

Other religious denominations

5.4.1   Consultations should be made through the local congregation with the appropriate religious authority, which will certify that the liturgical requirements stated in documentation to the planning authority are those of the particular religious denomination's worship and are in conformity with their traditions and customs.

Other religious communities

5.4.2   Consultations should be made through the local congregation with the appropriate leadership who will certify that the liturgical requirements stated in documentation to the local or planning authority are in conformity with their worship.

5.4.3   In order to ensure that these consultative mechanisms are as effective as possible, planning authorities and church authorities should begin the process as early as possible. Planning authorities may already have raised individual issues with the representative church bodies in their city or county area. Serious consideration should be given to establishing a continuing dialogue with those representative bodies, especially those with a number of protected structures, to devise a methodology that may be used in dealing with applications for declarations or planning permission. This should also allow the church bodies to give early indications where works are proposed to protected structures, and permit discussions on minimising the impact of proposed changes on the fabric of the protected structures in use for public worship.

5.5 Redundancy

5.5.1 The redundancy of a building as a place of public worship is a serious decision for a religious denomination. Several options can be considered including:

a) The religious denomination may wish to retain the building but for another purpose consistent with its own mission. In this case, an application for permission for a change of use could be treated sympathetically by the planning authority.

b) The protected structure may be loaned or sold to another religious denomination, assuring its continuance as a place of worship or building for use in accordance with the religious mission of the new occupant. If retained as a place of worship, incoming religious authorities may wish for alterations as required by its worship. In considering applications for declarations, or for permission to carry out internal works to make the structure suited to the new liturgical use, the planning authority shall respect liturgical requirements.

5.5.2 It may of course be decided to sell the protected structure. This may pose problems for the conservation of the building and its interior, especially where substantial works are proposed to accommodate the new use. In particular, consideration may have to be given to permitting the removal of some fixtures and fittings, which are of liturgical or devotional importance. These should be dealt with sensitively as set out in 5.5.3 below.

5.5.3 Changing liturgical requirements can have an impact on the spatial arrangements and the fixtures in a place of public worship. From a conservation viewpoint, liturgical fixtures that are no longer in liturgical use should not necessarily be removed. If it is necessary to remove them for liturgical reasons, it is important that they are removed with care so that they may be used or stored elsewhere, within the structure or otherwise, returned to the religious authority or donated to a museum. For example, the organ may be an important instrument that would merit efforts being made to find a new home for it.

The conversion of a redundant church to a socially-inclusive function is often a good way of retaining its central importance to the community as with this example of a former Presbyterian church which now houses a museum

Some redundant churches are also recorded monuments, or are within the area of constraint around the monument: they may be on the site of, beside or in the midst of ecclesiastical remains. This former Board of First Fruits church was built partly within the walls of a mediaeval church that is now a National Monument in state guardianship

Development Control

6.1   Development Control Policies and Objectives

6.1.1   Each development plan must include policy objectives to protect the architectural heritage in its functional area.[1] A primary policy should be to take the necessary steps to ensure the protection of the architectural heritage when exercising the development control function so that these structures retain their character and special interest and continue to contribute to the social and economic mix of the planning authority's functional area.

6.1.2   Suggested general policies to aid development control may include the following:

a)   identification of potential structures for protection within the functional area as a whole or within specified parts of the area, particularly where the NIAH has not yet been completed. This may be particularly appropriate in known areas of accelerated change;

b)   identification and designation of ACAs or ASPCs where areas of special interest exist within the functional area or where it is appropriate to protect the setting of a protected structure or protected structures;

c)   promotion of the reuse of redundant protected structures for their own economic benefit as well as that of the area in which they are located;

d)   requirement for development proposals to take account of the impact on protected structures, even where these are located outside the development site.

6.1.3   Policies to assist owners of protected structures and proposed protected structures, or buildings within ACAs at pre- and post-planning stage could include:

a)   offering pre-planning advice to owners and prospective owners of protected structures and proposed protected structures to complement formal development control policies;[2]

b)   promoting good standards of conservation in maintenance and development works including to protected structures in the planning authority's ownership;

c)   collating a database of conservation practitioners and craftworkers who operate within the functional area of the authority, to be available to owners and occupiers of protected structures or of buildings within ACAs;

d)   setting out the type of repair works or works to restore character that would be prioritised by the planning authority in disbursing grant-aid for protected structures;

e)   anticipating and encouraging, with financial support, the repair or redevelopment of those protected structures which are not obviously economically viable;

Policies could require that the impact on any protected structures adjacent to a development site be taken into account in development proposals

Development plan policies could be used to encourage the repair and reuse of protected structures or buildings in areas not otherwise economically attractive to private developers, through schemes such as Living over the Shop or LOTS

A best practice guide based on the experience gained in the restoration of these terraced buildings was subsequently published by the planning authority

[1] Section 10 (2) (f) and (g), 2000 Act

[2] Section 247, 2000 Act

Well-targeted financial assistance can mean the difference between the survival or gradual decay of vulnerable buildings

f) setting out the appropriate use of modern design and materials in works to protected structures;

g) establishing, when making an inventory or where queried, the extent of the curtilage of all protected structures and attendant grounds, if any, and mapping this information at an appropriate scale;

h) building up a comprehensive database of information on protected structures and ACAs as an aid to development control.

6.2 Planning Applications Step by Step

Pre-application consultations

6.2.1 Arrange these to provide general advice to developers regarding:

a) the availability of conservation expertise;

b) policy on, and standards for, conservation works for protected structures, proposed protected structures and the exteriors of buildings within ACAs and

c) the standard of documentation required for planning applications.

It would be useful to the planning authority to keep minutes of such meetings so that there is clarity on the matters discussed.

Requirements for planning applications

6.2.2 Ensure planning applications for protected structures and proposed protected structures are valid. By definition, this includes development within the curtilage of a protected structure or proposed protected structure. Planning applications should refer to the protected status on the public notices and adequately describe the potential impact of the proposals on the character of the structure by way of plans, photographs and any other necessary particulars.[3]

Notification to prescribed bodies

6.2.3 Send notification to the relevant prescribed bodies[4] as early as possible of applications that involve works to a protected structure, a proposed protected structure or a building in an ACA and also of applications for development which might detract from the appearance of any of these structures.

Consideration of application

6.2.4 Consider all written submissions or observations received within 5 weeks of the date of receipt of the application.[5] Take account of relevant information in RPS, declarations files and these guidelines. Consult with the conservation officer, where one is employed by the planning authority.

Consideration of impact on architectural heritage

6.2.5 Consider the potential impact of the development on the character of the protected structure, proposed protected structure or ACA when determining the application. Where demolition is proposed, consider whether exceptional circumstances apply.[6]

Further information

6.2.6 Seek further information where necessary to determine application.

Notification of decision

6.2.7 Issue the planning authority's decision to the applicant and notify the decision to all who made valid submissions.

Post-planning compliance

6.2.8 Assess submissions made in compliance with conditions of the permission. Refer to conservation officer for technical advice as necessary.

3 Article 23 (2), 2001 Regulations
4 Article 28 (1) (c), 2001 Regulations
5 Article 29 (1), 2001 Regulations
6 Section 57 (10) (b), 2000 Act

CHAPTER 6   DEVELOPMENT CONTROL

Enforcement

6.2.9 Inspect the development site to ensure that works are being carried out in accordance with the permission granted. Take appropriate action if unauthorised works or revisions have taken place that affect the character of the structure or endanger it.

6.3 Pre-Application Consultations

6.3.1 Planning authorities are encouraged to engage in pre-application consultation with owners and occupiers of protected structures and proposed protected structures in relation to proposed development.[7] This will offer an opportunity to direct an applicant's attention to the special requirements relating to the architectural heritage, including the type of information that must be submitted with the application and the resources that are in place to assist an applicant.

6.3.2 The conservation of historic buildings is a specialised discipline. An applicant should be advised that a level of specialised expertise may be necessary to guide on best practice in dealing with works to a protected structure. This will be increasingly important depending on the scale and complexity of works proposed to the structure or when considering the design and scale of new structures within the curtilage.

6.3.3. If the structure or site involved is also protected under the National Monuments Acts, it would be beneficial if both the planning authority and the applicant could apprise themselves of the fact at this stage.

If a protected structure is also a recorded monument under the National Monuments Acts (which may not always be obvious from its outward appearance), there are separate notification requirements under those Acts regarding proposed works

6.4 Information to Accompany Planning Applications

6.4.1 The 2000 Act provides for greater control over development that would affect the character of protected structures, proposed protected structures and the exterior of buildings within ACAs. Even apparently minor alterations to the fabric of these structures can impact on their character and special interest. But it is recognised that, over the lifetime of a structure, it may be necessary to accommodate appropriate change or new uses for a variety of reasons. In order to ensure that these changes have the minimum adverse impact upon the architectural heritage, the legislation requires additional procedures and information as part of the planning process.

6.4.2 The following guidance may aid in assessing the acceptable standard of planning applications relating to the architectural heritage, depending on the complexity and degree of intervention proposed to the structure.

Documentation to accompany an application

6.4.3 The level of documentation required to accompany a planning application works to a protected structure, a proposed protected structure or the exterior of a building within an ACA will depend on the scale, extent or complexity of the works involved. For example, works proposed to a confined area of a protected structure or works within the curtilage should not normally require extensive documentation regarding unaffected parts of the structure.

6.4.4 In the case of structures which have previously undergone inappropriate changes and which are now to be restored, emphasis should be put on describing the details of the proposed replacement elements and their interface with the historic fabric.

6.4.5 As indicated in the 2001 Regulations, a planning application for works to a protected structure or proposed protected structure must include (in addition to the normal requirements to supply maps and drawings) 'such photographs, plans and other particulars as are necessary to show how the development would affect the character of the structure.[8] The same requirements also apply to applications for permission for works to the exterior of a structure which is located within an ACA or an area it is proposed to designate as an ACA.

---

7 Section 247, 2000 Act

8 Article 23 (2), 2001 Regulations

CHAPTER 6 DEVELOPMENT CONTROL

Public notices

6.4.6 Public notices for any planning application that relates to a protected structure or a proposed protected structure are required to indicate this fact on public notices.[9] This includes both the required newspaper notice and the site notice.

Drawings

6.4.7 Additional drawings to those required under Article 23 (1) of the 2001 Regulations may be necessary to describe proposed works to a protected structure, or proposed protected structure. These drawings should be clear, comprehensible and may need to be to a larger scale. Where possible, drawings should be based on actual measurement and not on pre-existing plans. Except where the proposal involves little material alteration, separate annotated survey and proposal drawings can more clearly describe the changes.

6.4.8 The drawn information accompanying a planning application should concentrate on describing those parts or elements of the structure which will be impacted upon by the proposed development. The drawings should clearly indicate the location of works and the extent of alteration of the existing fabric. All works comprising proposed reconstruction, alteration or extension must be marked or coloured on the drawings to distinguish clearly between the existing structure and the proposed work.[10] Where interior works are proposed, every room or space to be affected should be annotated for ease of reference. Where there are separate survey drawings and proposal drawings, these should be set out and labelled for easy comparison.

6.4.9 It is a general requirement of planning applications that drawings of elevations should show the main features of any contiguous buildings.[11] The level of detail available may be dependent on access issues in specific cases. Ideally, in the case of a protected structure or a proposed structure, buildings and other features of interest within the curtilage should also be indicated on elevational drawings.

6.4.10 Planning authorities could consider requesting up to four additional copies of drawings to accompany an application relating to a protected structure or a building in an ACA; a total of ten sets of drawings for circulation to the prescribed bodies.

Photographs

6.4.11 While some general photographs will be necessary to set the context for the proposals, the photographs accompanying a planning application should concentrate on describing those parts or elements of the structure which will be impacted upon by the proposed development rather than provide an exhaustive survey of the development site.

Photographs accompanying a planning application should show the areas or elements proposed for alteration and be clear, focussed and legibly printed

6.4.12 All photographs should have clear captions identifying what they depict and, if necessary, should be cross-referenced to floor plans. The location and direction of the camera when the image was taken should be indicated on the survey drawings. Again it may be appropriate to seek additional copies of the photographs from the applicant for circulation to the prescribed bodies.

9 *Article 18 (1) (d) (iii), 2001 Regulations*
10 *Article 23 (1) (e), 2001 Regulations*
11 *Article 23 (1) (d), 2001 Regulations*

Other particulars

6.4.13 Article 23 (2) requires planning applications to be accompanied by 'other particulars as are necessary to show how the development would affect the character of the structure'. These other particulars are not specified but, depending on the circumstances and the nature of the proposed development, may include one or more of the following:

Written statement

6.4.14 A brief written statement is a useful tool as part of a planning application to help explain the rationale for the proposed development. This written statement could take the form of a cover letter. The statement could summarise the principal impacts on the character and special interest of the structure or site and describe how it is proposed to minimise these impacts. It may also describe how the works have been designed or specified to have regard to the character of the architectural heritage.

Architectural heritage impact assessment

6.4.15 For more extensive or complex works with a potential to have a major impact on the architectural heritage, a planning authority may require an applicant to submit a more detailed impact statement. This may be necessary to allow the planning authority to assess the full implications of the proposals and allow an informed decision to be made on the appropriateness of the development. An outline of the type of information that could be included in such an architectural heritage impact assessment is found in Appendix B of these guidelines.

Method statement and specification

6.4.16 A method statement and specification could be required for all works to the protected structure and any features of interest within the curtilage of the site which could affect their character and special interest.

Fire risk analysis

6.4.17 Works carried out in accordance with a fire safety certificate are not necessarily exempted development in the case of a protected structure or a proposed protected structure. Therefore careful consideration should be given in a planning application to any requirement for works to enhance fire safety. This could be done by way of a written summary describing the proposed works and setting out the way compliance with fire safety requirements could be achieved without adversely affecting the character of the structure, or how unavoidable impacts could be mitigated. In some cases, where the planning authority considers works proposed to enhance fire safety may necessitate an excessive amount of loss or disruption of historic fabric, the submission of a fire risk analysis could be required to accompany the application.[12]

6.5 Applications Required to be Accompanied by an EIS

6.5.1 Where a planning application is required to be accompanied by an Environmental Impact Statement, the EIS is required to include 'a description of the aspects of the environment likely to be significantly affected by the proposed development, including… the architectural and archaeological heritage, and the cultural heritage'.[13] The effect of this provision is to require that the architectural heritage, regardless of whether it has statutory protection or not, be taken into consideration when assessing the impact of these developments.

6.5.2 *Guidelines on the Information to be Contained in Environmental Impact Statements* were published by the Environmental Protection Agency in 2002. Those guidelines were followed by more detailed *Advice Notes on Current Practice in the preparation of Environmental Impact Statements* published in September 2003. The guidelines and advice notes are designed to assist developers in meeting the detailed requirements and to assist consent authorities in considering the adequacy of EISs submitted to them.

6.5.3 Note should also be taken of *Guidance for Consent Authorities regarding Sub-Threshold Developments* published by the Department of the Environment, Heritage and Local Government in August 2003.

6.5.4 The legislation relating to Environmental Impact Assessment is contained in Part X of the Planning and Development Act 2000.

6.6 Notification of Prescribed Bodies

6.6.1 Planning authorities are required by regulation to send notification to certain prescribed bodies when they receive planning applications which the planning authority considers would:

a) involve the carrying out of works to a protected structure or proposed protected structure, or to the exterior of a structure which is located within an ACA or a proposed ACA;

b) detract from the appearance of such a structure.[14]

6.6.2 It may not always be obvious when considering if notice should be sent to the prescribed bodies that the development site might be located within the curtilage of a protected structure or a proposed protected structure. A proposal might also detract from the appearance of a protected structure even if the protected structure is outside the lands under the control of the applicant and therefore is not itself identified in the submitted documents.

Adjoining buildings that are protected structures may be impacted upon, either directly or visually, although not actually part of the development site. This will be particularly obvious in the case of terraced buildings as in this example which has an important surviving mediaeval chimney stack on a party wall

6.6.3 Ideally, the notification to the prescribed bodies should include a copy of the planning application (including any EIS) together with submitted drawings, plans, photographs or other particulars.

6.6.4 The prescribed bodies for the purposes of Part IV of the Planning and Development Act 2000 are the Minister, the Heritage Council, An Taisce, the Arts Council and Bord Fáilte.[15]

6.7 Making Decisions on Planning Applications

6.7.1 A planning authority, or An Bord Pleanála on appeal, may impose any conditions relating to the protection of a protected structure or proposed protected structure without attracting compensation.[16] Any development that would materially affect the character of a protected structure or a proposed protected structure may be refused without attracting compensation.[17] Compensation is also excluded where a proposed development would adversely affect the character of an ACA.[18]

Framing conditions in a planning permission

6.7.2 A properly detailed planning application, as originally submitted or revised and/or clarified through submission of requested information, should obviate the need for the attachment of extensive planning conditions to a permission. However, where required, conditions could be attached with regard to:

a) agreement in writing with the planning authority of particular specifications which would be required in order to carry out a development in accordance with good conservation practice;

b) approval of samples of materials or workmanship prior to construction;

c) repair and retention of existing fabric and surviving material that contribute to the character of the structure, regardless of their age or condition;

d) recording or retention of concealed features or fabric exposed during works;

e) site supervision and project management by personnel suitably qualified in conservation during the progress of the works;

f) architectural salvaging;.[19]

g) reinstatement of features in the curtilage after temporary works;

h) protection of specified structures or features during the course of the works;

i) recording of the condition of building prior to development[20] (if not already requested as part of assessment process), or submission of an architectural heritage impact assessment to the planning authority for lodging with the Irish Architectural Archive;

j) monitoring of the works by an architect with conservation expertise and certification on completion that the works have been carried out in accordance with good conservation

14 *Article 28 (1) (c), 2001 Regulations*

15 *Article 52, 2001 Regulations*

16 *Fifth Schedule para. 34, 2000 Act*

17 *Third Schedule para. 3, 2000 Act*

18 *Fourth Schedule para. 13, 2000 Act*

19 *Section 34 (4) (p), 2000 Act and paragraphs 6.7.6 and 6.7.7*

20 *See paragraphs 6.7.3 - 6.7.5*

practice and in line with the conditions of the planning permission;

k) reinstatement of previously removed features to restore the character of the structure (with accurate detailing to be agreed if not already resolved);

l) phasing of work in a large-scale development so as to ensure that work to the protected structure is underway or will be completed in tandem with, or prior to, completion or occupation of new buildings.

Recording as a condition of permission

6.7.3 The demolition of a protected structure, or of elements which contribute to its special interest, may only be permitted in exceptional circumstances.[21] Where the dismantling or demolition of all or part of a protected structure is permitted, it may be a condition of permission that a record be made of the structure prior to the commencement of any works.[22] It should be considered that this is a permanent record which will have to substitute for the structure itself and should be capable of detailed analysis and interpretation.

6.7.4 Such archive-standard drawings should be produced on polyester film, linen, acid-free or rag paper, using permanent black ink. In these circumstances, dye-line prints are not acceptable, nor are copies of computer-aided design files. In addition to the full set of drawings, copies of original survey notes should be included with the report, as should copies of relevant earlier drawings, photographs with negatives (preferably dated), plans and maps.

6.7.5 Where a photographic record is to be made of all, or part of, a structure, the photographs should be of high quality. The use of a professional photographer should be considered and, where appropriate, the use of recording techniques such as rectified photography could be required. Black-and-white photography should be used when creating a permanent archive-quality record. Where it is essential to make an archive record of the colour of features, such as old or interesting wallpapers or painted decoration, colour slide film should be used and should be considered to be a supplement to, not a replacement for, black and white photography. Historic photographs should be identified by their archive name and negative number. One or more sets of legibly-sized prints should be included (for example, 20cm x 25cm).

Architectural salvaging as a condition of permission

6.7.6 The Act provides for making a condition of planning permission, where appropriate, the salvage of elements of special interest of a protected structure, or any element of a protected structure that is about to be altered or removed.[23] The removal of important or decorative elements should only be permitted where the developer has indicated how these elements will be used or maintained in the future, which, in order to mitigate the impact, should be relocated within the structure wherever possible. In such a case, the state of the structure or of the relevant interior spaces before dismantling should also be recorded, and two copies of the report sent to the planning authority (one for forwarding to the Irish Architectural Archive). All items permitted for removal and reinstatement should be tagged, photographed and stored securely, preferably on site.

6.7.7 In the case of the industrial heritage this may present particular problems, and expert advice should be sought, for example from the Industrial Heritage Association of Ireland.

6.8 General Types of Development

Extensions

6.8.1 It will often be necessary to permit appropriate new extensions to protected structures in order to make them fit for modern living and to keep them in viable economic use. Where the existing exterior appearance of a structure is of special interest, and its interior is of sufficient size, it may be possible to incorporate new functions or services within the existing envelope of the structure. With flexibility and imagination, it may be possible to use secondary spaces within the building, obviating the need to extend, where there would be minimal impact on fixtures and features of special interest. The cumulative effect of minor additions can compromise the special interest of a structure and the character of an ACA. The planning authority should consider this when assessing a proposal for even small extensions.

---

[21] Section 57 (10) (b), 2000 Act
[22] Section 34 (4) (p) (i), 2000 Act

[23] Section 34 (4) (p) (ii), 2000 Act

6.8.2   If planning permission is to be granted for an extension, the new work should involve the smallest possible loss of historic fabric and ensure that important features are not obscured, damaged or destroyed. In general, principal elevations of a protected structure (not necessarily just the façade) should not be adversely affected by new extensions. The design of symmetrical buildings or elevations should not be compromised by additions that would disrupt the symmetry or be detrimental to the design of the protected structure.

6.8.3   Generally, attempts should not be made to disguise new additions or extensions and make them appear to belong to the historic fabric. The architectural style of additions does not necessarily need to imitate historical styles or replicate the detailing of the original building in order to be considered acceptable. However, this should not be seen as a licence for unsympathetic or inappropriate work. Careful consideration of the palette of materials with which the works are to be executed can mediate between a modern design idiom and the historic fabric of the structure. Extensions should complement the original structure in terms of scale, materials and detailed design while reflecting the values of the present time.

6.8.4   In general, modern extensions to a protected structure do not have protected status themselves unless they contribute to the character of the structure. Therefore works to such an extension which do not affect the character of the protected structure itself, for example to the interior of the extension, would come within the normal rules relating to exemptions. However, new openings proposed from the principal structure into the extension would affect it. Care should be taken where works are proposed to extensions to ensure that they do not have an adverse effect on the character of the structure or its curtilage.

Well-considered extensions can be successfully integrated with a protected structure whether designed in a modern contrasting style (top) or in a matching historicist style (bottom)

6.8.5   In urban areas, careful consideration needs to be given to proposals for the construction of rear extensions to protected structures and buildings within ACAs. Rear elevations sometimes contain fabric that is useful in reading the history of the structure, for example surviving older windows or doors. The effect of extensions may have considerable impact on the appearance of buildings or on the setting of neighbouring buildings, or indeed on the appearance of the structure when viewed from a distance (or a set of similar structures such as in a terrace), and this should be considered by the planning authority when assessing applications.

6.8.6   The planning authority should discourage the infilling of gardens, lanes or courtyards of architectural or historical interest. Open spaces such as these have a function in the natural illumination and ventilation of a densely developed urban area. Where surviving plot-divisions remain in the older areas of towns, these can be of historic interest as indicators of the original layout of the area, for example the original burgage plots or defensive walls of mediaeval settlements (or line of the wall). They may even contain historic fabric and these structures and their precise alignment should be respected by any new development.

The size of new extensions should be in keeping with the scale of the protected structure

Extensions to the rear of a protected structure can have an impact on views of the building and also have the potential to affect the character of an ACA

Historic plot divisions can be an important aspect of the character of an area as with these burgage plots at Trim which survive from mediaeval times

6.8.7 There may be cases where the planning authority considers that additions cannot be permitted without seriously compromising the architectural significance of a protected structure or its setting; alternatively that they would be detrimental to the character of an ACA.[24] In such cases the proposals should not be permitted.

Material change of use

6.8.8 On the whole, the best way to prolong the life of a protected structure is to keep it in active use, ideally in its original use. Where this is not possible, there is a need for flexibility within development plan policies to be responsive to appropriate, alternative uses for a structure. A planning authority should carefully consider any proposed change of use and its implications for the fabric and character of the structure. A new use may have many implications for the structure which may not be immediately obvious, for example with regard to compliance with the Building Regulations.

[24] See also paragraph 7.13 'Avoiding Incremental Damage'

6.8.9   In considering an application for the material change of use of a protected structure, the planning authority will have to balance its continuing economic viability if the change is not permitted, with the effect on the character and special interest of its fabric of any consequent works if permission is granted. Where, having considered these issues, a planning authority considers that the alterations required to achieve a proposed change of use will not have an undue adverse effect on the special interest of the structure, the proposals may be granted subject to conditions as appropriate.

A material change of use can involve a large amount of alteration to the structure but may sometimes be necessary to ensure its future viability

6.8.10   Changes of use may lead to subsequent incremental proposals to change subsidiary features such as shopfronts, external signs, requirements for enhanced fire safety and the like. Impacts may arise to the curtilage of a protected structure from a change of use proposal, such as creating or increasing the need for car parking, creating or altering gateways or entrance arches for vehicular access. As many of these potential impacts as are foreseeable should be included as part of the planning application. If clarification is required of the implications of a change of use, this should be ascertained by way of a request for further information.

Some changes of use may lead to subsequent incremental changes. As many of these as possible should be anticipated and dealt with as part of the planning application. For example, extra storage space may be required (top) or additional entryphones (bottom). Any new signage should be kept to the necessary minimum (middle)

Demolition

6.8.11   The Act provides that permission may only be granted for the demolition of a protected structure or proposed protected structure in exceptional circumstances.[25] Where a proposal is made to demolish such a structure, it requires the strongest justification before it can be granted permission and will require input from an architect or engineer with specialist knowledge so that all options, other than demolition, receive serious consideration.

6.8.12   It may happen that the special interests of a protected structure have been damaged or eroded to an extent that demolition is permissible. In such cases, in order to avoid setting a precedent of permitting the demolition of a protected structure, it would be preferable to first remove it from the RPS. Any such cases should be carefully considered, as deliberate erosion of character or endangerment may be more appropriately tackled by enforcement action rather than permitting demolition.

25 *Section 57 (10) (b), 2000 Act*

6.8.13 Caution should be used when considering proposals to demolish parts of protected and proposed protected structures as these parts may be of importance to the cumulative historic interest of a building. Where partial demolition of a protected structure is proposed, the onus should be on the applicant to make a case that the part – whether or not it is original to the structure – does not contribute to the special interest of the whole, or that the demolition is essential to the proposed development and will allow for the proper conservation of the whole structure.

The demolition of a building's return can impact on neighbouring buildings also

Later extensions of little interest can be carefully demolished without adverse impact on the protected structure as with this later stair tower added to the rear of an eighteenth-century villa

6.8.14 There may be cases where an existing addition is of little architectural quality, or is even damaging, to the original architectural design. This may arise, for example, where a porch addition has obscured a fine entrance doorway or where a poor-quality extension has unbalanced a good symmetrical façade. Partial demolition may be permitted in such cases, providing it can be achieved without any adverse structural or architectural impact on the protected structure.

6.8.15 Where a protected structure has suffered fire or other accidental damage and substantial demolition is necessary, the elements that contribute to its special interest that have survived should be retained in any reconstruction or repair.[26]

6.8.16 The demolition of a protected structure or a proposed protected structure may be permitted if it has become a dangerous structure. However, if a protected structure has become dangerous, every effort should be made to retain its special interest by specifying works that limit, as far as possible, material damage or alteration to the character of the structure.

Façade retention

6.8.17 Façade retention, or the demolition of the substantive fabric of a protected structure behind the principal elevation, is rarely an acceptable compromise, as only in exceptional cases would the full special interest of the structure be retained. Such cases may occur if the building had previously been redeveloped behind the façade, in which event proposals for new redevelopment behind the façade could be favourably assessed, subject to receiving adequate assurances on how the historic fabric would be protected during the works.

The preservation of a façade, while permitting the demolition of the remainder of the building, is rarely an acceptable approach to conserving the architectural heritage

6.8.18 Any such permitted redevelopment should relate floor levels and room sizes to the fenestration of the façade, for example to avoid having open-plan office space behind a Georgian façade that would be visibly discordant seen from the exterior.

CHAPTER 6 DEVELOPMENT CONTROL

Outline planning permission

6.8.19 Outline planning permission cannot be granted for works to a protected structure or proposed protected structure.[27] This does not preclude an outline application for change of use, so long as such change of use does not require any consequential works or otherwise have a material effect on the character of the structure.

6.8.20 If outline planning permission was granted prior to 1 January 2000 for works that would have a material effect on the character of a protected structure, the planning authority should, in so far as possible, conform with the current legislative requirements to protect the special interest of the structure when a subsequent application for approval is being considered.

Permission previously granted

6.8.21 If full planning permission was granted for development relating to a structure that became a protected structure on 1 January 2000, and it is still valid and all other relevant permissions, certificates or licenses have been secured, the developer has the right to proceed with development. In cases where such development has not been commenced, but would have an adverse effect on the character of a structure that has become a protected structure, and the developer is prepared to consider it, the planning authority could facilitate devising alternative development proposals that would have a less negative effect. This may require a further application for planning permission.

6.9 Development by a Planning Authority within its own Functional Area (Part 8 Developments)[28]

6.9.1 Where a planning authority proposes to carry out works to a protected structure or proposed protected structure in its ownership and within its own functional area, it must take the same considerations into account as those expected of private developers. Regard should be had to these guidelines when preparing proposals for Part 8 developments and other works. In addition to indicating on the site notice and the development proposal document that the development is to a protected structure or proposed protected structure or the exterior of a building in an ACA,[29] the planning authority should ensure that information

on the impact of the proposed development on the structure is included in the information available to the public and the prescribed bodies.[30] It should be noted that planning authorities cannot carry out works that would contravene their development plans, including objectives to protect the architectural heritage.[31]

6.9.2 Works of maintenance and repair are not subject to the public consultation requirements under Part 8 of the Regulations, providing they would not materially affect the character of a protected structure or proposed protected structure.[32] However, planning authorities should ensure that where such works are being carried out to a protected structure or a proposed protected structure, they are done in a sensitive and appropriate way. In such cases the detailed guidance given in Part 2 of these guidelines may be of assistance, or the planning authority could seek the advice of the prescribed bodies, for example the Heritage Council. The Heritage Council has a particular role in this regard by virtue of Section 10 of the Heritage Act 1995.

A planning authority should promote good standards of conservation in development works to the protected structures in their ownership. This example shows the junction between a successful modern addition and the original local authority building

27 Article 21 (b), 2001 Regulations

28 Section 179, 2000 Act and Part 8, 2001 Regulations

29 Article 81 (2) (c), 2001 Regulations

30 Article 82 (2), 2001 Regulations

31 Section 178, 2000 Act

32 Section 179 (6) (a), 2000 Act

6.10 Development by Certain State Authorities (Part 9 Developments)[33]

6.10.1 Certain classes of development carried out by state authorities are not subject to the normal requirements of planning permission. The classes of development specified in Part 9 of the Regulations, such as the provision of prisons, Garda stations, barracks etc. are excluded from the normal planning process for reasons of public safety or order, the administration of justice, national security or defence. The state authority may instead be required to give notice of the proposed development, asking for observations, which it must take into account in deciding whether or not to modify or carry out the development. The Regulations specify that the consultation procedures must be followed in cases where the proposed works are to a building that is a protected structure or proposed protected structure, even where it would not otherwise be required.[34]

6.10.2 In addition to the normal notification requirements of Part 9, where the development includes works to a protected structure or a building in an ACA, the authority concerned must, in addition, send notice to the Minister.[35] The plans and particulars must, in the case of works to a protected structure or proposed protected structure, include drawings and particulars showing how the proposed development would affect the character of the structure.

6.10.3 Where state authorities are proposing to carry out works to a protected or proposed protected structure, it is advisable to consult in advance with the Architectural Heritage Advisory Unit of the Department and, where appropriate, with the conservation officer of the planning authority.

6.11 Exempted Works to Monuments

6.11.1 The Minister may carry out works under the National Monuments Acts 1930 - 2004 in relation to national monuments or any particular monuments as before, without seeking planning permission, whether or not such structures are protected under Part IV of the 2000 Act.[36]

6.12 Compliance

6.12.1 In many cases it is acceptable to allow particular, small-scale aspects of a permitted development to be clarified after a grant of permission is made, by attaching a condition requiring the submission of drawings or other documents. Such matters could include details which would not have a substantial impact on the nature or extent of the development, as those should be resolved prior to deciding the case.

Certain building types such as Garda Stations, subject to the provisions of Part 9, are also protected structures

---

[33] *Section 181, 2000 Act and Part 9, 2001 Regulations*

[34] *Section 181, 2000 Act and Part 9, 2001 Regulations*

[35] *Article 88 (2), 2001 Regulations*

[36] *Section 260, 2000 Act*

6.12.2 The submission of some architectural details may be necessary at compliance stage if, for example, they could not be finalised prior to gaining full access to the property or if selected areas had first to be demolished or made safe. All drawings should, as normal, be sufficiently legible and well annotated to show clearly the appearance and materials, with samples of materials submitted or sample elements constructed as necessary. If architectural details are meant to copy previous or original elements, supporting visual information might be necessary to confirm the accuracy of the new work. Specifications or method statements should follow recognised conservation procedures. The Department of Environment *Conservation Guidelines* or Part 2 of these guidelines may help to establish if the proposed works are appropriate. Agreement should not be given until it is clear that the character of the protected structure will be protected in the work.

6.12.3 Where works commence on receipt of planning permission, the planning or conservation officer should visit the site whenever feasible to ensure that the project is proceeding in compliance with the permitted plans and conditions. If it is a condition of permission that a conservation specialist is to oversee the project on site, this person should be on hand to discuss progress and answer queries. Where reports have been required to set out progress at specified stages of the project, these should be submitted and approved. Not all of the personnel who are involved in even a relatively small contract may be aware of the significance of the structure being modified; however, an ongoing relationship with the planning authority officials should improve communications.

6.12.4 A developer may seek discussions on the procedures to take if concealed features have come to light during initial works.[37] The best way to proceed depends on the importance of the features, how their retention would affect the development, whether or not a small-scale redesign would require a further grant of permission or could be resolved by writing a declaration and if the features could be satisfactorily recorded or relocated within the structure. The conservation officer, where available, should be involved in these decisions.

6.13 Enforcement

6.13.1 The Act gives new and clarified powers of enforcement to planning authorities.[38] The consistent enforcement of the legislative and regulatory provisions and conditions attached to planning permissions are intended to effect a positive change in the public perception of the impacts of development, and to assure the credibility of the system of planning and development control.

6.13.2 A quick response to complaints about the nature of the works by members of the public during the course of development projects affecting protected structures is desirable.

6.13.3 It is of course impossible to replace lost historic fabric. Damage to or demolition of protected structures therefore irredeemably damages our architectural heritage. In cases where an owner or occupier of a protected or proposed protected structure has knowingly and unlawfully demolished or damaged that structure, or a part of that structure that contributes to its special interest, immediate consideration should be give to enforcement action by the planning authority, and the site closed down if necessary.

6.13.4 The seriousness of the infringement and the willingness (or not) of the owner to respond should guide the planning authority as to the most appropriate step to take. Relatively small-scale unauthorised works such as inappropriate window replacement can often be mitigated by their removal and replacement by correctly detailed elements. This can be achieved by the owner or occupier applying for retention permission or by the planning authority issuing a notice requiring the restoration of character of the structure.[39] If an owner is unwilling to comply, enforcement action should be considered. Where retention permission, or a Section 60 restoration notice, would be inadequate to remedy the damage immediate enforcement action is advisable. This may arise, for example, where a protected structure, or a substantial part of it, has been demolished or altered without consent, where ongoing development is not being carried out to the approved standards such that it is endangering the structure, or where important fixtures and features have been damaged or removed during the works.

37 See also paragraphs B5.14 and B5.15 in Appendix B

38 Part VIII, 2000 Act

39 See also paragraph 6.16 'Restoration of Character'

6.14 Retention Permission

6.14.1 Some protected structures have been previously altered in an unauthorised and unsatisfactory way. In some cases it will be desirable and possible to restore structures to their original character by identifying their previous design from careful inspection of the fabric and from historical evidence such as old photographs. In cases where some or many of the external features of the structure (such as original doors and windows) have been removed, or an unauthorised extension or new structure has been built within the curtilage of the structure, retention permission with mitigating conditions attached could be acceptable, depending on the individual circumstances.

6.14.2 Where an application for retention of unauthorised works to a protected structure is lodged, a planning authority should apply the same consideration to the works as for planning applications and should, if considering granting permission, seek to ensure that the works for which retention permission is granted have the minimum possible impact on the character of the structure.

6.14.3 Where in a particular case inappropriate works have been carried out, and in the opinion of the planning authority it is possible to restore its character by the carrying out of works, the authority could also consider refusing permission and using the enforcement provisions to require removal of the unauthorised works. Alternatively the planning authority could consider issuing a notice to require restoration of character.[40]

6.14.4 It should be noted that the planning legislation has been found to make no provision for applications to be made to 'retain' the demolition of a structure, that is, after an unauthorised demolition has taken place. Therefore, a planning authority that receives an application for the retention of the demolition of a protected structure should not consider that application. Consideration instead should be given as to whether enforcement action is appropriate.

6.15 Endangerment

6.15.1 'Endangered' is defined by the Act as 'exposed to harm, decay or damage, whether immediately or over a period of time, through neglect or through direct or indirect means'.[41] Protected or proposed protected structures that appear to be endangered may come to the attention of the planning authority in the course of normal planning duties or if informed by a member of the public. The state of a structure may also be brought to notice of the planning office by the sanitary authority prior to the issue of a notice in relation to a dangerous structure under the Local Government (Sanitary Services) Act 1964.

6.15.2 A structure may be endangered by structural interventions such as the removal of internal floors and/or partition walls, breaking new openings in external walls, removal of or damage to roofs and chimney stacks, removal and boarding up of windows and doors, excavation of the ground in close proximity to the structure without adequate shoring up or other protection for the structure, or the demolition of parts of a structure without shoring or protecting it. Indirect endangerment could include allowing a building to fall into disrepair, leaving structures open to the elements and possible vandalism, or the removal of temporary safeguards which had secured a vacant structure, such as temporary roof-coverings, security fencing or blocked openings.

Derelict buildings can become targets of vandalism if not properly safeguarded

---

[40] Section 60, 2000 Act

[41] Section 2, 2000 Act

6.15.3   Immediate action should be taken to require the owner to stabilise or secure the structure, using either Section 59 (which may be a quicker option if the owner is amenable to carrying out the works) or the regular enforcement procedures in Part VIII of the Act. Either way, the planning authority should specify the works that are required to prevent continuing endangerment. The detailed guidance given in Part 2 of these guidelines or the Department of Environment *Conservation Guidelines* should, where necessary, be reinforced by advice from an engineer or architect with conservation expertise.

6.16   Restoration of Character

6.16.1   A Section 60 notice can be served on the owner or occupier of a protected structure to require the restoration of its character where unauthorised removal, alteration or replacement of particular elements has taken place and where the original character (or a documented previous state) can be restored without needing retention permission. This solution is limited to works that would not otherwise require planning permission as they would not materially affect the character of the structure. For example, unauthorised and inappropriate windows or doors could be replaced with correctly profiled windows or doors, the details based either on surviving fragments or examples measured from a directly comparable structure. The restoration of character is best achieved by the agreement of all parties on the details of the necessary works and a time-frame for compliance.

6.16.2   The restoration of character could also mean the straightforward removal of items that detract from the character of the structure, for example inappropriate shop signage, aerials or air-handling units. If the notice relates to the removal of items that have an economical or physical function in the structure, their replacement in some form may be necessary. An acceptable replacement item should be discussed among all parties and the details agreed in advance of a planning application, to facilitate a quick decision.

Restoration of character can sometimes be achieved simply by the removal or relocation of inappropriate additions (bottom). However, where original elements such as windows have been lost (top) they can only be replaced in replica but this may be necessary to restore the character of the overall building or area

Table VIII   An Outline of Planning Application Procedures for Works to Protected Structures

1. Is the planning application valid?
> The protected status of the structure should be correctly referred to on public notices
> The required plans, drawings and maps should be included
> The potential impact on the character of the architectural heritage should be adequately described by means of photographs, plans and other particulars
> The application should be for full permission

NO

1a. Return to applicant stating why it is invalid

YES

2. Consultation and notification
> Notify the prescribed bodies as soon as possible after validation
> Place the details of the application on the public file in the planning office
> Publish weekly list indicating where development relates to a protected structure or a proposed protected structure
> Consult with the conservation officer, where one is available

3. Evaluate the proposed development and its potential impact
> Consult the relevant information in the RPS file and any declaration issued regarding the protected structure
> If a pre-planning meeting was held, consult the minutes of that meeting
> Consider any submissions made within 5 weeks of validation
> Consult Part 2 of these guidelines

4. Is the information contained in the application sufficient to allow an decision to be made on the proposed development?

NO

4a. Request the applicant to provide further information

YES

4b. Process and evaluate the further information received
> Notify the relevant people/bodies of the receipt of further information as required
> Consider any submissions made on the further information
> Evaluate the application as a whole

Further information received within 6 months

5. Is the proposed development consistent with proper planning and development?

NO

YES

6a. Consider granting permission

5a. Can negative impacts be mitigated by conditions of permission?

YES

NO

7. Decision:
> If the decision is made to grant permission, draw up any conditions necessary to mitigate negative impacts or to ensure the works are properly completed
> If the decision is made to refuse permission, draw up the reasons for the refusal
> Send notice of the decision to the applicant
> Send notice of the decision to those who made observations during the planning process

6b. Consider refusing permission

Detailed
Guidance Notes

PART 2

Conservation
Principles

CHAPTER 7

7.1 Purpose of the Detailed Guidance Notes

7.1.1 The purpose of the detailed guidance notes in Part 2 is to assist planning authorities in the identification of structures or parts of structures which are of special interest, in the writing of declarations and in the consideration of applications for planning permission involving works to protected structures and to buildings within ACAs. The aim is to achieve a consistency of approach to the conservation and protection of the architectural heritage and to set out the standards of architectural conservation supported by the Minister for the Environment, Heritage and Local Government.

7.1.2 The advice contained in these detailed guidance notes falls into two categories. Guidance included under the sub-headings 'Identifying special features for protection' is intended to assist a planning authority in identifying structures or parts of structures which are of special interest. It draws attention to features of a structure which may contribute to its character and/or the character of an ACA. Identification of such features will help in the selection of structures for inclusion in the RPS and in writing declarations.

7.1.3 The guidance sub-headed 'Consideration of proposals' is intended to assist a planning authority in meeting its development objectives of protecting the architectural heritage and preserving the character of ACAs. It will aid the assessment of the potential effects of development applications on the character of a protected structure and/or the character of an ACA. It is also intended to guide a planning authority in writing conditions which may be attached to a grant of permission.

7.2 Conservation Principles

7.2.1 Conservation is the process of caring for buildings and places and of managing change to them in such a way as to retain their character and special interest. Historic structures are a unique resource. Once lost, they cannot be replaced. If their special qualities are degraded, these can rarely be recaptured. Damage can be caused to the character of a historic structure as much by over-attention as by neglect. Over-restoration can harm the special qualities of a building with the loss of details, materials and craftsmanship which, while sometimes seeming of little significance in themselves, can contribute to the character of the building and make it special. For this reason, it is vitally important

that proposals for works to protected structures, and within ACAs, be examined at a detailed level. It is intended these detailed guidance notes will draw attention to the importance of the seemingly minor details of a historic building that nonetheless play an important part in establishing its character.

Over-restoration or poorly specified replacement elements can be as much a threat to the character of historic structures as neglect or wilful damage. In this case, the datestone of 1736 is one of the few surviving original features on the exterior of this house

7.2.2 Entry into the Record of Protected Structures does not mean that a structure is forever frozen in time. Good conservation practice allows a structure to evolve and adapt to meet changing needs while retaining its particular significance. The challenge facing owners, planning authorities and all others involved in architectural conservation is to identify how and where change can occur and to ensure that the heritage is not damaged by inappropriate intervention. Additions and other interventions should be sympathetic to the earlier structure and of quality in themselves and should not cause damage to the fabric of the structure, whether in the long or short term.

7.3 Keeping a Building in Use

7.3.1 It is generally recognised that the best method of conserving a historic building is to keep it in active use. Where a structure is of great rarity or quality, every effort should be made to find a solution which will allow it to be adapted to a new use without unacceptable damage to its character and special interest. Usually the original use for which a structure was built will be the most appropriate, and to maintain that use will involve the least disruption to its character. While a degree of compromise will be required in adapting a protected structure to meet the requirements of modern living, it is important that the special interest of the structure is not unnecessarily affected. Where a change of use is approved, every effort should be made to minimise change to, and loss of, significant fabric and the special interest of the structure should not be compromised.

7.3.2 Where a protected structure is a ruin and does not have an active use, it may nonetheless be of special interest. It may be a local landmark or contribute to the character of an ACA. In such cases, it may be more appropriate to allow it to continue to stand in a ruined state and be repaired or consolidated where necessary.

7.4 Researching and Analysing

7.4.1 Before formulating proposals for works to a protected structure, the developer should research its historical development and understand thoroughly the present condition of the structure. The research should encompass not only the main structure and its interior but also its curtilage and attendant grounds, where relevant, and any structures or features within them which contribute to the special interest of the protected structure. The contribution of the setting of the structure to its special interest should also be assessed, as should any other relationships which add to the appreciation of it.

7.4.2 The research should include an analysis of the physical fabric of the site, and any available documentary or other evidence. The work should only be undertaken by those with the appropriate knowledge and skill. The results of the research should be analysed in order to understand the reasons for any decay and to inform future proposals.

Buildings should be kept in active use, preferably the original use. Where this is not possible, permitted changes of use should aim to minimise the impact on the character of the structure, as with this former gaol observation tower, which is now in education-related office use

Some protected structures such as bridges, follies and other iconic landmarks are strong, self-contained compositions that may be difficult to alter without affecting their character and special interest

7.5 Using Expert Conservation Advice

7.5.1 Building conservation is a specialised discipline and the method of work needs to be specified by experts with a knowledge and experience of historic buildings. Planning authorities, when discussing proposals with the owners or occupiers of protected structures, should encourage them to seek expert advice when considering undertaking works to their buildings. Where a protected structure is of particularly high quality or rarity, the use of conservation expertise by an applicant could be a condition of any grant of planning permission.

7.5.2 The input of expert advice should not be confined to the planning application process. In order to ensure that the works are competently and correctly completed, continued expert involvement may be necessary in the management and site supervision of the project, using experienced and skilled workers with proper and adequate supervision.

7.5.3 Planning authorities should ensure that they themselves have access to appropriately qualified, competent specialist advice on any development likely to impact on a protected structure. This advice might come from in-house conservation staff or from independent consultants.

7.6 Protecting the Special Interest

7.6.1 The character and special interest of a protected structure can be damaged by inappropriate works. Most obviously, a structure can be demolished or partly demolished. It can also be stripped of its value and distinctiveness by neglect and decay, unsuitable alteration, uninformed repair or over-restoration.

7.6.2 The blanket application of standard solutions to historic buildings is not appropriate, nor can old buildings be expected to perform in the same way as modern buildings in terms of structural strength, durability of materials or thermal insulation. But old buildings have qualities which modern structures may not have. For example, handmade building materials are evidence of dedication and craftsmanship perhaps no longer achievable today. Other materials, such as a particular type of stone, may no longer be obtainable. Above all, historic buildings have a patina of age which is irreplaceable and cannot be replicated.

7.7 Promoting Minimum Intervention

7.7.1 The principle of promoting minimum intervention in a protected structure is best summed up by the maxim 'do as much as necessary and as little as possible'. Dramatic interventions in a protected structure are rarely appropriate. The best work in conservation terms is often that which is low key, involves the least work and can be inexpensive.

7.7.2 In granting planning permission, a planning authority should be satisfied that works are necessary, whether these be repair works to the fabric of the building or adaptations to the structure to allow it to perform a new or enhanced function. Over-restoration of historic buildings can be detrimental to their character and value. Old buildings both charm and inform for the very reason that they are old. Bulging or leaning walls, unevenness and bowing are not necessarily imperfections to be ironed out but are evidence of the building's antiquity. Such evidence of a patina of age is irreplaceable and should be preserved where possible with appropriate professional advice.

Uninformed works, even where carried out with care, can irreparably damage the character of a building as with the installation of these inappropriate modern timber windows. Here also the original render has been stripped from the building, a current fashion at odds with the original design intention which furthermore leaves the structure vulnerable to damp ingress

Evidence of the quality of materials and craftsmanship can endure through years of neglect. Where they survive, every effort should be made to retain and repair features of importance to the character of a protected structure or an ACA

Good conservation works should aim to do as much as necessary, yet as little as possible, to a protected structure. The advice of experienced conservation professionals is invaluable and minimal intervention may often prove less expensive than comprehensive refurbishment

7.7.3　Conjectural restoration of a protected structure, or part of a structure, should generally only be permitted where there is sufficient physical or documentary evidence of the earlier state of the structure or element or where restoration is necessary to enhance the appreciation of other elements that contribute to the character of the structure. For example, if a Georgian house has in the past had its original roof replaced with a flat roof, the reinstatement of an appropriately designed pitched roof to the building will enhance the appearance of the façade and possibly of a whole terrace of buildings. Similarly, a case may sometimes be made to reinstate a symmetrical composition part of which has previously been lost. The practice of 'restoring' a building or structure to an appearance at some notional date in its history should generally not be permitted, nor should the practices of moving buildings or of reducing them to mere façades be permitted except in exceptional circumstances.

7.7.4　The replication of a lost feature may be appropriate in some circumstances where the essential form and detailing are still evident, so that the physical evidence can be used to re-establish the feature as an integral part of the works. For example, where a carved bracket is missing from a shopfront, the profile and material of the missing feature may be determined from a surviving bracket elsewhere on the same shopfront. A replacement feature should harmonise with its surroundings and it should be a condition that the incorporation of any replacement feature is not to the detriment of later work of quality or interest. Any reconstruction of details should be permitted on a selective rather than a systematic basis.

7.7.5　Another acceptable option to replace a lost element would be to incorporate, as a new feature, a design that is sympathetic with the remaining historical features of the building. Where this is permitted, it should be a condition that the new feature take into account the size, scale and material of the building itself, and care should be taken to avoid creating a false historical appearance.

The demolition of all but the façade of a structure will inevitably result in a loss of character and should rarely be considered acceptable. In cases where the façade is the sole surviving feature of a building, any proposal to construct a new building behind that façade should respect the location, not only of existing openings, but also of the original floors and internal walls to avoid an adverse impact on the external appearance of the building

This mid-eighteenth-century house had lost its original windows and the opening sizes had been altered (left). These works had damaged a carefully proportioned classical design. Detailed research, including an analysis of surviving original windows, led to restoration of the openings to their original proportions and the fabrication of historically accurate sashes and frames (above)

Where elements of a composition have been lost, new work should generally avoid creating a false historical appearance while respecting the scale and materials of the surviving fabric, as has happened here in the conversion of a shop to office use

7.8 Respecting Earlier Alterations of Interest

7.8.1 Alterations and additions to a structure can themselves be an irreplaceable part of a unique history. Different periods of alteration can inform the social and architectural history of the built heritage. For example, the subsequent addition of porches, balconies, shopfronts and returns can say much about changing fashions in architectural design and social aspiration, as can alterations or embellishments such as the addition of bargeboards, window and door surrounds or dormer windows.

7.8.2 In order to appreciate the integrity of a structure, it is important to respect the contribution of different stages of its historical development. Concentration on whether or not various parts of a building are 'original' can obscure the fact that later alterations and additions may also contribute to the special interest of the structure. Of course there may be alterations or additions which have not contributed to the special interest of the building, and which may in fact have damaged it.

7.8.3 Where new alterations and additions are proposed to a protected structure, it should be remembered that these will, in their turn, become part of the structure's history and so it is important that these make their own positive contribution by being well designed and constructed.

Alterations of different periods may contribute to a knowledge and appreciation of the history of a structure. The application of plaster hood-mouldings to earlier buildings was fashionable at the end of the nineteenth century. While they may now appear anachronistic, they can also be seen as part of the unique history of that building

The conversion of this 1762 Charter School nursery to a store in the nineteenth century involved partially blocking the window openings, thereby altering its character. Restoring the openings would be possible using surviving evidence in the fabric and employing historically accurate detailing. This approach is appropriate where the character of an architectural composition can be restored by undoing later alterations of little interest

New alterations – as in this conference room with tiered balconies constructed within a mediaeval castle tower – should respect their context and be of high-quality design and specification. In time, such interventions will contribute to the history of the structure

7.9 Repairing Rather than Replacing

7.9.1 It should be the aim of good conservation practice to preserve the authentic fabric which contributes to the special interest of the structure. Good repair will arrest the process of decay of a structure and prolong its life without damaging its character and special interest. Where a damaged or deteriorated feature could reasonably be repaired, its replacement should not be permitted.

7.9.2 Many historic structures date from a time when the majority of building materials were wrought by hand. These materials have a variety and vitality that cannot be matched by machine-made materials. Tooling and chisel marks on stonework, undulations in blown-glass panes, and adze marks on timber elements supply a wealth of irreplaceable information about the people and the times that produced these structures. Also, through time, a structure and its components acquire a patina of age that cannot be replicated. The unnecessary replacement of historic fabric, no matter how carefully the work is carried out, will have an adverse effect on the character of a building or monument, seriously diminish its authenticity and will significantly reduce its value as a source of historical information. Replacing original or earlier elements of a building with modern replicas only serves to falsify the historical evidence of the building.

7.10 Promoting Honesty of Repairs and Alterations

7.10.1 To promote good conservation practice in line with the recommendations of international charters, repairs to a protected building or structure should generally be carried out without attempt at disguise or artificial ageing. This does not mean that the repair should be obtrusive or that inappropriate materials should be used in order to contrast with the historic fabric. A good repair, carried out with skill, leaves an interesting record of works done. Deliberately obscuring alterations confuses the historical record that is the building. New repairs should not detract from the visual integrity of the structure but should be discernible on closer inspection.

The careful repair of a damaged feature such as a cast iron balustrade contributes much to preserving the character of a structure (shown here before and after repair). Where elements are not capable of repair, the new work should accurately reproduce the detail of the original. Entire sections should not be replaced if only a part is damaged

Good conservation practice encourages the honesty of repairs and alterations which may be discernible to the expert eye but not visually obtrusive. This new hopper head was designed to match the style of the structure but is recognisable, on close inspection, as a new element from its 1999 date

7.11 Using Appropriate Materials and Methods

7.11.1 Only appropriate materials and methods should be used in works to a protected structure. In early restoration works of the past, untested materials and techniques, such as the use of cement repointing and of some surface consolidants, actually resulted in the accelerated decay of the building fabric on which they were applied as part of conservation works. The use of modern materials and techniques should only be permitted where their appropriateness is supported by firm scientific evidence or where they have proved themselves over a sufficient period and where traditional alternatives cannot be sourced.

7.11.2 When dealing with planning applications for works to a protected structure, materials, details and specifications for works should be approved by the planning authority prior to the commencement of any works.

7.12 Ensuring Reversibility of Alterations

7.12.1 The use of processes which are reversible, or substantially reversible, when undertaking works to a protected structure is always preferable as this allows for the future correction of unforeseen problems, should the need arise, without lasting damage being caused to the architectural heritage. For example, filling structural voids with concrete would be an irreversible process while a loose fill could easily be removed at a later stage. Similarly, scribing new partitions around an existing cornice or skirting allows for the earlier work to remain intact, possibly to be re-exposed at a future time.

7.12.2 Not all works can be made reversible and a judgement will have to be made by the planning authority where irreversible works are proposed. Ideally, permitted works which affect the character and special interest of a protected structure should be reversible and such works considered temporary, to be reversed when circumstances allow. Such works might include the subdivision of important rooms or spaces within the interior of a protected structure.

7.12.3 The reversibility of proposals is an important conservation principle but should not be used to justify inappropriate interventions.

The restoration of the pioneering cast- and wrought-iron glasshouses at the National Botanic Gardens was preceded by technical and scientific research to ensure that the proposed ironwork repairs would be appropriate in terms of materials and construction

Alterations, particularly those which impact on important elements of a protected structure, should as far as possible be reversible. Internally this can be achieved by scribing partitions around cornices, dado rails and skirting boards. However, the reversibility of a proposal should not be used to justify inappropriate works

7.13 Avoiding Incremental Damage

7.13.1 Thought must be given by the planning authority to the potential cumulative impact of minor works to the character of protected structures and of ACAs. The quality and character of both can be damaged by incremental alterations. In the case of protected structures this applies to both internal and external works.

7.13.2 In an ACA, this principle can apply to a street or area where a precedent becomes established for the removal of architectural features or the addition of extensions. For example, the proposed alteration of the external railings of an individual house and the conversion of its front garden to accommodate car parking may at first appear minor and acceptable. However, the planning authority must consider the effect on the character of an ACA and the setting of other protected structures should substantial numbers of properties also alter historic railings and lose their gardens. Similarly, proposals to demolish existing returns to replace them with larger extensions should be treated with caution.

7.13.3 It can sometimes be difficult to refuse permission for minor works, but a point may be reached when the combined impact of all the small alterations will be considerable and detract substantially from the architectural quality and character of the building or of an area.

7.14 Discouraging the Use of Architectural Salvage from Other Buildings

7.14.1 In granting planning permission for works to historic buildings, including all protected structures, the planning authority should not encourage the use of architectural salvage from other buildings for two reasons. Firstly, the re-use of architectural features from elsewhere can confuse the understanding and appreciation of a building, casting doubt on the authenticity of even the untouched parts of the fabric. Secondly, creating a market for salvaged building materials promotes the dismantling of other old buildings, for example the removal of slates or cut-stone elements from a building for re-use elsewhere.

7.14.2 The planning authority could use the planning process to discourage the use of architectural salvage from other buildings. Promoting the use of newly produced materials such as stone or wrought iron could help to keep them in production or encourage the revival of the craftsmanship associated with these materials. There may be occasions where suitable traditional materials are no longer in production and their production cannot be revived. In such cases, the use of salvaged materials may be appropriate after their provenance has been ascertained.

7.15 Complying with the Building Regulations

7.15.1 The Building Regulations are designed to secure the health and safety of people in and around buildings. The Regulations are set out in twelve parts (Parts A - M, excluding I). They are expressed in performance terms and are backed up by relevant Technical Guidance Documents (TGDs) which give guidance regarding compliance. Apart from a limited number of exemptions, they apply to all works involving new construction, extensions to buildings, material alterations to existing buildings and material change of use of such buildings.

It can often be difficult to resist proposals for minor works which seem of little consequence such as the replacement of windows, doors and roof coverings or the conversion of front gardens to parking bays. However the cumulative effect of such alterations can be destructive to the special interest of a protected structure or of an ACA

This salvaged portico is obviously not a part of the structure it now fronts. However it is not clear if it survives from a previous building on this site or was imported from elsewhere. This has the effect of blurring the historical record. The use of salvaged items can promote the practice of dismantling of other structures capable of repair and it is important to establish the provenance of salvaged material before use

7.15.2 Works carried out in accordance with the guidance in the TGDs will, prima facie, indicate compliance. However, the adoption of an approach other than that outlined in the guidance is not precluded, provided the relevant requirements of the Regulations are complied with. Parts of the Building Regulations which are particularly relevant to works in relation to historic buildings include Part A (Structure), Part B (Fire Safety), Part L (Conservation of Fuel and Energy) and Part M (Access for People with Disabilities). However, some parts of the Regulations do not apply to a material change of use, for example the requirement in Part A dealing with disproportionate collapse or the requirements of Part K dealing with stairways, ladders, ramps and guards.

7.15.3 Alterations, extensions and material changes of use affecting historic buildings may present particular problems, and approaches other than those contained in the TGDs may be appropriate in order to ensure compliance while protecting the character of the building. The difficulties that may arise in the application of the Building Regulations to existing buildings is acknowledged in the preamble to each TGD, where it is stated:

> In the case of material alterations or changes of use to existing buildings, the adoption without modification of the guidance in this document may not, in all circumstances, be appropriate. In particular, the adherence to guidance, including codes, standards or technical specifications, intended for application to new work may be unduly restrictive or impracticable. Buildings of architectural or historical interest are especially likely to give rise to such circumstances. In these situations, alternative approaches based on the principles contained in the document may be more relevant and should be considered.

7.15.4 In the interest of conserving the character of buildings of outstanding architectural and historical importance, the enhanced thermal performance requirements introduced in the 2002 amendment to the Building Regulations do not apply to works (including extensions) to existing buildings which are protected structures or proposed protected structures under the Planning and Development Act 2000. In that amendment it is also acknowledged that the application of this part may pose particular difficulties for habitable buildings which, although not protected structures or proposed protected structures may be of architectural or historical interest, and the following guidance is included in the TGD:

Works such as the replacement of doors, windows and rooflights, the provision of insulated dry-lining and damp-proofing to walls and basements, insulation to the underside of slating and provision of roof vents and ducting of pipework could all affect the character of the structure. In general, the type of works described above should be carefully assessed for their material and visual impact on the structure. Historic windows and doors should be repaired rather than replaced, and dry-lining and damp-proofing should not disrupt or damage historic plasterwork or flagstones and should not introduce further moisture into the structure. Roof insulation should be achieved without damage to slating (either during the works or from erosion due to condensation) and obtrusive vents should not affect the character of the roof. In specific cases, relaxation of the values proposed may be acceptable if it can be shown to be necessary in order to preserve the architectural integrity of the particular building.

7.15.5 Specific issues in relation to Parts B and M of the Regulations are dealt with respectively in other chapters of these guidelines. Provision is also made in the Building Control Act for the granting of a dispensation or relaxation in relation to specific works or materials by a Building Control Authority where the case for such dispensation or relaxation is accepted by the authority.

Walls and Other Structural Elements

CHAPTER 8

8.1   Introduction

8.1.1   The structural system of a historic building and its elements play a major role in defining its character. Structural elements may include external and internal load-bearing brick or masonry walls, mud walls or timber-framed walls; columns of stone, cast iron or concrete; stone, brick or concrete vaults; timber, iron or steel beams, trusses, girders and many others. Structural elements may be important as early examples of the use of certain materials such as cast iron or concrete. Even where interesting structural elements are not exposed, they are nonetheless of significance and contribute to the character of the building.

8.1.2   The structure of the building may be clad externally and the type and appearance of the cladding materials used may also contribute to the character of the building. Common cladding materials include metal sheeting such as corrugated iron, slate-hanging, tile-hanging, timber boarding and terracotta or faïence units.

8.1.3   Any finishes applied to the structure of a building may also be of importance. Rubble stone walls were often finished with a render coating. This may have been applied as a roughcast coat or with a smooth, trowelled finish sometimes ruled and lined to resemble ashlar blocks. Smooth or roughcast renders may have been limewashed, painted or self-finished. Small stones or other materials may have been pressed into the wet coating after application to provide a pebble-dashed finish.

8.1.4   When assessing the contribution of structural elements, including walls and associated features, to the character of a protected structure or of an ACA, the planning authority should ask:

a)   What is the original structural system of the protected structure?

b)   Has this been altered in the past? If so, are the alterations of interest or have they damaged the appearance or the structural integrity of the building?

c)   Are there early or original structural elements of particular interest?

d)   Are there likely to be any concealed elements of interest?

e)   Is the present structural material, cladding or finish original?

f)   If not, is it of interest or does it conceal an original surface or earlier finish beneath?

g)   If there is an original surface or earlier finish beneath, should it be investigated or were there reasons why it was covered over, such as poor quality materials or unsightly alterations?

h)   If there is a later finish, is it causing damage to the earlier surface? If it is causing damage, would the process of removing this finish lead to further damage? For example, the removal of a strong cement-based render could take away parts of the earlier surface below.

i)   Is the structure part of a group or terrace of similar buildings? If so, would any alterations to one of the terrace affect the quality or character of the entire group, such as uncoordinated façade cleaning, painting or repointing?

j)   Is there any original architectural detailing such as string courses, pilasters, cornices or quoins? Are there any later embellishments or alterations of interest? How will these be protected and conserved during the works?

k)   Are there any elements such as balconies, verandas or balconettes attached to the walls? Do these contribute to the special interest of the building?

l)   Are there any other features or fixtures of interest attached to the walls such as plaques or fire marks?

Structural elements, such as masonry walls, may play a major role in defining the character of the structure. Here the granite and brickwork wall retains its original pointing. This wall was never rendered, but where finishes were originally used they almost always contribute to the special interest of the structure

8.2 Alterations to Walls and Other Structural Elements

8.2.1 In identifying the important qualities of the walls and other structural elements of protected structures, all original architectural detailing should be respected, as should later additions, embellishments or remodelling of definite quality. There may be cases where alterations are of little interest in themselves or which positively detract from the architectural quality of the whole by reason of their poor design or their poor relationship to the rest of the building. Past alterations may also have damaged the structural integrity of the building or structure. In such cases, the planning authority may consider it desirable to encourage the reversal of unsatisfactory alterations that disfigure or conceal earlier work of greater merit or have caused physical problems or deterioration. This should only be done after careful consideration of all the consequences. Any works carried out on this basis should always be based upon firm evidence and an assessment of the original state and detailing of the structure.

Structural Stability

8.2.2 The analysis of the structural stability of a historic building generally requires the skill and experience of a specialist structural engineer rather than one who is a general practitioner. Where an application is made to demolish or dismantle a protected structure (whether in whole or in part) based on reasons of structural instability, the onus is on the applicant to prove that the proposals are valid and all relevant matters have been properly addressed. In some cases, the planning authority may need to commission its own independent advice on structural matters.

8.2.3 Where alterations are proposed to walls or other structural elements of a protected structure, the planning authority should be satisfied that the proposals are based on a proper knowledge and understanding of the existing structure. Many old buildings suffer from minor structural defects but will continue to perform satisfactorily providing they are not subject to major disturbance. Alterations such as the creation of new openings, changes to the interior spaces or the installation of new services and equipment could overload an existing structural system and, where this is a possibility, the proposals should be reconsidered. In these circumstances, specialist advice may be required.

Evidence of minor structural defects such as cracking should be investigated but may be symptomatic of structural movement or settlement that happened long ago and may now have stabilised. Cracks should be monitored over a period of time to establish if movement is continuing and is sufficiently serious to warrant action

8.2.4 Repair works to a protected structure should generally be permitted only where they are low key and involve reinstatement or strengthening of the existing structure. It is preferable to repair rather than rebuild structural elements. But where it is considered acceptable to permit part of a structure to be taken down and rebuilt, the planning authority should make it a condition of the permission that the existing work be thoroughly recorded prior to any works taking place and that rebuilding incorporate as much of the original material as possible.

Settlement

8.2.5 Proposals which have the potential to cause settlement in a historic building should be given careful consideration. Excavation or re-grading of ground levels adjacent to or within a protected structure could cause its foundations to settle or fail. The structural integrity of old foundations may also be undermined by previous inappropriate alterations or extensions, by the planting of certain types of tree close to the building or by the saturation of adjacent ground by poor drainage design.

8.2.6 Settlement of the foundations of a structure in the past may have resulted in loads being transferred onto previously non-load-bearing partitions. Therefore proposals to remove all or part of any walls of old buildings should be treated with great caution as these may adversely affect the structural integrity of the building. Intensification of use or seemingly minor alterations can cause settlement and have an adverse effect on the structural integrity of an old building.

Works in connection with damp-proofing

8.2.7 Works in connection with damp-proofing may materially alter the appearance or character of a protected structure or have implications for its structural stability. Inappropriate works can lead to the unnecessary destruction of large amounts of fabric such as external render, internal plasterwork, panelling or flooring. Where there would be such an adverse effect on the structure, the proposals should be not be permitted. Likewise, any proposals which would involve the removal of large amounts of historic finishes, such as plasterwork, are not likely to be considered acceptable.

8.2.8 In assessing applications for planning permission involving damp-proofing works that could have an adverse effect, the applicant should show that the works are in fact necessary. There may be other solutions to the issue which should be first considered. The fabric of older buildings was usually designed to allow absorption of moisture from the ground or from rainwater and its subsequent evaporation from the surface. Later alterations or neglect may have interfered with the original drying-out process of the structure. Also, damp problems may be caused by condensation.

8.2.9 Reversing inappropriate later alterations may be sufficient to alleviate the problems of damp and are generally less destructive to the fabric of the building. Such works could include reopening blocked-up windows or vents, removing later impervious surface finishes from walls or floors, ensuring that ground levels around the building are appropriate, or locally re-grading the ground surrounding the building to ensure that surface water drains away from the external walls. The location of vapour-generating activities within a building such as cooking or showering should be carefully considered and, if necessary, relocated.

8.2.10 A proposal to install a new damp-proof course into a protected structure is likely materially to alter the appearance or character of the structure or have implications for its structural stability. If it has been determined that the installation of a damp-proof course is the only solution to problems in a protected structure, the method proposed should be carefully considered. The insertion of a continuous lead, slate or other damp-proof course is probably the most effective method but only if a complete physical barrier can be achieved. This may not be possible without unacceptable disruption or damage to the fabric of the structure and the added possibility of settlement-cracking in the future.

Damp problems arise more often from poor maintenance or poorly-executed repair works than from inadequate original detailing.

The injection of a damp-proof course may result in visually obtrusive pockmarks on the external walls of the building and is unlikely to be fully effective in rubble walling

This method is usually only successfully achieved in walls of coursed stone or brickwork.

8.2.11 The planning authority should be aware that the injection or infusion of a chemical damp-proof course will require injection holes drilled into the walls which may be visually unacceptable in an historic wall and can often be ineffective. The efficacy of electro-osmotic systems is doubtful. Furthermore, such systems may involve the use of metals, such as iron or copper, which are likely to rust or to stain the fabric of the building.

Adding flashings

8.2.12 Lead flashings can be provided to prolong the life of decayed projecting features but should generally only be used where this can be achieved unobtrusively. New flashings should not visually distort the proportions of important mouldings or other features.

Surface treatments

8.2.13 The covering of walls of a protected structure with a water-repellent coating should not normally be permitted. Traditional buildings were designed to 'breathe', that is, to absorb a certain amount of ground or atmospheric water, allowing it to evaporate at a later stage rather than to repel all water from an impervious surface.

8.2.14 The inappropriate use of surface consolidants prevents the evaporation process. Any cracks which develop in the surface layer will allow the entry of water trapping moisture and salts against or behind the wall surface, so promoting decay and endangering the character and fabric of the protected structure. Such treatments, where permitted, should only be carried out by experts after detailed consultation.

Cladding in synthetic materials

8.2.15 Permission should not normally be granted for the cladding of any part of a protected structure in synthetic materials, such as artificial stone.

8.2.16 The addition of external insulation to historic buildings should not be permitted where this would adversely affect important features.

8.3 Walling and Other Structural Materials

Stonework
IDENTIFYING SPECIAL FEATURES FOR PROTECTION

8.3.1 There is a wide variety of building stones to be found in Irish buildings, usually locally produced limestone, granite and, to a lesser extent, sandstone. In addition, imported stones such as Portland stone, red sandstone and marble were often used in architecturally significant buildings.

8.3.2 Cut stone, or ashlar, was used extensively in construction. Many prominent buildings are entirely faced in finely worked ashlar, while even humbler buildings can include cut-stone elements such as sills, string courses, copings or quoins. Other buildings and many boundary walls were constructed of rubble stonework, which was often finished in plain or roughcast render.

8.3.3 The original ashlar surface was often tooled or polished and this distinctive texture should always be respected as a part of the building's character. Carved work, where it exists, should be identified and protected. Masons' marks, where found, should also be protected. These are symbols or initials incised into stonework by the mason originally responsible for executing the work.

Architectural detailing, tooling, masons' marks and carving – ranging from lettering and vermiculation to bas-relief sculpture– should always be noted and protected

Even durable stones such as granite and limestone can be irreparably damaged by inappropriate works. The cement mortar used in repointing this wall is stronger than the stonework. As a result, structural movement in the wall could not be absorbed by the mortar and instead the stone has fractured. The impermeability of the mortar may cause future additional damage, as any water entering the wall through this fracture will be unable to escape

CONSIDERATION OF PROPOSALS AFFECTING STONE WALLING
Specification of repair works

8.3.4 Stone is generally a very durable material but inappropriate repairs and poor workmanship can accelerate its decay. It may be better that masonry be left untouched rather than allow proposals which could result in incorrect treatment and consequent damage.

8.3.5 Stonework repairs require detailed specification and the applicant should be required to supply all necessary information to allow an assessment of the proposals. In some cases, the planning authority may need specialist advice to satisfy itself that due care has been exercised and that all relevant matters have been properly addressed in the application.

8.3.6 Where repair works are proposed to stone walls, particularly ashlar walls, of a protected structure the information required as part of a proposal could include:

a) identification of the existing stone;

b) the specification of any replacement stone;

c) a sample of that stone;

d) the proposed surface finish of any new ashlar;

e) the method of coursing;

f) the specification and extent of any proposed repointing;

g) the techniques to be used in carrying out the works, and

h) the experience and expertise of the people who will be responsible for the work.

Indenting

8.3.7 Indenting is the replacement of an individual decayed stone where that stone has been damaged or decayed to the extent that its structural integrity is in doubt. The term is also used to describe the cutting out and replacement of a decayed part of a stone.

8.3.8 The need to indent all or parts of stones may arise from the existence of iron cramps originally used to fix the stonework. Iron is susceptible to rust and expands on rusting, resulting in the cracking or spalling off of parts of the surrounding stone. Where this has occurred, it may be necessary to take remedial action to remove the cramps, replace them with a non-ferrous cramp and repair the damaged stonework.

8.3.9 Any proposed indenting should be carefully assessed, as indented stones can be visually intrusive. Leaving the damaged original stone may often be a more acceptable option. New indented stones should be finished by hand, where appropriate, to provide a finish which would blend in with the existing stonework while allowing it to be clear on close inspection that this is not the original material.

Redressing of stonework

8.3.10 Redressing an ashlar façade involves the removal of the original face of the wall. This can cause considerable damage to the appearance and character of the building with the loss of original tooling patterns, moulded detail and the patina of age.

8.3.11 There may, however, be exceptional circumstances where redressing could be permitted, for example:

a) where so many stones are decayed that no other solution is possible;

b) where the face of the stones has become badly disfigured by spalling;

c) where the deterioration is so severe as to pose a threat to the general public.

Where there has been mechanical damage or spalling of a stone, it can be repaired using a small indent, tooled to match the surrounding stone. The indented stone should respect the original joint lines of the wall

Iron cramps were traditionally used to hold stones in place. However, iron is susceptible to rusting and, on rusting, expands, often cracking the surrounding stone which spalls off so exposing the iron to further rusting. In severe cases, such as here, it may be necessary to remove the iron cramp and replace it with a non-ferrous metal such as stainless steel or phosphor bronze and repair the damaged stonework

The repair of stonework using specialised mortars may be permissible if appropriately specified. However, the long-term effect of weathering and other interventions should inform a decision as to its suitability. In this case the erosion of the face of the stone following grit-blasting has left an old mortar repair standing proud; it will inevitably fail taking more stone with it

8.3.12 Redressing should generally not be permitted, especially where there is carved detailing to the stonework. In many cases where redressing of stonework is proposed, it may be necessary to encourage the applicant to accept the existing appearance of the stonework.

Mortar repairs to stonework

8.3.13 Damaged stonework can be repaired using specialised mortars, sometimes known as 'plastic repair'. Extensive mortar repair work should not normally be permitted unless the façade has already been painted and is likely to continue to be painted.

8.3.14 Where mortar repairs are proposed, the work should be carried out by specialists and be appropriate to the fabric and appearance of the original stonework. The applicant should be able to satisfy the planning authority that the specification of the work will not promote further damage of the stonework. For example, the use of hard cement-based mortars will accelerate decay in many cases. The use of large elements of cast stone (sometimes described as 'reconstituted' or 'artificial' stone) should not generally be permitted as a replacement for original stonework. Cast stone rarely possesses the same visual or performance properties of the surrounding stonework and will look and weather differently.

Repointing of Stonework

8.3.15 Repointing has the potential to cause physical damage to the fabric of the building, radically alter its appearance and substantially detract from its character and quality. A proposal to repoint stonework of a protected structure, which would materially alter its character, requires planning permission; and, where permitted, the work should be carried out by experienced people and under the direction of a specialist with a working knowledge and experience of historic buildings.

8.3.16 Repointing should be considered a repair which replaces lost or damaged fabric with that of a compatible and appropriate mix (or series of mixes), material and appearance, providing always that the existing pointing is not inappropriate or damaging to the stonework. Comprehensive repointing of a structure is rarely necessary, unless the existing pointing has deteriorated and is causing damage to the stonework or other fabric. It should be a condition that sound old pointing is left undisturbed as it is an essential part of the fabric and character of a historic building or structure and should not be removed unnecessarily.

8.3.17 Visually, any new pointing should be subservient to the stonework and for this reason obtrusive pointing methods such as ribbon, weatherstruck or strap-pointing should not be permitted unless it is proven that that was the original design intention and not merely a previous unsuitable intervention. Care should be taken to preserve the original pattern of work in cases where the joints contain pinnings (spalls) or galleting. Any pinnings (spalls) dislodged in raking out should be retrieved and re-used.

8.3.18 Existing mortar should not be cut out with inappropriate mechanical cutters, such as angle-grinders, as these will inevitably damage the arises

Repointing which is inappropriately specified and carried out will not only damage the appearance of stone walling but may accelerate the decay of the stone. Sound old pointing should not be removed unnecessarily but, where repointing is unavoidable, the mortar used should generally be slightly weaker than the stone to avoid damage to the historic fabric

The use of mechanical cutters such as angle-grinders to remove existing pointing should be avoided because of the potential to damage the arrises of the stones and widen joints as is the case in this illustration. Needing to rake out historic joints with power tools is often a sign that the pointing has not failed. Mechanical tools, used by specialist conservators, may be appropriate for the removal of later cement repointing

The cleaning of one building in a terrace can lead to a patchwork appearance; on a detailed level it can result in ragged edges where chemical washes or blasted grit have been sprayed onto the neighbouring structure

of the ashlar, widen the joints and so materially alter the appearance of the stonework. The use of mechanical tools in the hands of specialist conservators may be appropriate for the removal of later cement repointing.

Stone cleaning

8.3.19 The cleaning of stonework can materially affect the appearance of a protected structure or the character of an ACA. The potential of stone cleaning to cause irreversible damage means that where works would materially affect the character of such a structure, these works will require planning permission. Unco-ordinated cleaning can create aesthetic problems where a building forms part of a terrace. Where a proposal is made to clean a building that is part of an architectural composition and would result in an unacceptable patchwork effect, damaging the architectural integrity of the group of buildings, permission should normally not be granted. But if the stonework of the group in general is being damaged by dirt deposits, the planning authority may consider it necessary to encourage the simultaneous cleaning of all the relevant buildings to the same specification.

8.3.20 The applicant should be able to justify the necessity of cleaning the stonework of a protected structure. The most frequent reason is on aesthetic grounds. Cleaning is also undertaken to identify necessary repair works or to remove encrustation which is thought to be facilitating decay. It should be considered whether the appearance of the building would be improved by cleaning, which may reveal previously hidden patches or repairs that were specifically coloured to blend with the dirtied appearance of the building.

8.3.21 While a well-executed programme of cleaning may expose detailing of high quality and reveal a building's true architectural merit or can remove damaging encrustations, incorrect decisions can lead to irreversible damage being caused to the building together with a loss of fabric, architectural detailing and character. In some cases, an inappropriate cleaning method will accelerate decay in the stonework. Grit-blasting can be particularly problematic. The proposed cleaning methods should be examined in detail and the planning authority should inform itself on whether the proposed cleaning technique is appropriate and all relevant matters have been properly addressed.

8.3.22 Proposals for the removal of localised stains will require careful consideration. Such stains can include organic growth, graffiti or paint. The use of biocides to remove organic growth should be treated with caution as inappropriate use can cause damage to stonework. Graffiti and paint can be difficult to remove successfully from porous stone surfaces. A variety of methods such as poulticing, steam stripping and abrasion may be used but expert advice should be a requirement of such proposals.

8.3.23 A sample of each of the cleaning techniques should be approved by the planning authority before work commences. The applicant should be able to prove, to the satisfaction of the planning authority, that the proposed works have been specified by experts and would not damage the fabric of the building by:

a) promoting outbreaks of wet or dry rot,

b) creating surface staining due to the release of iron deposits within the stone,

Inappropriate grit-blasting or chemical cleaning methods may ultimately shorten the life of stonework by removing the protective skin of the stone, exposing it to greater environmental damage, or may damage the appearance of the stonework by blurring arrises, tooling or carved work, as has happened in this example

These adjoining houses of the 1770s both retain original brickwork. On the right, the brickwork has an applied red wash and penny-struck pointing; the brickwork on the left retains its original flush pointing, now needing repair

c) causing damaging salt migration through the stone or

d) distorting the architectural detailing, removing tooling marks and blurring arrises.

Brickwork

IDENTIFYING SPECIAL FEATURES FOR PROTECTION

8.3.24 Brick has been used in the construction of buildings in Ireland for several hundred years. Early examples of brick walls used soft handmade bricks, sometimes of irregular shape. Where examples of these exist they should be identified and protected. Specialised pointing methods such as tuck-pointing, the use of coloured mortars and the like should also be noted.

8.3.25 As the nineteenth century progressed, the manufacture of bricks became industrialised and bricks were usually mechanically cut, resulting in sharp arrises. The use of various coloured bricks became popular and these were often used decoratively in patterned courses. Moulded bricks were extensively used in architraves, string courses, cornices, plinths and in decorative panels. Where these exist they will normally contribute to the architectural character of the wall and they should be protected.

CONSIDERATION OF PROPOSALS AFFECTING BRICK WALLING

Specification of repair works

8.3.26 Many of the considerations that apply to the repair of stonework apply equally to brickwork. Brickwork repairs need detailed specification and an applicant should be required to provide the planning authority with all necessary information to allow an assessment of the proposals. This information could include:

a) the specification of any replacement bricks;

b) a sample of the replacement brick;

c) the specification and extent of any proposed repointing;

d) the techniques to be used in carrying out the works, and

e) the experience and expertise of the people who will be responsible for the work.

8.3.27 In some cases, the planning authority may need to seek specialist advice to ensure that all relevant matters have been thoroughly investigated by the applicant.

Replacement of bricks

8.3.28 The replacement of individual decayed bricks may be permitted where bricks have been damaged or decayed to the extent that their structural integrity is in doubt. It should be a condition that decayed bricks are cut out in a way that causes the minimum disturbance to the surrounding sound bricks. If an unacceptable amount of disturbance is likely, the use of brick slips may be permitted as replacements rather than full-depth bricks, providing the structural stability of the wall is not compromised and the adhesion of the slips is guaranteed.

8.3.29 Any replacement bricks should match the original as closely as possible in size, durability, texture and colour. For example, where the original bricks are soft handmade bricks, the use of machine-made replacements are likely to be inappropriate. In special cases, it may be necessary to have new bricks made in order to achieve an appropriate match. Any replacements should be laid with the same bond, joint size and joint colour as the original. Where the brickwork is patterned or coloured, the replacement bricks should match the pattern and colours of the originals.

8.3.30 Matching second-hand bricks should normally only be used where they have been weathered similarly to the existing bricks and providing that the replacement bricks have not been taken to the detriment of another building.

The decay of the soft handmade bricks of this façade has been accelerated by the use of extensive and poorly-executed cementitious mortar repairs coupled with strap pointing

Where the repointing of historic brickwork is proposed, the specification of the mortar and the style of work to be used in repointing should be provided. Where specialist work will be required such as wigging and tucking, demonstrated here, the work should be undertaken by experienced personnel

Mortar repairs to brickwork

8.3.31 Damaged brickwork can be repaired by patching using specialised mortars, a technique also known as 'plastic repair'. Extensive mortar repair work is not appropriate in brick walls. The technique should normally only be permitted where small amounts of work are required and where specialists will carry out the work. Mortar repairs should not be permitted in cases where it is seen merely as an inexpensive alternative to brick replacement.

8.3.32 The applicant should be able to show that the specification of the work will not promote further damage of the brickwork. For example, the use of cement-based mortars will accelerate decay in many cases.

Repointing of brickwork

8.3.33 Repointing which is poorly executed or uses unsuitable techniques or materials can cause physical damage to the fabric of the building, materially alter its appearance and substantially detract from its character and quality. A proposal to repoint a protected structure, which would materially alter its character, will require planning permission. The planning authority should make it a condition of permission that the work is carried out by experienced people under the direction of a specialist with a working knowledge and experience of historic buildings.

8.3.34   Repointing should be considered a repair that replaces lost or damaged fabric with a compatible and appropriate mix (or series of mixes), material and appearance, provided that the existing pointing is not inappropriate or damaging to the brickwork. Comprehensive repointing of a structure is rarely necessary unless the existing pointing is causing damage to the brickwork or other fabric. It could be a condition that any sound pointing is left undisturbed, as it is an essential part of the fabric and character of a historic building or structure and should never be removed unnecessarily.

8.3.35   Visually, pointing should always be subservient to the brickwork and for this reason obtrusive pointing methods such as ribbon, weatherstruck or strap-pointing should never be permitted unless it is proven that that was the original design intention and not merely a previous unsuitable intervention. Where examples of pointing exist, such as tuck-pointing or lime putty used in gauged brickwork, as much as possible of the original material should be retained and should not be lost in a comprehensive repointing of the wall.

8.3.36   Again, as with stonework, existing mortar should not be cut out with inappropriate mechanical cutters, such as angle-grinders, as these will inevitably damage the arrises of the bricks, possibly widen the joints and so damage the appearance of the brickwork. The use of mechanical tools in the hands of specialist conservators may be appropriate for the removal of later cement repointing.

Brick cleaning

8.3.37   As with stonework, the cleaning of brickwork can materially affect the appearance of a protected structure or the character of an ACA. The potential of brick cleaning to cause irreversible damage means that where the works would materially affect the character of such a structure, these works will require planning permission. Unco-ordinated cleaning of buildings, which are part of an architectural composition, can create a patchwork effect, damaging the architectural integrity of the group of buildings. In such cases, permission should normally not be granted. But if the brickwork of the group in general is being damaged by dirt deposits, the planning authority may consider it necessary to encourage the simultaneous cleaning of all the relevant buildings to the same specification.

The conservation work carried out to the left-hand house – new tuck pointing and cleaned brickwork – appears to have been well specified and executed, however the architectural integrity of the terrace as a whole may suffer from the patchwork effect of unco ordinated works

8.3.38   The method of cleaning a brick building should be considered carefully. In some cases, the cleaning method may in fact accelerate decay in the brickwork. On the other hand, a well-executed programme of cleaning may expose detailing of high quality and reveal a building's true architectural merit. As with stone cleaning above, proposals for the removal of localised stains, such as organic growth, graffiti or paint, will require careful consideration. A variety of methods such as poulticing, steam stripping and abrasion may be used but expert advice should be a requirement of such proposals.

8.3.39   Before any works are undertaken, careful research and a full assessment are needed and the onus should be on the applicant to satisfy the planning authority that cleaning will benefit the protected structure and that the methods used will not damage its fabric or character.

8.3.40   The planning authority should approve a sample of each of the proposed cleaning techniques before work commences. The risk of damage to the fabric should be assessed. Unlike certain types of stonework, brickwork is usually unaffected by dirt deposits except in its appearance. Water-washing, if incorrectly used, may saturate the fabric and cause outbreaks of wet or dry rot within the structure or cause damaging salt migration through the brickwork. Inappropriate abrasive systems such as grit-blasting will damage the outer surface or fireskin of the brick and accelerate the decay process. Specialised pointing methods, such as tuck-pointing, will be damaged by inappropriate cleaning processes.

Timber

IDENTIFYING SPECIAL FEATURES FOR PROTECTION

8.3.41   Timber is found as a structural element throughout traditional buildings whether as framing, posts, beams, lintels, wall plates, rafters or trusses. Timber pieces are also found set into masonry walls as bonding and levelling pieces, fixing points or simply as filling. Early timber-framed external walls are extremely rare in Ireland and where they are found they should be identified and protected. Timber stud internal walls can be either structural in function, sometimes trussed, or acting as non-structural partitions.

8.3.42 In addition to their interest as evidence of original or early structural systems, old timbers are of importance where they can be used, by means of dendrochronology (tree-ring dating) or by means of the construction method used, to date periods of construction. Where original or early timber structural elements exist, such as timber flitch beams, cruck trusses and other trussed construction methods, they should be identified and retained.

CONSIDERATION OF PROPOSALS TO REMOVE OR REPLACE DECAYED STRUCTURAL TIMBER

8.3.43 While a great quantity of historic timber fabric can been lost through the processes of decay, a great deal more can be lost in the process of treating it. The appropriate treatment and repair of timber decay in old buildings involves careful detailing, experience and an understanding of the decay processes. The use of chemical treatments is no substitute for good detailing and workmanship.

8.3.44 The timbers used in structures built before the twentieth century generally came from slow-growing, often virgin, forests and as such are a non-renewable resource. This timber is usually denser (often having greater load-bearing capacity than modern timber), more durable and more resistant to fungal infection and insect attack. In many cases original timber elements can outlast pre-treated modern timber repairs exposed to the same decay factors.

8.3.45 Where timber is a significant part of the structure's fabric, the applicant may be required to provide detailed independent survey reports and methodologies for dealing with timber decay issues in a way which would minimise the damage to, and loss of, historic fabric.

8.3.46 The removal of original or early timber from a protected structure should generally not be permitted or, where proven to be necessary, should be kept to a minimum. The removal of important timber structural elements or joinery simply as a precautionary measure against possible fungal infection should not be permitted. Where an unavoidable risk has been identified, monitoring can

Original or early structural timbers contribute to the character of a structure. Rare elements of structural timber, such as this seventeenth-century brick-nogged partition, are extremely important and should be identified and protected

The localised removal of bonding or levelling timbers within a masonry wall may be appropriate where there is good reason to suspect that they have significantly decayed. However locating these timbers and removing them can involve the destruction of large amounts of historic fabric particularly plaster

be used as an alternative to the removal of timber. The only justification for the removal of original or early timber should usually be where structural decay has occurred and repairs require its removal. This is normally confined to bearing ends.

8.3.47 Proposals may be made to remove large areas of render, plasterwork or other finishes in order to expose structural timber, often resulting in a significant loss of historic fabric. These proposals should not be permitted unless the applicant can prove there is good reason to suspect that significant decay has occurred to concealed structural timber. If concealed timber is present, but is not structural, a case can often be made for its retention in situ. Stripping large areas of wall plaster in the pursuit of concealed bonding timbers can often be avoided by simply tapping the plaster surface and listening for voids. Localised removal and replacement with a non-timber element can then be carried out where necessary.

Fungal attack

8.3.48 Structurally significant timber decay is generally only found where the timber is embedded in, or is in contact with, saturated masonry. Timber decay fungi in buildings are commonly grouped into 'wet rots' which includes a range of fungal species and 'dry rot' (Serpula lacrymans) a single fungal species. Although the typical conditions in which each thrive and the patterns of decay vary, the remedial actions required are the same. In the recent past, treatments of dry rot have tended to be very destructive of the existing fabric of buildings. These treatments often require the cutting out and destruction of all timber within a specified radius of the infection and the introduction of large amounts of fungicidal chemicals into the surrounding fabric. In light of a greater understanding of the processes of fungal decay in buildings, this type of treatment is now considered inappropriate. The removal of timber should be confined to that which is structurally decayed.

8.3.49   Proposed opening-up works and treatments that require the extensive disturbance or loss of fabric (such as ceilings, floors and finishes) and the widespread removal of uninfected timber should not be permitted and are not necessary to control a fungal attack. Dry rot requires water and masonry in order to decay timber. When the source of water has been removed, the fungus will die back naturally once the timber has dried out.

8.3.50   Where proposals are made to treat fungal attack within a protected structure, the applicant should be able to show that the sources of moisture (past and present) have been identified and that proposals have been made for remedial action such as the drying-out of masonry, ventilation, repair of structurally decayed timber and the isolation of existing and new at-risk timber, with a minimum disruption of the historic fabric.

8.3.51   Proposals to irrigate walls of any structure with fungicidal chemicals should be treated with caution. In cases of dry rot decay, the drying out of the structure, the provision of adequate ventilation and appropriate detailing of repairs will be sufficient to control the infection. Where the structure is difficult to dry out, for example where there are thick masonry walls, the detailing and monitoring of the moisture contents of critical timbers, localised ventilation and, occasionally, the use of dehumidification can control rot during the drying-out period. This may arise particularly in cases where the fabric of a building has been saturated as a result of fire-fighting or flood damage.

Insect infestation

8.3.52   Only two types of wood-boring insect are commonly found in structures in Ireland: woodworm, which is the larval stage of a beetle (Anobium puncatum) and wood-boring weevils. Wood-boring weevil damage, unlike woodworm, is caused by the adult weevils. Conditions required for weevil damage include persistently wet timber partially (and often substantially) decayed by fungi.

Where an outbreak of fungal attack in timber has been identified, the removal of historic fabric should be confined to timber directly infected by the rot or structurally weakened by it. Once the source of water has been removed and adequate ventilation provided, the fungus will die back naturally, thus avoiding the need for the wholesale stripping out of timber

Where timbers contain flight holes from past infestation by wood-boring insects, it is important to establish whether or not the infestation is current. In this case a furniture beetle, or woodworm, is visible on the surface of the timber beam, indicating ongoing attack

8.3.53   Wood-boring insects require timber of a high moisture content to survive, so the elimination of dampness and the provision of appropriate ventilation should usually be sufficient to control the infestation. Appropriate remedial action to deal with wood-boring insect damage is to cut out and replace structurally affected timber and to isolate replacement timber from the moisture source, combined with clearing dirt and debris from relevant voids and the provision of ventilation to protect against future infestation.

Mud and sod walling
IDENTIFYING SPECIAL FEATURES FOR PROTECTION

8.3.54   Unbaked earth was used throughout Ireland in the construction of vernacular buildings, usually where free stone was not available in sufficient quantities or quality for the construction of rubble walls. Mud-walled houses can be substantial single or two-storey buildings. Clay from the subsoil was mixed with chopped straw, water and other materials to form the building material. The mud walls were constructed off a plinth of stone and the walling built up in layers, sometimes using timber shuttering to support the work. Often the cross walls of the house containing the chimney stacks were built in stone or brick but they could also be constructed of wickerwork plastered with daub. Clay and mud were also used as mortar materials.

8.3.55   Because earth walling was traditionally covered with lime-based roughcast or limewash coatings and sometimes a stone facing, the construction of these buildings may not always be readily identifiable. Their increasing rarity means that the preservation and maintenance of the surviving examples is extremely important.

8.3.56   Sod walling is another form of vernacular walling where trimmed lumps of topsoil were used as building blocks. These blocks were sometimes pegged together or bound together with a clay mortar. Examples of this type of construction are extremely rare and any surviving examples should be identified and protected.

CONSIDERATION OF PROPOSALS AFFECTING MUD AND SOD WALLING

8.3.57   Alterations or extensions, that might endanger the stability of an earthen structure should not be permitted. Where alterations or repairs are proposed to mud-walled structures, expert advice needs to be taken by the applicant.

8.3.58   The strength of mud walling is dependent on its moisture content. Consequently, the introduction of damp-proof courses should be avoided as these may lead to a drying out of the wall and to instability in the structure. For the same reason, strong and impervious cement renders or plasters should not be permitted to the exteriors or interiors of these walls as these damage the walling material's ability to breathe and can lead to its failure.

8.3.59   The addition of impervious building materials, such as the insertion of bricks and concrete blocks into the fabric, should always be avoided as these can undermine the structural stability of the walling.

Iron and other metal structures
IDENTIFYING SPECIAL FEATURES FOR PROTECTION

8.3.60   Wrought or cast iron are found in use as structural elements in a variety of protected structures, including industrial buildings and conservatories. Because of technical advances during the nineteenth century in the production of iron, iron structural elements were used extensively in many Victorian industrial buildings such as railway stations and warehouses. Wrought iron has a high tensile strength and so tends to be found in beams. Cast iron on the other hand, has little tensile strength but considerable compressive strength and so was commonly used in posts and columns. Both forms of iron, and a combination of the two, were also used in architectural embellishments such as balconies, verandas, cresting and railings.

Mud walling was generally built up in layers or occasionally using unbaked blocks of clay. Mud-walled buildings are not always readily identifiable as they were usually finished with a roughcast render coating of mud or lime mortar. It is in the nature of the material that mud-walled buildings tend to decay rapidly unless well-maintained and promptly repaired when damaged

The early twentieth-century cast in situ concrete repair to this mud-walled house at Mayglass, Co. Wexford was the subject of careful consideration during recent conservation work, but was left in place once stabilised. Unbaked brick was used elsewhere for repairs to the walling

Structural ironwork is found in a large range of building types where it is usually clearly identifiable. However, cast-iron elements were also formed in imitation of masonry, as in this balustraded bridge parapet, and the material used may not always be obvious

CONSIDERATION OF PROPOSALS AFFECTING
IRON STRUCTURES

8.3.61 In situ repairs will usually cause less damage to historic ironwork than dismantling and re-erecting. However it may be necessary for the planning authority to permit partial dismantling and re-erection of an iron structure in cases where movement or distortion of the structure has occurred, in order to effect repairs. Dismantling may also be necessary in order to apply rust treatment to inaccessible areas.

8.3.62 Where dismantling of an iron structure is permitted, it should be conditional on the structure being recorded in detail before work commences by means of drawings and photographs, with each element tagged and numbered and cross-referred to the relevant drawing. As much of the existing material as possible should be retained and consolidated rather than renewed. Additional and appropriate material may be added, where necessary, to reinforce or to support the existing material where this would not adversely affect the fabric or appearance of the protected structure.

8.3.63 When permitting the removal of paint prior to repair, it must be realised that this action eradicates the paint history of the ironwork, where this survives, thus making it impossible thereafter to determine the original or earlier colour schemes. Where the planning authority considers important evidence of an earlier paint scheme may exist, it could be a condition of permission that a small area of ironwork be left unstripped or a proper paint analysis carried out before an appropriate method of paint stripping takes place.

8.3.64 Where small elements of ironwork are missing, a case could be made for restoration or replication of the missing element. However, such restoration should be based upon firm evidence of the original element using old photographs, drawings, or other reliable information and should not be conjectural. Where it is necessary to replace wrought-iron structural members, recycled wrought iron should be used or new wrought iron obtained, if available. This is preferable to introducing a replacement material, such as mild steel with its different physical properties, such as thermal expansion coefficient, which may be potentially damaging to the structure.

While it may sometimes be necessary to carefully dismantle an ironwork structure for repairs, some structures may consist of iron-clad sections on timber and masonry supports and may be more difficult to successfully dismantle and reassemble

Early mass- and reinforced-concrete structures, as well as early blockwork and cast or reconstituted 'stone' structures may be of technical interest. This silo of 1905 is constructed of reinforced concrete using the pioneering Hennebique technique and is one of the few such structures surviving in Ireland

Mass concrete and reinforced
concrete structures
IDENTIFYING SPECIAL FEATURES FOR PROTECTION

8.3.65 Mass concrete has been used for construction in Ireland since the middle of the nineteenth century. Although the use of iron, and later, steel rods to strengthen concrete began in the eighteen-fifties, the use of reinforced concrete in Ireland is primarily found in buildings of the twentieth century.

8.3.66 Both mass and reinforced concrete were commonly used in the construction of engineering structures such as bridges. In the twentieth century, mass concrete was often used as a walling material which was commonly rendered or clad. Concrete was also used as a self-finished material sometimes board-marked from the shuttering to give the finished concrete a textured appearance. Early mass or reinforced concrete structures will be of interest and should be identified and may often be worthy of protection.

CONSIDERATION OF PROPOSALS AFFECTING CONCRETE STRUCTURES

8.3.67　Where repair works are proposed to concrete structures it is important to ensure that the applicant has carried out adequate investigations to determine the cause and extent of damage. An incomplete understanding of the mechanisms of decay can lead to inadequate, or possibly damaging, repairs.

8.3.68　Where voids in the surface of exposed concrete allow water to enter and cause spalling, these will need to be filled. However, superficial methods of repair to concrete, such as spraying with new concrete, should generally not be permitted without assessing and treating the underlying problem of rusted reinforcement. Spraying on new concrete may be visually unacceptable where it will alter the profile of the concrete components of a protected structure. Specification and methods of repair should be approved by the planning authority prior to works commencing.

8.4　Cladding Materials

Plain and roughcast render
IDENTIFYING SPECIAL FEATURES FOR PROTECTION

8.4.1　Plain and roughcast renders are traditional coatings applied to rubble, brick and other structures throughout the country and usually form an integral part of a building's weathering system as well as its designed appearance.

8.4.2　Roughcast renders were the traditional external coatings applied to rubble-walled buildings. These were made of a mixture of lime putty and sand with other additives, including animal hair, creating a relatively soft and porous render which was applied by throwing the mixture at the wall resulting in a gentle, undulating finish. Roughcast render was usually finished with layers of limewash, reapplied on a regular basis. Where original or early lime-based roughcast finishes are identified, they may be worthy of protection.

8.4.3　The late eighteenth and nineteenth centuries saw much experimentation with render mixes leading to the development of a number of patented renders

The repair of concrete structures should be carried out so as to resolve the underlying problem without a visually obtrusive result. In this illustration the repair to the reconstituted 'stone' will tone down in time although the strap repointing is inappropriate

Render is a traditional coating which contributes both to the weathering performance and appearance of a structure. This house has been partially faced in Roman cement in imitation of rusticated ashlar and, while not the original finish, clearly contributes to its character

including oil mastic stuccoes and Roman cement. The patenting of Portland cement in England in the early nineteenth century allowed for the production of harder, more brittle coatings which could be applied by trowel and finished to provide a smooth surface.

8.4.4　Plain renders are found on buildings throughout the towns of Ireland and often on the minor elevations of high quality ashlar or brick-faced buildings. Plain render is a harder and smoother material than roughcast render and often included the use of cement. In many cases, the render was ruled and lined out to imitate the pattern of ashlar blocks.

8.4.5 Later, more elaborate, uses of render included the formation of imitation rustication, cornices, string courses, window and door surrounds and shopfronts. Although often not original to the building, render embellishments can be of great interest and form part of the character of a building.

8.4.6 Pebble-dash is another form of render coating usually dating from the late nineteenth and early twentieth centuries. Also known as dry-dash, this finish is achieved when natural or artificial pebbles are pushed or thrown onto wet render and left exposed.

CONSIDERATION OF PROPOSALS AFFECTING RENDERS
Proposals to remove plain or roughcast render

8.4.7 Early or original, plain or roughcast render contributes to the character of a protected structure and should generally not be removed. The stripping-off of existing render, merely to expose rubble or brick walls that were not originally intended to be seen, should generally not be permitted. Not only does the stripping-off of the original finish greatly diminish the architectural quality and character of the building, it also seriously threatens the watertightness of the entire fabric. Removing the original finish also eradicates part of the history of the building, making it impossible thereafter to determine the material or mix of the original coat and any paint history of the applied finish.

8.4.8 It can be sometimes proved, using old photographs or similar, that a coating is a later addition to the structure. However, in such cases it should be borne in mind that the coating may have been added in order to cover up alterations, damage or decay in the original wall surfaces, which it may not be desirable to re-expose.

8.4.9 Where it is permitted to strip off and replace a plain or roughcast render finish, the planning authority should require as a condition that any evidence of the history of the building or structure, revealed by stripping off plain or roughcast render coatings, be carefully recorded before the application of the new finish. Where it is permitted to remove a lime-based roughcast, the planning authority should normally make it a condition that it is replaced on a like-for-like basis and not with a cement-based coating. The specification, mix and finish should be approved by the planning authority before any work commences.

Embellishments in render were popular as a cheap alternative to cut-stone decoration; some craftsmen took the form to its creative epitome, notably the McAuliffe family of Listowel, active in the early twentieth century at the height of the Celtic Revival

The removal of render from surfaces originally rendered not only significantly alters the architectural character of the structure but removes the weathering layer provided by the render. In most cases the rubble stone or stone-and-brick mix, now exposed, was never meant to be visible. In this example, the removal of external render has also affected the visual integrity of the entire row of buildings

Hard cement-based render can cause lasting damage due to its impermeability. Any cracks and gaps which develop in the render allow moisture into the fabric behind, which cannot then easily escape, so saturating the wall. In the case of this mediaeval window surround, moisture, and the salts carried by it, is forced to evaporate through the historic stone so setting up conditions for decay. It can often be difficult to remove cement render without causing damage to the underlying masonry

8.4.10 Where a building is covered with an inappropriate cementitious render, which is causing damage to the fabric beneath, the opportunity could be taken to use a more appropriate replacement coating. However, where the removal of a later render is likely to cause damage to the material below, it may be better to leave it in place. Testing and assessment should be carried out and decisions made based on this information.

Proposals to apply plain or roughcast render to buildings not currently rendered

8.4.11 Walls should not normally be rendered unless the surface was originally finished in this way. Permission should not be given for such surfaces to be faced with new cosmetic treatments which would be difficult or damaging to remove, such as cement render, stone facing, Tyrolean render, dry or pebble-dashing or cement-based paints.

8.4.12 In cases where the original walling is of a very poor weathering quality and a severe degree of decay has occurred, it could be appropriate to permit the application of plain or roughcast render when the only alternative would be to reface the structure completely. Permission should only be granted after careful consideration of all the implications.

Repairing plain or roughcast render finishes

8.4.13 Most old renderings fail from problems associated with water penetration, either from lack of maintenance, inadequate protection from the elements, salt contamination from the backing material or because of poor materials or techniques employed in the original application.

8.4.14 Where the coating has separated from its backing, only the loose material should normally be removed. The sound areas of coating should be retained and patched with new material which matches in terms of colour, material, texture and strength of the original finish. The number and thickness of coats should also be matched.

8.4.15 Where the wall has an undulating surface, as with rubble stonework or earth, it could be a requirement that no attempt be made to dub out the surface in order to achieve a flat mechanical finish, unless there is evidence that this was so originally. Original details at corners and at openings should usually be replicated. Where render has been lined out in imitation of ashlar, care should be taken in setting out so that the original pattern is replicated. The lining of window arches should be set out from a centre-point or points and window and door openings should be detailed so that blocks or half-blocks rather than closers appear at the architraves.

Localised re-rendering should be carefully specified to match the existing material. In this example, while the strength and texture may be adequate, the unmatched colouring of several patches is visually obtrusive

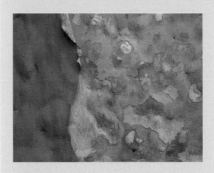

The way that limewashed render weathers contributes greatly to the patina of age: as it rubs away layers of different colours may be exposed. New coats of limewash can be applied as necessary without removing the existing layers

8.4.16 Where areas of pebble-dashing are to be repaired or replicated, the type, size, shape and colour of the exposed stones should blend with the original while allowing it to be clear on close inspection that the work is not original.

Cut-stone details

8.4.17 Where stone quoins, string courses, cornices, or other architectural details were originally left exposed, permission should not normally be given for these to be covered over by new coatings except shelter-coating.

Painted façades
IDENTIFYING SPECIAL FEATURES FOR PROTECTION

8.4.18 Decorative or other painted façades, which contribute to the character of a protected structure or of an ACA, should be identified and protected.

8.4.19 Limewash was the traditional finish for lime-based roughcast or renders and a variety of traditional building materials. It was usually applied in multiple coats and reapplied on a regular basis to maintain the fabric. Where there is evidence of limewash on surfaces, these surfaces should preferably continue to be maintained with limewash and the use of alternative paint systems discouraged, particularly where they would have an adverse effect of the substrate by limiting the porosity of the wall.

CONSIDERATION OF PROPOSALS AFFECTING PAINTED FACADES

8.4.20 Proposals to paint façades not previously painted should be carefully scrutinised. Permission should not normally be given for previously unpainted walls of protected structures to be painted over (except for the addition of shelter-coating). The use of cement-based or other waterproof and hard gloss paints should not be permitted on surfaces covered with traditional render, as they will cause damage to the historic fabric. Similarly, the partial painting of brick or stone façades around shopfronts or to display advertising material should be avoided.

8.4.21 Plain render was often left unpainted with a grey-brown self-coloured finish, but over the years paint finishes have tended to be applied to such render. Where these are not harming the fabric, for example by restricting the porosity of the wall, no issue should arise.

Metal cladding
IDENTIFYING SPECIAL FEATURES FOR PROTECTION

8.4.22 Many nineteenth and twentieth-century structures incorporate metal sheeting or metal-faced panels in various materials including iron, steel, lead, copper and zinc. Corrugated-iron sheeting (in fact, generally made of steel) has been used as a cladding for many vernacular buildings such as barns and outbuildings, and even churches, since the eighteen-fifties. Where this material exists on a protected structure, the profile of the corrugations should be noted and the type and colour of the finish used. Good examples of corrugated-iron-sheeted structures should be identified and protected.

CONSIDERATION OF PROPOSALS AFFECTING METAL CLADDING

8.4.23 Existing metal cladding should be repaired rather than replaced. Where works are proposed to a corrugated-iron structure or any metal-clad structure, any proposed new sheeting should match the existing in terms of weight, profile and finish. Existing details should be replicated, except where the original cladding had inherent faults which led to failure, such as the use of overlarge metal sheets or incorrect fixings that caused cracking of the cladding. Where there was an inherent design fault, the metal cladding will require replacement to an improved design. Cracks should not be repaired with solder or with sealant, as these repairs will often cause further problems at a later stage.

Applying impermeable paint to render or masonry can inhibit the necessary passage of moisture through the fabric. Unsuitable paints may peel off, sometimes shortly after application

Metal sheeting consisting of flat or corrugated panels of iron, steel, lead, copper or zinc was used to clad many types of buildings, including places of worship such as this small church. Early metal sheeting is often of technical interest and should be identified and, where necessary, repaired, unless an inherent design fault requires its replacement to an improved specification

Coade stone, a proprietary fired clay, was used for fine decorative detailing. It generally makes a significant contribution to the character of the structure it adorns

Terracotta, faïence, Coade stone and ceramic tiling
IDENTIFYING SPECIAL FEATURES FOR PROTECTION

8.4.24 The external use of terracotta and faïence cladding on buildings in Ireland generally dates from the late nineteenth and early twentieth centuries. Good quality design and craftsmanship and examples of decorative detailing may be suitable for protection.

8.4.25 Coade stone is a proprietary fired-clay material used for the production of architectural ornament such as plaques, friezes, statues etc. This highly durable material was produced at a factory in Lambeth, in south London between c.1770 and c.1840. Where this type of ornament exists on a protected structure, it is a feature that should be identified and protected.

8.4.26   The external use of glazed ceramic tiling, faïence or glazed terracotta is generally associated in Ireland with shopfronts, although there are examples of glazed brick used as external facing. Where examples of tiling contribute to the character of a protected structure or an ACA, they should be retained.

CONSIDERATION OF PROPOSALS AFFECTING SUCH CLADDING

8.4.27   These products are generally long lasting provided water penetration can be prevented. If the fireskin of a fired clay unit is breached, there can be a rapid deterioration of the weaker underbody of the element. The fireskin or the glazing can be defective due to poor original firing, but they will also be damaged by aggressive cleaning methods such as grit-blasting.

8.4.28   Repairs or cleaning of fire clay products, where necessary, should be carried out only by specialist conservators. Painting of these elements or their replacement in alternative materials should not normally be permitted. Large-scale repairs with mortar are not appropriate nor is the facing-up of damaged terracotta with mortar followed by overall painting, as this will materially alter the character of the building and may cause further damage and deterioration to the fabric.

Slate-hanging

8.4.29   Slate-hanging was often applied to exposed external walls and chimney stacks to provide extra protection from the weather. Where slate-hanging exists it should be preserved and carefully repaired. Particular care should be taken to identify and protect any slates that are of decorative shape or carved with dates or initials.

Arts-and-Crafts wall cladding

8.4.30   Late nineteenth and early twentieth century buildings of the Arts and Crafts style experimented with a variety of cladding materials and methods. These included clay tile-hanging, exposed timber framing, pebble-dashing, timber weather-boarding and others. These finishes are essential to the character of these buildings and all original materials and their detailing should be identified, and retained.

Terracotta, faïence and glazed ceramic tiles are all used to good visual effect in cladding or decorating the walls of buildings

Materials such as terracotta and faïence tend to be very durable. However, they can be damaged by aggressive cleaning methods. In this case, a later paint finish, together with the original fireskin of the terracotta, have been removed, exposing mortar repairs and old defects and leaving the ceramic vulnerable to future accelerated weathering

Cladding walls with slate was often done to protect structures, or parts of structures, on elevations exposed to prevailing winds. Slate-hanging often includes decoratively-cut slates or banding using fishscale patterns. Its use may be a regional characteristic

Slate-hanging should be carefully repaired where necessary using slates of a matching size and colour, with additions such as downpipes and vents carefully sited and fixed in order not to cause damage

8.4.31 Where repairs are necessary to such cladding materials they should be carried out in accordance with the relevant section of these guidance notes.

8.5 Exterior Fixtures and Features

8.5.1 Protection includes all fixtures and features which form part of the exterior of a protected structure and contribute to its special interest. In some cases it may be difficult to establish whether or not a particular object or feature is a fixture. Although not defined in the Act, the term 'fixture' implies a degree of physical annexation together with indications that the annexation was carried out with the intention of making the object an integral part of the structure. However, free-standing objects may be considered fixtures if they were placed in position as part of an overall architectural design. For example, the external walls of a public building may contain statues or other carvings within niches which, while they may or may not be physically fixed to the building, were designed or made to fit a specific space to form part of the design. In some cases, the planning authority may need to take expert advice on assessing the contribution of the object to the character of the protected structure where there are proposals to alter or remove that object.

IDENTIFYING EXISTING FIXTURES AND FEATURES FOR PROTECTION

8.5.2 Exterior fixtures and features of architectural metalwork on walls such as railings, cresting, balustrades and anchor plates are usually an essential part of the character of a protected structure.

8.5.3 Balconies and verandas can be important original architectural fixtures and features on many buildings, usually dating from the nineteenth and twentieth centuries. They may also be additions to earlier buildings. Where these are original features or additions of quality, they should be retained. Because fixtures and features such as balconies by definition tend to be exposed elements, they often give rise to maintenance problems and, as a result, have been removed. Surviving features are therefore increasingly rare and should be preserved, where possible.

8.5.4 Other fixtures and features such as date-stones, fire insurance plaques, commemorative plaques and carvings, statues, inscriptions, coats of arms etc. are equally part of the history of a building, even where they are later additions, and should be retained in situ. Old lettering and shop signs may be more

Arts and Crafts style cladding can feature a variety of materials and cladding types. As shown here, materials such as brick, half-timbering and tiles are juxtaposed to form visually attractive patterns

Exterior fixtures and features vary widely in size, function and materials. Some, such as the lead gas lamp illustrated here, have been adapted to electric light and continue in use. But, even where redundant, such fixtures and features are often important to the character of a structure or area, in addition to being well-crafted items in themselves

Carved stone plaques are found most often on the walls of public buildings such as schools and churches – as with this wall monument - but many domestic buildings also have datestones. Whether or not the structure has changed use or the carving is now illegible, efforts should be made to retain interesting plaques or monuments in situ

difficult to retain when premises change ownership, but efforts should be made to identify and retain examples that are of particular interest or quality.

CONSIDERATION OF PROPOSALS AFFECTING FIXTURES AND FEATURES
Existing exterior fixtures and features

8.5.5 The appearance of a protected structure or any other historic building will be materially altered by the removal of architectural features from walls such as balustrades, string courses, brackets and others. The removal of such features would be detrimental to the character of the building. Where works to a structure require the temporary removal of a feature or fixture, it should be replaced in its former position within a time frame specified by the planning authority.

8.5.6 The removal of elements such as balconies, balconettes and verandas should not be permitted without careful consideration of the potential effects on the character of the building. Where these elements are later additions to a structure and they cut across or conceal work of a higher architectural quality, a judgement will have to be made on whether or not to remove the later work. In such cases, where the addition is relatively recent and of little architectural merit, it may be acceptable to permit careful removal. Proposals to glaze in balconies, verandas and the like, where they were originally intended to be open, should be treated with caution as this may adversely affect the appearance of a protected structure or the character of an ACA.

New items fixed to the exterior of the building

8.5.7 Careful consideration needs to be given to proposals to fix new items to the exterior of a protected structure. Permission should usually only be given for fixtures that respect the architectural design of the structure and do not detract from its appearance. Examples of types of fixtures which may be proposed could include floodlighting, entry phones, name plates or signboards, information plaques, alarm boxes, satellite dishes, window-cleaning eyes, or plastic utility boxes such as gas and electricity meters.

8.5.8 The applicant should be able to satisfy the planning authority that matters such as the location of fixtures, associated cable runs, light fittings and so on have been properly considered and would not detract from the appearance of the protected structure, the setting of other protected structures or the character of an ACA. Consideration should be given to the effect the methods of fixing proposed may have. Many fixing methods will cause damage by staining or fracturing the material into which they are fixed. The presence of a fixture which requires painting, cleaning or lubrication will usually result in splashing or staining of the adjacent building fabric. If the fixture is changed or removed, holes left may remain visible even after careful repair. Fixing should be carried out in a manner that minimises the visual impact upon the building and avoids physical damage to the fabric. Fixing into existing joints or holes may be acceptable.

8.5.9 Automatic teller machines, where their installation is permitted, should be accommodated within existing openings wherever possible. Proposals to create new openings for such machines should be discouraged. Those which cut through important architectural features or disturb elevational symmetry, should be refused permission. The use by major retailers or commercial organisations of

Fixtures or features fitted without thought as to their visual impact can adversely affect the character of a structure or area. The removal – or resiting – of such items should be encouraged whenever possible. The method of fixing should be reversible and, on stone or brick façades in particular, made into existing joints rather than through the masonry to avoid scarring

The removal of signs may cause or exacerbate existing problems. In this case rusticated masonry was cut out to recess the sign. Now that the sign has been removed, the damaging consequences of the work are all too obvious

corporate colours and lettering on the walls of a protected structure is not appropriate in most instances and should be discouraged.

External plumbing, flues, vents and cabling

8.5.10 The appearance of many historic buildings will be marred by the addition of external plumbing, especially where it cuts through or across architectural features or disturbs the symmetry of an elevation. Planning applications for works to protected structures or buildings within ACAs should include on the drawings the location of all proposed external plumbing, flues, vents and cabling to allow for a complete assessment of the proposals. The planning authority should be aware that some proposed changes of use will require additional flues and pipework.

8.5.11 Change of use or upgrading can lead to a proliferation of pipework associated with new kitchens or bathrooms. Every effort should be made to avoid the introduction of new external pipework or cabling, particularly on the primary elevations. Proposals that include kitchens and bathrooms on these elevations should therefore be discouraged, if the pipework cannot be satisfactorily accommodated internally.

8.5.12 The addition of external flues should be avoided wherever possible and not be allowed to interrupt important elevations. Vent pipes should not generally be permitted on the roofs of principal elevations. In cases where new external pipework or flues are agreed, the additions should be painted to blend in with the wall surfaces so as to minimise their visual impact.

8.5.13 Where the opportunity arises, the removal or rationalisation of any existing added pipework and cabling that disrupts architectural features or elevations should be considered. The use of extruded aluminium or plastic drainage and rainwater goods and their associated fittings on a protected structure is rarely appropriate and should generally not be permitted.

The ill-considered fixing of new items such as pipework to the principal elevations of structures can adversely affect their architectural quality and cause physical and irreversible damage, as has happened in this case where a fine architectural element has been cut through to facilitate the location of a new pipe

Roofs

The character of a roof relates to its profile and pitch, whether gabled or hipped; the cladding materials; use or not of dormers; the style, materials, siting and number of stacks; the use of decorative bargeboards or rainwater goods; and the way all of these together contribute to the overall character of the structure or area

9.1 Introduction

9.1.1 In many buildings, the roof is a major element that gives the building its distinctive profile. The aspects of a roof, which may contribute to the special interest of a protected structure or a structure within an ACA, include the profile and structure of the roof, the cladding materials used and other details associated with the roof. Specialist advice may be needed in order to identify the special characteristics of a roof.

9.1.2 To help assess the potential contribution of a roof or its components to the special character of the structure, several questions may be considered:

a) Is the roof structure, or any of its component parts, original to the building?

b) If not original, is the roof structure nevertheless of architectural merit or of other interest?

c) If not of interest in itself, does it contribute to or detract from the perception or appreciation of other, more important, parts of the structure?

d) Is there the possibility of an earlier structure existing below later alterations?

e) What are the existing cladding materials? Do these contribute to the character of the building?

f) Are the details such as dormer windows, chimney stacks etc. original to the building? Are they part of a later remodelling? Do they contribute to the interest of the building?

g) Where it is proposed to upgrade the thermal insulation of an existing timber roof, what effect would this have on the appearance of the roof? How is it proposed to ventilate the roof? Where are proposed vents to be located? Would their size, shape or location adversely affect the appearance of the building?

9.2 Profile and Structure

IDENTIFYING SPECIAL FEATURES FOR PROTECTION

9.2.1 When identifying the special characteristics of the profile of a roof it should be considered whether or not the roof retains its original profile and structure. If the present profile is not likely to be the original, then it should be decided whether the present roof profile is of any architectural or other interest or is a later alteration which detracts from the appearance of more important elements of the building.

9.2.2 The structural elements of the roof should be examined. The roof structure should, wherever possible, be viewed from within the roof space and evidence of any part of an earlier structure noted. Structural elements are of importance when they are original to the building, are evidence of earlier alterations or are examples of unusual or innovative design. Wrought and cast-iron roof structures, particularly those with applied decoration, are also of importance. Early mass or reinforced-concrete roofs are of interest as examples of civil engineering design.

CONSIDERATION OF PROPOSALS TO
ALTER A ROOF STRUCTURE

9.2.3 Unevenness and undulations of a roof surface are often part of the character of an old building. Where they exist, it should be established whether or not they affect the watertightness or structural integrity of the building, if it is proposed to replace the roof.

9.2.4 The unnecessary removal of a roof, or part of a roof, in order to replace it in replica, should not generally be permitted. Where this is proposed, the applicant should be required to demonstrate the necessity for the proposed works.

9.2.5 Roofs of structural interest should generally not be altered. Any original, or early, roof structure or structural members should be retained. In cases where the construction of a new roof is unavoidable, the planning authority could make it a condition that the earlier roof construction is retained below the new roof.

The structural components of a roof may contribute to its character. Here a seventeenth-century pegged oak roof structure survives largely intact, with the carpenter's numbers visible on some timbers

Undulations and previous repairs of good quality may all contribute to the character of a roof. Any necessary works should leave intact original detailing such as this raised archway roof, as it provides definition to the entrance bay

Old roof timbers should not be routinely stripped out as this can lead to a loss of character and the destruction of important historic elements. In this case, a roof structure, dated to the 1580s using dendrochronology, remains intact and, although no longer capable of taking the weight of cladding, is preserved beneath a new metal structure

9.2.6   Proposals to alter the shape of the roof of a protected structure or of a structure within an ACA will have a potential impact on the character of the structure and its surroundings. It should not be permitted without careful consideration of the circumstances.

9.2.7   Roofs of protected structures should retain their original form and profile and not be radically altered, for example, to provide extra accommodation in the form of a mansard roof. The insertions of lift-motor rooms, plant rooms and dormers can also materially alter the character and profile of a historic roof and should be carefully scrutinised. Similar alterations to other structures in an ACA should only be permitted after careful consideration of any effect that the alteration could have on the character of the ACA or on the setting of adjacent protected structures.

9.2.8   Where the original shape of the roof has been previously unsympathetically altered, the opportunity could be taken to reinstate the earlier form of the roof, thus restoring the integrity of the structure. However, any such restoration should be based upon firm evidence of the original state. Where a new roof is proposed, the design of the replacement should be sympathetic to the character and special interest of the building and not detract from the overall appearance.

9.2.9   Where a roof or its components have been removed, poorly repaired or altered inappropriately, the reversal of unsatisfactory later work could be undertaken. However, any such restoration work should be based upon firm evidence of the original state of the roof or element using old photographs, drawings, or other reliable information. Where it is proposed to re-roof a ruinous structure, the applicant should use expert advice to identify fabric or other evidence of the previous roof construction. Care should be taken that this evidence is not lost in the restoration works and is either recorded in detail or preferably retained in situ. A new roof should be appropriate to the character of the protected structure but this need not necessarily preclude the use of modern materials providing these do not damage the fabric or appearance of the building.

Inappropriate alterations to roof shapes and details detract from the character of a structure; in this case the new roof has overhanging eaves with uPVC fascias, soffits and rainwater goods - an incorrect design using inappropriate materials on this former Board of First Fruits church

The placing of service plant and lift overruns on roofs that are visible from either near or far can seriously detract from the character of a protected structure or of an ACA

The original roof of this eighteenth-century dovecote was lost; however sufficient evidence survived to design a new roof which complements the structure

Valentia slate, famed for its qualities during the nineteenth century and again being quarried on a commercial basis, is here used on a conservation project. The use of regional slate types can be an important aspect of local distinctiveness and research indicates that slate native to a region generally performs best in the climatic conditions of that area. When undertaking restoration works to important roofs, the feasibility of reopening a local quarry to supply new slate should be investigated

9.3   Cladding Materials

9.3.1   The type and nature of the cladding materials used on a roof have a significant impact on the appearance and special interest of a building. There are a number of types of roof cladding commonly found on historic buildings. The most common ones are described below.

9.3.2   The retention of traditional roofing materials and the development of new sources of these materials should be encouraged. The dismantling of other buildings for salvage materials, such as slate, should however be discouraged as this promotes the destruction of old buildings.

9.3.3   Any proposals that involve the removal, partial removal or alteration of the roof cladding materials of a protected structure will require careful scrutiny. The insertion of large areas of glazing or numbers of openable rooflights into prominent slopes of roofs is generally not appropriate. The covering of historic roofs with waterproof membranes such as bitumen or tar should not be permitted, except to those roofs originally covered with such materials.

Slates

IDENTIFYING SPECIAL FEATURES FOR PROTECTION

9.3.4   Slate is the most common covering material found on older roofs in Ireland. From the beginning of the eighteenth century until the mid-twentieth century, it was used on most buildings of consequence. Eighteenth-century slates that survive in situ are increasingly rare. Where they exist, these slated roofs contribute to the character of the building and are usually worthy of protection.

9.3.5   In the nineteenth century, the design of slate roofs became more elaborate with patterns formed in different colour variegated slates or courses of clipped or scalloped-edged slates. Such elaborate uses of slate are found on many churches and houses. Where such patterning is found, it should be identified, assessed and retained.

9.3.6   Slate roofs that have been laid in diminishing graduated courses should also be identified, as should the existence of unusual or large-sized slates.

9.3.7 In principle, sound slates should be carefully retained in situ. The stripping of traditional slate roofs should be discouraged because of the resulting loss of historic material such as the slates themselves, associated timberwork and parging (a lime mortar coating applied to the underside of slates). An applicant should be required to justify proposals by providing evidence of widespread failure of fixings or the poor condition of slates, battens or structural elements before stripping the roof. Where the work is permitted it should be carried out by experienced craftsmen, in order to maximise the preservation of the original material. Breakages can be minimised by good work practices such as the avoidance of double handling and by keeping slates in proximity to the work. As many as possible of the removed slates should be re-used on the more prominent slopes of the roof, with matching new materials on other, concealed slopes. The roof should be photographed prior to commencement of works to allow for its correct reinstatement. Where the existing slates are laid in patterns or in diminishing courses, such features should be retained. Any repairs should be carried out with care.

9.3.8 New cladding materials used in repair works should be compatible with the existing ones in terms of colour, size, texture, thickness and durability. The use of concrete tiles and fibre-cement tiles (sometimes referred to as 'artificial slate') should not be permitted in conjunction with, or as a replacement for, natural slate as the weathering characteristics, durability and appearance of these materials are very different from those of natural slate.

Thatch
IDENTIFYING SPECIAL FEATURES FOR PROTECTION

9.3.9 There are two distinct forms of historic thatched roof: the vernacular thatched roof, now most often found on traditional cottages, and the architect-designed, cottage-orné thatched roof. The vernacular thatched roof was common throughout the country until the early twentieth century, but is now becoming increasingly rare. While many thatched roofs have been replaced in other materials, others have been simply covered over with corrugated iron sheeting above the thatch. Where there is a possibility that a building was thatched, care should be taken to identify, record and protect evidence of the original roof-covering.

Regional slate varieties, by reason of their colours and distinctive sizing differences, contribute to the character of their structures, and indeed whole areas, although they are becoming increasingly rare. The unnecessary disturbance or comprehensive stripping of a slate-clad roof should be avoided as such works can result in breakages which may be difficult to replace. Exceptional circumstances may require the stripping of a slate roof such as failure of the roof structure due to rot, or if the roof is 'nail sick'

Bands of different colour slate, variegated patterns or the use of decorative clipping of slates in diamond or fishscale shapes contribute to the character of a roof

Parging, a traditional method of sealing and securing the underside of slates using a coating of lime mortar, is inevitably lost when a roof is stripped. In advance of any proposals to repair or renew a slate roof, the roof should be surveyed internally and externally to identify the types of slates used and existence of details such as parging, and to ascertain areas of local failure of the covering and of the structural elements

9.3.10 Thatch was a pervasive feature of the Irish landscape, as it provided a plentiful locally available roofing material. The traditional thatched roof has become symbolic of the vernacular heritage and is considered to be the indigenous roofing material.

9.3.11 Although the predominant material used was straw, there are regional variations in thatching style and materials used. Wheat straw, a farming by-product of food production, was used wherever it was produced. Rye is to be found on the Aran Islands, Co. Galway. Flax was used in Ulster. Heather, oats, potato hulm and marram grass are also to be found. Reed is used in particular locations where there were supplies from nearby riverbanks and lake margins.

9.3.12 In the vernacular tradition, thatched roofs are detailed functionally to withstand the elements and to make efficient use of scarce resources. The roof structure is often of unwrought wood. In coastal or other exposed locations, the roof structure was not a simple 'A' frame (which would necessitate a sharp ridge and excess concentration of wind pressures), but was truncated and made of four members to create a rounded profile. In these areas too, netting from ridges to eaves was employed as a restraint, as well as ropework tied back to pegs at the top of the wall and ridge scallops. In midland, eastern and southern areas, hipped- or half-hipped roofs replaced the gables to avoid excessive wind pressure. The roof structure often supported sods of earth, into which the thatch was fixed. When re-thatching, it was expedient only to replace the upper layers, and lower layers can thus represent an important record of agricultural life in an area and retain features such as old varieties of straw and older fixing techniques. Scallop-thatching used wooden rods to fix the straw, and thrust thatching required the knotted straw bundle being forced tightly into the layer below.

9.3.13 The cottage-orné style of thatching differs greatly from the vernacular tradition, having a separate language of detailing featuring verandas, elaborate cresting to the ridge and patterned eaves fixings together with a sculptural treatment of chimney stacks and windows to attic rooms.

CONSIDERATION OF PROPOSALS AFFECTING THATCH

9.3.14 Thatch presents special conservation issues, for two reasons. As a material it has a relatively short life, requiring to be renewed on a ten to thirty-year cycle. Secondly, thatch tends to be found on modest buildings whose accommodation may be inadequate for modern expectations. Hence there

Irish vernacular thatching is simple in its construction and detailing, addressing, in the choice of roof profile, structure, materials and weathering details, the prevailing climatic conditions and available materials

Unwrought or partially-wrought roof structures, however simple or slight they may seem, are part of the historic vernacular fabric. Repairs should aim to support the existing structural elements with new timbers rather than replace them

Thatched roofs can decay quickly once neglected. Therefore it is important to make their repair a priority if grant assistance is available and to ensure that a thatcher, experienced in methods traditional to the region, is employed

There are local variations in thatching techniques and some details are particular to individual thatchers. In areas of the country, chickenwire is a traditional cover over thatch; whether over the entire roof or over vulnerable details requiring extra protection. Here a wire covering is about to be applied to finish off the ridge

are economic barriers to the conservation of this roofing material. Planning authorities should bear this in mind, and give consideration to any assistance that it may be possible to offer.

9.3.15 Re-thatching should, according to best practice, follow regional characteristics of materials, form and detail. Permission should not normally be granted for replacement of thatch with other materials, or of one type of thatch material with another. Complete stripping of thatch is rarely required and defective thatch should only be removed to a sound base. It is acceptable for a roof to have a variegated appearance following repair. Where anti-fire devices are introduced for thatch, they should be visually acceptable.

9.3.16 Proposals to reinstate thatch, on a roof that is known to have been thatched, should be carefully assessed. Surviving evidence from the building itself and information provided by old photographs and other records should be used to ensure accurate reinstatement of features.

9.3.17 Re-thatching a simple traditional vernacular roof using elaborate ridge or eaves details from the cottage-orné style is not appropriate. When re-thatching a cottage-orné roof, however, it is important that the original detailing is respected. Where a thatched roof has been covered, for example with corrugated metal sheeting, the opportunity to re-expose the traditional material could be taken.

Metal sheeting

IDENTIFYING SPECIAL FEATURES FOR PROTECTION

9.3.18 Lead and copper were traditionally used on buildings of quality for flat roofs, roof-walks, gutter-linings or cladding for domes and cupolas. Both materials, together with zinc, were also used extensively for flashings. Dates or inscriptions can be found carved into lead. Where these exist they are often important features which should be preserved and, if possible, incorporated into the new roof-covering.

9.3.19 Corrugated-iron and profiled steel, zinc or aluminium sheeting is also to be found on a variety of buildings and it should be noted where they are likely to be the original cladding material.

CONSIDERATION OF PROPOSALS AFFECTING METAL SHEETING

9.3.20 Lead and copper roofs should, where possible, be repaired rather than replaced. A correctly detailed and well-executed lead or copper roof can last for several hundred years without problems. There are examples, however, where the design of the original roof may have had inherent faults. These were most often caused by the use of overlarge sheets of the material or incorrect fixings that can lead to cracking of the sheets. Where there is an inherent design fault, the roof covering will require replacement to an improved design. Cracks should not be repaired with solder or with sealant, as these repairs will often cause further problems at a later stage. In addition, repairing metal sheeting with solder creates a fire hazard as most metal sheeting is supported by timber below.

Stone 'slates'

9.3.21 So-called stone 'slates' are in fact thin slabs of limestone or sandstone dressed simply to rectangular shapes and used in a manner similar to slates. Stone 'slates' were usually laid in diminishing courses. There are very few remaining examples of stone 'slates' in Ireland and any examples should be preserved in situ with a minimum amount of disturbance.

Clay tiles

9.3.22 Clay tiles were rarely used traditionally in Ireland after the middle of the eighteenth century and are now usually only seen in buildings of the late nineteenth or twentieth century. They can be found as flat tiles, pantiles or profiled interlocking tiles. Clay tiles should be retained on buildings or additions where they are the original roof-covering. Examples of clay roof tiles predating the twentieth century are

Lead or copper sheeting were traditionally used on flat roofs or as a cladding to domes or cupolas. Lead, if properly specified and laid, can last several centuries in situ. Lead flashings can sometimes be cut with decorative finishes. Leadwork may have dates or inscriptions scratched on as graffiti, which is now of historical interest

Corrugated iron sheeting may degrade through cracking or rusting (caused for example by sea spray in maritime areas) to a point where replacement is necessary. This recently-reclad harbour-master's office has replaced the original, but rusting, corrugated iron with a modern profiled metal sheeting

Moher 'slates', a regional type of roof cladding once common in Co. Clare, are in fact thin slabs of limestone dressed as slates. Stone 'slates' are rare survivors and, wherever possible, should be maintained in place with minimum intervention

Clay roof tiles, though widely used in other countries, in Ireland rarely date from before the latter half of the nineteenth century. Either flat or profiled (pantiles) they can be decoratively shaped, as in this instance

valable historical and architectural survivals and should be retained in situ. Clay and terracotta are however found extensively in ridge tiles.

Glazed tiles

9.3.23 A distinctive feature on some roofs of the mid-twentieth century is glazed tiling. Glazed tiles should be retained on buildings or additions of that period where they are the original roof-covering.

Concrete tiles

9.3.24 Concrete tiles were used on roofs of the late twentieth century and should be retained on buildings or additions of that period where they are the original roof covering.

Shingles and shakes

9.3.25 Shingles are thin, sawn or cleft pieces of timber used as roof, and sometimes wall, cladding. Shakes are shingles which are split on at least one face. Shingles and shakes were rarely used as a roof-covering in Ireland after the end of the seventeenth century and where examples are found they should be identified and are generally worthy of protection. In addition to their use as roof cladding, shingles and shakes are sometimes found as cladding to roof lanterns and similar features and as cladding to walls. Shingles and shakes were usually made of cedar, but chestnut and oak are among the timbers also used.

9.3.26 Where shingles and shakes are found, they should be retained. Where replacement shingles or shakes are required, these should match the original ones on a like-for-like basis, while allowing it to be clear on close inspection which is the original material.

Asphalt, bitumen and other membranes

9.3.27 Where this is the original type of covering it should be retained, but, if necessary, replaced with a like material, as membranes can be difficult to repair effectively.

9.4 Roof Details

9.4.1 The architectural detailing of roofs is often of importance not only to the individual building, but can also contribute to the character of a town or surrounding countryside.

Glazed roof tiles are part of the architectural design of some mid twentieth-century structures. They are unusual and should be retained where found. In this example, the purple colour of the glazed tiles contrasts strongly with the green copper cladding of the dormer surrounds and the creamy colour of the faïence wall cladding to make a strong architectural statement

The use of shingles and shakes is rare in Ireland. Where it is necessary to replace parts of a shingled roof or wall cladding, the new shingles should match the original and should not be lighter in weight than the originals. Both shingles and shakes need ventilation to their undersides and roofs and walls clad in these materials should not be altered to include felt underlays

A visually interesting roof, such as this one with multiple gables, decorative stacks, turrets, cresting, finials and elaborate dormers, is a very important feature not only of the structure itself but may also act as a landmark in the local townscape or landscape

9.4.2   Architectural details are important features of the roofscape and their removal should rarely be permitted where they are in good condition or are capable of repair. The removal of details of interest will have implications for the special interest of the structure, as they contribute to the quality and character of a roof. Where the structure forms part of a unified terrace, the alteration or removal of roof details from one structure will affect the character of the entire group and this should be borne in mind when considering a proposal for planning permission.

9.4.3   Where inappropriate earlier changes have been made, the reinstatement of missing features in replica may be appropriate, where there is sufficient evidence for their original form, or otherwise with an appropriate new design. Evidence for the original design might be found in adjacent buildings, for example, where the building is part of a terrace.

Decorative and functional details of roofs that contribute to its character should be protected. In this instance, the original crenellated parapet, in place until recent years, has been removed, significantly detracting from the character of a rare late-mediaeval townhouse

Ridges, ridge-combs, cresting, finials and weathervanes

IDENTIFYING SPECIAL FEATURES FOR PROTECTION

9.4.4 Ridges were traditionally finished with clay, terracotta, lead or stone capping. In the latter part of the nineteenth century the treatment of the ridge became more elaborate with terracotta ridge-combs, finials or iron cresting being used. Original or early weathervanes are of particular interest and contribute to the character of the structure.

CONSIDERATION OF PROPOSALS AFFECTING RIDGES, ETC.

9.4.5 Modern ridge tiles should not be permitted as a substitute for clay, terracotta, stone, lead or zinc. Where possible the original or early ridge details should be retained and repaired. Where replacement is considered appropriate they should be replaced to match. Original or early weathervanes should be retained and repaired as necessary.

Associated masonry detail

IDENTIFYING SPECIAL FEATURES FOR PROTECTION

9.4.6 The masonry details associated with a roof may include crowsteps, kneelers, scrolled springers, bell-cotes, gargoyles, decorative water-spouts, eaves cornices, blocking courses, parapets, balustrades and other ornaments.

CONSIDERATION OF PROPOSALS AFFECTING MASONRY ROOF DETAILS

9.4.7 Masonry details are important features of roofs and their removal should rarely be permitted where they are in good condition or are capable of repair. The repair and conservation of these details should be in accordance with the guidance notes given for stonework in Chapter 8 above.

Domes, cupolas, lanterns, decorative roof-ventilators, spires and steeples

IDENTIFYING SPECIAL FEATURES FOR PROTECTION

9.4.8 These roof features are not only important architectural features of the structure itself; the silhouette of such features contributes to the character of the surrounding landscape or townscape.

CONSIDERATION OF PROPOSALS AFFECTING DOMES ETC.

9.4.9 The removal of domes, cupolas, lanterns, ventilators, spires or steeples, or their replacement with simpler forms, should generally not be permitted.

Ridge tiles, finials, iron cresting and weathervanes are found on many structures and give a building its distinctive outline against the sky. Repairs should follow best practice for each particular material

Where it is proposed to ventilate roof spaces, important architectural details should be retained intact; in this example a pierced ceramic tile has been replaced by a new vent tile which disrupts the line of the ridge comb and damages its visual integrity

Masonry details associated with roofs may be functional or not. Whether they are plain or decoratively detailed, they add character to a roof and, even if now redundant, should be retained

The visual impact of domes, lanterns, steeples and other prominent architectural features can extend well beyond their immediate setting and their removal may affect a wide area even where they are unused or unnecessary to the current use of the building

Chimneys, shafts and pots

IDENTIFYING SPECIAL FEATURES FOR PROTECTION

9.4.10 Chimney stacks and pots are important elements of the roofline of a building. They can be indicators of the date of a building and of its internal planning. In Victorian buildings in particular, chimneys are usually an integral part of the architectural design.

CONSIDERATION OF PROPOSALS
AFFECTING CHIMNEYS

9.4.11 Chimney stacks or pots, finials, or cresting should usually be repaired and retained. Only if they are decayed to the extent of being dangerous, should their rebuilding or replacement be permitted. Even when they are perceived to have no further use, chimneys should be retained together with their pots where their appearance is important to the appreciation of the building as a whole. While their main purpose is to remove smoke from open fires, chimneys also function in providing permanent ventilation to the building and, particularly in older buildings, they serve, or may have come to serve, a structural function. They also contribute visually to the architectural composition and massing of a building. Redundant flues should be capped but never fully sealed.

Eaves, verges and parapets

IDENTIFYING SPECIAL FEATURES FOR PROTECTION

9.4.12 The architectural treatment of the edges of a roof often gives a distinctive character to the entire structure. The eaves may be flush, or almost flush, with the wall below or there may be a projecting stone or brick course at the head of the wall to support the eaves gutter. Alternatively, the eaves may overhang the wall supported on projecting, exposed rafter ends, or on boxed-in rafter ends. Projecting eaves may be supported on plain or decorative timber or metal brackets.

9.4.13 There may be a parapet wall that rises above eaves level with a concealed gutter behind. Parapets can be balustraded or plain.

9.4.14 The verges of the roof may be flush with the wall and the gaps between the slates or tiles filled with mortar. The wall may rise above the plane of the roof and form a gable parapet. Alternatively, the verge may overhang the wall in which case the edges may be trimmed with bargeboards. Bargeboards can be relatively plain timbers or elaborately carved or pierced.

Chimneystacks, whether simple or elaborate, are integral to roofs of most periods and make a vital contribution to the silhouette of the structure. This terrace of early nineteenth-century cottages has simple stacks set diagonally in a revival of a Tudor detail

Work to this chimneystack has included coating the stone cladding of the right-hand stack with render and adding a new clay pot. The new work contrasts badly with the original well-crafted ashlar stack with chamfered sides and carved mouldings

Curvilinear 'Dutch-Billy' or Queen Anne Revival style gable parapets are relatively uncommon in Ireland, especially elaborate terracotta examples such as this dating from the late-nineteenth century. These decorative elements make a contribution to the townscape as well as largely redefining this pair of Georgian houses

CONSIDERATION OF PROPOSALS AFFECTING
EAVES ETC.

9.4.15 Alterations to the treatment of the eaves and verges of a roof, which materially alter the character of the roof and the entire structure, should not be permitted. Exposed rafter ends should not be enclosed with the addition of fascia boards and soffits, as this alters the appearance of a roof, and possibly the entire façade. Overhanging eaves and verges are a distinctive architectural feature of many buildings and should not be truncated.

9.4.16 The covering of previously uncovered parapets and blocking courses with lead or an other weather-proofing material should generally not be permitted where it would tend to distort the proportions of the building. The upper surfaces of cornices should only be covered by a lead flashing if the porosity of the stone or the absence of saddle joints makes this unavoidable. In such instances, the depth of the drip at the edge of the cornice should be kept to a minimum to avoid the presence on the façade of a dark line where none was intended and similarly with any upstand at the back of the cornice. The planning authority should approve details in advance of works commencing.

9.4.17 Where decorative bargeboards, consoles, valances or brackets are in good condition or capable of repair, they should be retained and repaired. The addition of fascia boarding to provide fixing for gutter brackets should not be permitted as this will alter the appearance of the building.

Dormer windows, access hatches, skylights and rooflights
IDENTIFYING SPECIAL FEATURES FOR PROTECTION

9.4.18 Original or early dormer windows, external access hatches, skylights and rooflights are features of importance on a roof. Dormer windows used during the late eighteenth and early nineteenth centuries tended to be confined to secondary elevations. Surviving early eighteenth-century dormers are very rare and should be considered for protection. Cast-iron framed rooflights should be identified and retained wherever possible.

9.4.19 Dormer windows, skylights or rooflights may retain old glass, whether coloured or painted, or early plain glass such as crown glass. Bargeboards, finials, ridge tiles, ridge combs and other details associated with individual dormer windows should also be identified and protected as part of the character and special interest of the building.

The application of proprietary spikes or wiring may be necessary to deter birds congregating as their droppings damage masonry. Such additions to architecturally significant buildings should be designed to be unobtrusive and reversible

The eaves of a building can be vulnerable to weather-related problems, typically parapet walls become saturated as they are exposed on both sides to rain. Problems will also arise where the blockage of the gutter concealed behind a parapet may not be readily noticed. However, where they exist, parapet walls are usually an important architectural feature of the building

Original dormer windows were usually designed as part of the architectural vocabulary of a structure and may contain a wealth of detail such as finials, ridge tiles, bargeboards and slate-hung or glazed cheeks

CONSIDERATION OF PROPOSALS AFFECTING DORMERS ETC.

9.4.20 Proposals to remove or alter original or early dormer windows, access hatches, skylights and rooflights from a protected structure will affect the character of the structure and should be carefully scrutinised. Alterations to these features will affect the overall appearance of the structure and, in some cases, the appearance of an entire terrace of buildings.

9.4.21 Original dormer windows should be retained and repaired rather than replaced. The enlargement of existing dormers and the linking of dormers should not be permitted where this would adversely affect the external appearance of the building. Old or interesting glass, whether coloured, painted or plain, should be conserved when repairing skylights, rooflights and dormer windows.

9.4.22 Where it is proposed to install new dormers or rooflights, the extent of potential damage to historic roof structures should be considered. If the building is part of a terrace, the proposed addition may upset the balance of the whole architectural composition. New rooflights and dormers on minor or concealed slopes may be considered acceptable in some cases. Low-profile 'conservation-type' rooflights with a central glazing bar should be used in preference to standard modern types. Where a large increase in natural lighting is required in the roof space below, it is usually preferable to permit the use of patent glazing in place of the existing roof cladding rather than the use of excessive numbers of rooflights which would disrupt the visual appearance of the roof.

9.4.23 Where it is proposed to reinstate a lost dormer or to replace a later unsympathetic alteration, this may be permitted, provided sufficiently accurate evidence exists either from an adjacent dormer or from old photographs or drawings. However, if such an alteration would result in an obtrusive patching of the roof-covering, it may not be appropriate to permit it.

Rainwater goods

IDENTIFYING SPECIAL FEATURES FOR PROTECTION

9.4.24 Rainwater goods which contribute to the special character of a structure can include plain or decorated lead or cast-iron hopper heads, profiled or half-round gutters, square section or round downpipes and decorative fixings and brackets. The fixing methods of the gutters should be identified. Traditional gutters are either supported on iron straps or brackets which project from the eaves, or they may rest on a projecting stone or brick course at the head of the wall.

While well-designed new dormers may be acceptable where they do not conflict with the architectural character of a structure, the profusion of many different-sized dormers on a terrace usually detracts from the character of the area as well as that of the individual structures (top). New rooflights may also have an adverse effect, particularly when installed on a principal elevation or where several are grouped or spread out over the roof (bottom)

Original lead rainwater goods (bottom) are rare survivors and often incorporate dates or impressed or embossed marks. This example is embossed with a fleur de lis and a Tudor rose. In the Victorian period the design of rainwater goods came to be an intrinsic part of the design of the structure (left). The style of the fixings – some with decorative clasps – may also be integral to this design

9.4.25 A roof may retain evidence of interesting early water-collecting systems on or within the structure such as tanks, cisterns, pipework, internal guttering and the like. Such features should be identified and, even where subsequent alterations have rendered them redundant, efforts should be made to retain them in place.

CONSIDERATION OF PROPOSALS AFFECTING RAINWATER GOODS

9.4.26 The character of the structure will be altered by the removal of early rainwater goods. In many buildings, particularly Victorian buildings, the design of rainwater goods was an integral part of the overall design. In other structures the existence of early and original details adds to the special interest of the building. Many buildings, often cottages and farm buildings, were designed without rainwater goods and proposals to install gutters and downpipes on such structures will require careful consideration.

9.4.27 Original or early lead, iron or more modern pressed steel rainwater goods and their associated features should be retained. The use of extruded aluminium or plastic rainwater goods and associated fittings on a protected structure is rarely appropriate and should not be permitted.

9.4.28 Where the repainting of rainwater goods is proposed, the colour used should be sympathetic and appropriate to the character of the building. In cases where a profiled cast-iron gutter is mounted above the moulded brickwork of an eaves cornice to form the corona, the gutter should be painted to blend in with the brickwork thus visually completing the cornice. Lead gutters, hopper heads and downpipes should not be painted.

9.5   Insulation of Roofs

9.5.1 The insulation of a traditional roof can have far-reaching effects on the way in which the roof performs. The performance of a traditional roof was designed to rely on the ventilation of the roof space by the movement of air through gaps between the slates and tiles or through thatch. Insulation of a traditional roof to enhance energy efficiency will generally bring about the need for additional ventilation, requiring alterations to the eaves and ridge or the addition of vents in order to prevent the timbers within the roof space from being damaged through excessive moisture build-up and condensation. The location and type of vents and any proposed alterations to eaves and ridges should be carefully considered. Insulation of the roof space should only be undertaken where it can be achieved without damage to the fabric and appearance of the roof. The effect on cladding materials, such as slates, thatch or lead sheeting, should be assessed whether during the course of the works or from subsequent erosion due to condensation.

Industrial complexes and country houses often had their own systems of rainwater collection and may retain water cisterns, usually of cast iron but occasionally of lead. Even where these are now redundant they may be features of social and technical interest which should not be unnecessarily lost

Galvanised steel gutters and downpipes are prone to damage and rust attack; their use, along with rainwater goods of extruded aluminium and uPVC, is generally inappropriate on a historic structure, such as this courthouse. It is doubtful whether these rainwater goods are performing adequately, given the apparent warp and rust

Any necessary ventilation required as a result of insulating a roof should be carefully designed to be visually unobtrusive and appropriately sited, usually in locations concealed from principal views of the structure, such as behind parapet walls. In this case ridge vents project a minimal amount, and are just visible on the skyline

Openings
Doors and Windows

CHAPTER 10

Whether grand or simple, doors and windows are usually the main elements that, on first glance, establish the character of a structure. Their design, materials and arrangement can tell much of the use, history or status of the building

10.1 Introduction

10.1.1 Doors, windows and the openings that contain them are important architectural features of an elevation. The design of doors and windows and the materials used can be of significance in establishing the special character of a structure. The way in which the openings are formed and their architectural treatment is also important, as are the proportions of the openings themselves and the proportion of opening size to wall area.

10.1.2 In order to assess the qualities of openings that contribute to the character of a structure, the following should be considered:

a) Are the openings original to the particular part of the building?

b) If not, are they of interest as being part of a later remodelling of the structure?

c) Have the proportions of the openings been altered? Have they been widened or the sills dropped?

d) If the openings have been altered, are the alterations of interest or do they distort the proportions of the wall or façade?

e) Have any openings been blocked up or made redundant by previous alterations? Were any of these blocked openings designed as dummy, or blind, windows?

f) Have any openings been added and, if so, are they of interest or do they distort a previously symmetrical or well-balanced elevation?

g) Are the windows and doors original to the building?

h) If not, do they contribute to the character of the building or do they detract from it because of unsympathetic design or use of materials?

i) Are there other features associated with the openings? These might include porches, canopies, entrance steps and landings, railings, bootscrapers, fanlights, overlights, shutters, blind boxes, balconettes, window boxes and many others.

153

j) Are these features original? If not, do they nonetheless contribute to the character of the building or ACA?

k) Do the windows or doors contain any original, early or interesting glass?

10.2 Openings in Structures

IDENTIFYING SPECIAL FEATURES FOR PROTECTION

10.2.1 The manner in which structural openings are formed and decorated is important to the architectural character of a structure. Head details of special interest may include arches of rubbed bricks, stone voussoirs, and iron or timber lintels. There may be important associated features such as carved or decorated keystones. Sills may be of cut stone, brick, rendered brick, timber or metal. The treatments of the reveals should also be noted, whether these are rendered or not, or of cut stone or moulded brickwork. Surrounds to openings of decorative render should be identified and protected. The depth to which window and door frames are recessed within a wall is also an important feature and alterations to this relationship, when inserting replacement windows or doors, will affect the appearance of a building.

CONSIDERATION OF PROPOSALS AFFECTING STRUCTURAL OPENINGS

10.2.2 Careful consideration should be given to proposals to alter openings in a protected structure or in any structure within an ACA. The architectural quality of a historic building may be compromised if the size of openings is altered; if existing openings are blocked up; if new openings are formed; or if door openings are converted to window openings and vice versa. Where the openings are a conspicuous part of the architectural design and this design would be marred by the proposed alterations, permission should rarely be given. Similarly, on prominent elevations, planning permission should not generally be given for the conversion of window openings to doorways or vice versa where this would be detrimental to the overall design of the structure. Consideration also needs to be given to the effect of alterations on the interior of the building.

10.2.3 The removal, partial removal or replacement of important features associated with the formation of the opening, such as arches, sills, keystones or architraves may adversely affect the character of the structure.

The treatment of structural openings may add considerably to the character of a building; here the elaborate brick and terracotta detailing and the arched window-heads add architectural distinction to the opening

Openings that were later created or remodelled can contribute to understanding phases of the history of the structure. The late eighteenth-century fashion of lowering windowsills altered many earlier openings, but they can now be seen to represent a valid phase in the structure's history. Restoring these windows to the original proportions would require the loss of later fabric of historical interest and should only be undertaken in exceptional circumstances, based on sound evidence and after all alternatives and potential consequences have been fully explored

The inaccurately-detailed alteration of doorcases or other features will, in most cases, be to the detriment of the structure and often affect the character of an ACA also

10.2.4 Proposals to block up, in whole or in part, the existing openings in symmetrical or well-balanced elevations should only be permitted in exceptional circumstances. Proposals to insert new openings in such walls should generally be refused although it may be considered permissible on minor or random elevations. Any new openings should be sympathetic with the architectural character of the building in terms of materials, design, scale and proportion.

10.3 Doors

10.3.1 The details associated with the doors of a building are of importance to the special character of a historic building. Types of doorways may range from major entrances with elaborate architectural treatment to simple secondary doorways or entrances to minor structures. It is important to identify and protect the features of doors and doorways that contribute to the special character of the protected structure.

10.3.2 Inappropriate works to its doorways will damage the special interest of a structure and this should be a consideration when assessing a planning application for works to a protected structure. Proposals to remove, replace or otherwise inappropriately alter features of interest should be treated with great caution. The complete replacement of historic doors, and their associated elements, in protected structures should rarely be permitted where they are capable of repair.

Doorcases
IDENTIFYING SPECIAL FEATURES FOR PROTECTION

10.3.3 In buildings of high architectural quality, there may be doorcases and door surrounds of timber, stone, render or cast iron. They may incorporate columns, pilasters, pediments, cornices, consoles or other carved or moulded detail. All these details should be identified and retained and, where necessary, repaired appropriately.

CONSIDERATION OF PROPOSALS

10.3.4 In cases where an entrance has, or will, become redundant because of alteration, the doorcase, door and other details of special interest should be retained in situ. This is particularly important in buildings where the doorway is a prominent feature of an elevation and where its removal would therefore alter the character of the building. Retaining the doorcase in place allows the possibility of its future reinstatement as an entrance.

Doors and door frames
IDENTIFYING SPECIAL FEATURES FOR PROTECTION

10.3.5 Original door leaves and frames should be protected, as should any later replacement work of obvious quality and good design. Most doors associated with historic buildings are constructed of timber and these may be panelled, match-boarded, ledged-and-braced or flush-sheeted doors. Other structures may have metal-framed doors with glazed panels or plain metal sheeting.

While early, well-executed conversions of doors to windows, and vice versa, may now merit a place in the history of a structure, the entire removal of the principal entrance and its replacement with a window can rarely be considered acceptable, particularly where the works are carried out using inappropriate materials and to a poor-quality design

Doorcases often contain details of surprising beauty and craftsmanship, such as these tiny carved caryatids which date from the early nineteenth century

Front doors are traditionally strongly constructed from high quality materials. Panelling styles or applied decoration, seen in this ornate and well-maintained example, can be characteristic of an area or region

10.3.6 The quality of the original materials and craftsmanship of much historic joinery means that it is usually capable of repair. Throughout the country, many doors survive which are over two hundred years old and still capable of giving good service. Joinery that is original to a building or a replacement of definite quality should be retained. Original or early doors may be disguised by the later application of sheeting or boarding to the faces of the doors and may conceal panelling beneath.

CONSIDERATION OF PROPOSALS

10.3.7 The installation of modern replacement doors, which have inappropriate design features such as integral fanlights, should not be permitted in a protected structure. The installation of doors of inappropriate materials will also damage the appearance of the building. For example, the use of uPVC or aluminium doors in an old building will affect its character and damage its special interest, as will the replacement of solid door panels with glass and vice versa.

10.3.8 An inappropriate finish applied to a replacement door or to an existing historic door will affect the appearance of a building. Most doors associated with protected structures are made of timber. Until the mid-twentieth century external joinery was generally given an applied finish such as paint. Sometimes the paint finish was grained or scumbled to resemble unpainted timber. Unpainted hardwood or stained or varnished softwood doors are therefore not appropriate for use in a historic building unless it can be proven that this was the original finish.

10.3.9 Where repair works are to be carried out to historic joinery, only the minimum amount of timber should be replaced using timber of a matching species and grain type. New pieces, where required, should be carefully jointed in. The profiles of decayed sections of moulded work should be copied exactly and spliced precisely into the existing work. Large-scale renewal of frames or sections of door joinery should always be avoided.

Ironmongery
IDENTIFYING SPECIAL FEATURES FOR PROTECTION

10.3.10 Where there is original or interesting ironmongery associated with a door, it should be retained in place, even where it has become redundant. Such ironmongery includes hinges, knockers, letter plates, lockcases, escutcheons, bell-pulls, handles, door-pulls, nameplates and numerals.

Modern replacement doors of inappropriate design, materials or finishes should not be used. Where such doors now exist, as here, their replacement by an accurately profiled door, informed by research, should be encouraged. Alternatively a high-quality well-designed contemporary solution, which would not adversely affect the character of the historical design, may be acceptable

Previous repairs to this door and doorframe included the piecing-in of new material to the ends of the stiles. This fine and barely visible repair work has retained the original sturdy, clouted door hinge

Redundant items of door furniture such as locks, knockers, hinges and bell-pulls are sometimes removed in the course of refurbishment works and often sold as antiques. However, where items of original and early door furniture are fixtures included in the protection of a building, their removal may require planning permission.

CONSIDERATION OF PROPOSALS

10.3.11 Original or interesting items of ironmongery associated with a door should be identified and retained in situ. If security issues arise, they may be augmented with sensitively placed modern locks or hinges rather than replaced.

Fanlights, overlights and sidelights
IDENTIFYING SPECIAL FEATURES FOR PROTECTION

10.3.12 Fanlights and overlights may be integral parts of the doorcase or may be housed in separate openings above the doorway. The doorway may also incorporate lights to the sides of the opening. These sidelights can not only be important decorative features of a protected structure but also play an important role in providing natural light to entrance halls. Some were designed to be openable to provide ventilation. Others contain integral lanterns. Fanlights, overlights and sidelights may be plain single openings, have simple timber glazing bars or contain elaborate metal-framed decorative glazed panels usually with lead cames on a zinc armature within a timber subframe. Some may have original iron security grilles internally, often decoratively worked.

CONSIDERATION OF PROPOSALS

10.3.13 Fanlights, overlights and sidelights of interest should be retained and repaired as appropriate to the materials. In situ repair is the least disruptive method and should generally be preferred. However, in some cases, it may be necessary for a specialist restorer to remove the light to a workshop for repair. Where works are proposed to fanlights, overlights and sidelights, the opportunity should be taken to re-route any later cables away from their subframes wherever possible. Internal iron grilles, where they exist, should be kept in position.

Porches and canopies
IDENTIFYING SPECIAL FEATURES FOR PROTECTION

10.3.14 Original or early porches and canopies are important architectural features on many buildings and should be identified and retained. They may be constructed of timber, wrought or cast iron, brick, stone, glass or concrete. A similar feature is a porte-cochère which is a large porch designed to permit the through-passage of carriages or cars.

10.3.15 A porch or portico is an important feature of an elevation, particularly where it is associated with a significant entrance. Canopies over entrance doors are often important features in smaller, humbler buildings. Porches and canopies can be important features contributing to the character of an ACA.

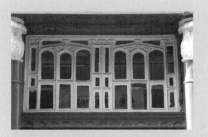

Fanlights, overlights and sidelights may be integral parts of the design of a doorcase, contributing a decorative appearance as well as providing light to the interior; many are unique and, as they were handmade in small batches, fanlight details may be particular to a single street, square or town

Cabling should not be routed into a building through a fanlight frame, as the drilling causes damage and can exacerbate problems that arise at the bottom rail – already vulnerable to rain-driven moisture – eventually making repair inevitable. There are also obvious adverse impacts on the appearance of the fanlight from such cabling

Porches, although functional items, are often decoratively designed. Whether original or later additions, porches, such as the one illustrated here, often contribute to the special interest of a structure

10.3.16   Because features such as porches and canopies are usually exposed, they tend to suffer maintenance problems and, consequently, many have been demolished. Others may have undergone insensitive alteration in the past which has disguised their importance such as the installation of replacement roofs or windows. Surviving features are increasingly rare and are usually worthy of protection.

CONSIDERATION OF PROPOSALS

10.3.17   Where there is an open porch of a high architectural quality, as in many Neo-Classical or Gothic-Revival buildings, it should in principle not be glazed in but left open as originally intended. Where such glazing is proposed, it should be of considerable quality and reversible if possible. Where inappropriate glazing-in has occurred, its removal should be considered.

10.3.18   The removal of original canopies above entrances, whether constructed of timber, metal, glass or concrete, should not normally be permitted. Where porches or canopies are later additions to a structure and where they cut across or conceal work of a higher architectural quality, a judgement will have to be made on whether or not to remove the later work. However, if the later work has cut through a stone or brick façade, the visual appearance of the building following removal of the porch may not be desirable. In cases where a new porch or canopy is considered acceptable, it should be appropriate in design and materials to the existing building and should not detract from its quality and appearance.

Entrance steps and landings

IDENTIFYING SPECIAL FEATURES FOR PROTECTION

10.3.19   Many historic structures have steps or ramps up to the entrance. These may range from highly detailed flights of stone steps with railings or balustrades to simple stone, concrete, brick or tiled single steps or thresholds.

10.3.20   Where bootscrapers survive, these should be protected. Different types may be free-standing, mounted adjacent to the doorway or incorporated in the wall of the building or into the railings.

CONSIDERATION OF PROPOSALS

10.3.21   Where the structure includes important entrance steps and landings, these features should be retained, even if the doorway they serve is no longer in use. They should generally be considered for removal only if they are modern alterations or additions subsequent to a subdivision of the building. Where there are worn or damaged stone

This porch has undergone at least one phase of alteration, although several elements of interest survive, such as point-arched cast-iron windows, strapwork gates and stone steps. Any proposed restoration of a porch such as this should be well detailed, based on good evidence and incorporate surviving features of interest

This aluminium canopy is an inappropriate addition to the early nineteenth-century doorcase. Any proposal to remove it should ascertain if the fixings have damaged any cut stonework that might survive beneath the modern render

Most flights of steps are designed to complement a doorcase, whether immediately fronting it or including a landing or terrace leading to the entrance. Balustrades, railings, flagstones or tiling, where found, are usually integral parts of the design

steps and landings which it is necessary to repair, the existing stone can be redressed by a skilled mason or indented with compatible stone. The maximum amount of the original stonework should be conserved. However, damaged steps and landings should not be built up in cement screed or similar inappropriate artificial compounds as this would alter their appearance.

10.3.22　Where there is a weathering problem connected with entrance steps and landings, specialist advice should be sought to overcome this. It should not be solved by covering the stone steps and landings with any waterproof coating material which would adversely affect their fabric or appearance.

10.4　Windows

IDENTIFYING SPECIAL FEATURES FOR PROTECTION

10.4.1　The design of windows and the materials used in their construction make a significant contribution to the appearance and special character of a structure. Windows have historically been subject to changing fashions and advancing technology of glass manufacture so that an old building may exhibit a variety of window sizes and glazing patterns. Where different window types are important evidence of the building's history and contribute to its character and interest, no attempt should be made to standardise the fenestration. Surviving original proportions of glazing patterns should always be respected, even if these now differ from the adjoining buildings of similar style and date.

10.4.2　While most windows in older buildings are made of timber, windows are also found dating from the late-eighteenth century onwards made wholly of iron or which incorporate iron or brass frameworks. The traditional use of lead-based paints and the quality of the close-grained timbers used in the eighteenth and nineteenth centuries have ensured the survival of many historic windows. Many are well suited to being carefully repaired. Generally, paint is the correct finish for external joinery on buildings over fifty years old and for all historic metal windows, including fanlights. Staining and varnishing are rarely traditional finishes for external surfaces although scumbling (or wood-graining) is occasionally found. There may be rare cases where external joinery was originally unpainted, generally oak or mahogany, and where this is so it should be identified and protected.

Bootscrapers and other entrance features add character to the structure and are of social interest in themselves. Many have interesting design details and, like other handcrafted items, may be particular to a single street or area

The indenting or redressing of decayed or damaged step nosings may occasionally be necessary. Such work should be carried out by an experienced mason. In cases of minor damage, and providing there is no threat to the safe use of the steps, it may be sufficient simply to smooth broken edges and avoid major intervention

Coating stone steps in a waterproof material in an attempt to solve damp problems in the room below is rarely a successful solution. Apart from the unsightly nature of such work, it may cause the stone to decay from condensation from within the building or from moisture ingress through cracking of the coating

10.4.3 A variety of window types will be found in protected structures and buildings in ACAs. Some of the common types are listed below. In all types of windows, where regional characteristics exist, these should be identified and retained. The internal joinery associated with window openings is discussed in Chapter 11 below.

Sash windows

10.4.4 Vertically sliding timber sash windows are probably the most common type of window found in older buildings in Ireland. Many original sashes and frames survive which are over two hundred years old and still give good service. The quality of the original materials and craftsmanship of these windows means that they are usually capable of repair and, if so, this should be encouraged.

10.4.5 Examples of horizontally sliding sash windows are now rare and any survivals should be retained in situ.

Sash windows were used in Ireland for most building types from the end of the seventeenth century until the middle of the twentieth. In general the glazing pattern, the profile of the sash bars and the materials used reflect architectural fashions, the social status of the building (or its builder) and the available materials. The high quality and density of the timber available in the eighteenth and nineteenth centuries means that most of these historic windows are still capable of repair

The majority of sliding sash windows found in this country slide vertically and sashes that slide horizontally are rare; they are usually, but not exclusively, found in smaller structures such as cottages

Clues to the different phases of a building's development can often be found on subsidiary elevations; this house retains a very early eighteenth-century sash window on the top right of this photograph; the differences in opening sizes and sash details of the other windows are the result of several later phases of work

10.4.6 The number, arrangement and proportion of panes, the details of the glazing bars and frames and the presence or absence of horns, are important features of sash windows that should be respected, as should the opening methods. In many early windows, only the lower sash was weighted and the upper fixed. Where early examples of sash windows with exposed sash boxes survive they should be retained and not replaced with rebated windows. Late eighteenth and early nineteenth century Georgian-Gothic sash windows in pointed arched openings often had curvilinear glazing bars to the upper sash. Where these survive they should be retained. Later styles included the use of smaller glazed panes to the edges of the sashes called 'margin lights'. The margins are often, but not always, glazed with coloured or patterned glass. Where these survive, they are of interest whether or not they are original to the building or to the opening.

The use of arched openings and the arrangement of glazing bars in decorative patterns helps to enliven facades and adds character to a structure

Casement windows

10.4.7 Early lead-glazed casement windows, predating the arrival of the sash window in the late seventeenth century, are extremely rare in Ireland and every effort should be made to retain surviving examples in situ. The use of casement windows was revived in the nineteenth century and examples are to be seen in late-Georgian, Victorian and later buildings with timber or metal frames. These are often glazed with small diamond or square quarry panes. French windows are a version of a casement window where the casements are carried down to the floor level and open like doors. Where casement windows are original or early replacements of quality, they should be retained, and repaired where necessary.

Casement windows, although widely used in many countries, were seldom used in Ireland after the arrival of the sash window in the late-seventeenth century. Eighteenth- and nineteenth-century casement windows, whether of timber or metal, generally open inwards, excepting French windows, which open out onto terraces or balconies

Blocked, blind and dummy windows

10.4.8 Blind or dummy windows are a feature of many important buildings and structures. These are imitation window openings, usually the size and shape of adjacent openings and with similar head, sill and reveal details. They were used as a decorative device to give symmetry to the façade of an asymmetrically planned building. The blind or dummy window may contain a plain rendered, brick or stone panel. More elaborate versions can contain fully glazed fixed timber sashes set in the masonry panel. Where blind or dummy windows exist, they are usually an integral part of the elevational design and should be retained.

10.4.9 Blocked-up window openings are of historical interest particularly in informing an understanding of previous uses or forms of the building. Where they exist their presence should be recorded and analysed.

Fully-glazed blind windows such as this example are rare; they may be deliberately designed to ensure symmetrical fenestration (for example, where the plan form did not permit a window), or could represent later blocking of openings. It is commonly thought that openings were blocked to avoid paying window tax, which was in force between 1799 and 1851, however in Ireland there is little evidence to support this theory

Mullioned windows

10.4.10 Mullions can be found in conjunction with transoms in cross-windows or as the vertical dividers in tripartite or bipartite windows or in bay windows. These mullions can be of stone, rendered brickwork or of timber, sometimes decoratively treated. The lights can be fixed, casement or sash. The proportioning of the subdivisions of mullioned windows is an important element in the overall design of a building and should be conserved.

Metal windows

10.4.11 Seventeenth-century leaded lights were glazed into wrought iron frames and are now extremely rare. Cast-iron windows first appeared in Ireland in the early nineteenth century. These are commonly glazed with diamond quarries in casement or pivot lights, although wholly cast-iron sash windows are also occasionally found.

10.4.12 Most examples of steel-framed windows in Ireland date from the first half of the twentieth century. Steel-framed windows with horizontally proportioned panes were characteristic features of buildings of, or influenced by, the Modern Movement in architecture. When these window frames are removed and replaced with frames of different materials, proportions or sectional profile, much of the architectural character of the building is lost. Where metal-framed windows are important to the character and quality of a structure that is protected, they should be repaired or, if beyond repair, their replacement on a like-for-like basis should be encouraged.

Window ironmongery

10.4.13 Original sash fittings include meeting rail catches, weights and pulleys, or quadrant catches where weights were not used. Casement latches, hinges and fasteners, where they survive, are features of interest. They should be identified and retained in situ. If security issues arise, existing window ironmongery could be augmented with sensitively placed modern locks rather than replaced.

Balconettes, window boxes, external blinds

10.4.14 Wrought or cast-iron balconettes, window boxes and sill guards are important architectural elements contributing to the interest of a building and should be retained. Other features such as early or original external shutters, blind boxes and window canopies should be identified and retained.

Mullions, sometimes together with transoms, were used to divide larger openings into manageably-sized sashes or casements. As with these Arts and Crafts style leaded casements, mullioned windows were usually designed consciously to contribute to the appearance of the structure

Cast-iron sash, casement, pivot and fixed windows were often designed more for function than beauty, but occasionally cast-iron windows of subtle elegance are found and where this is so, they may be the most important element of the façade

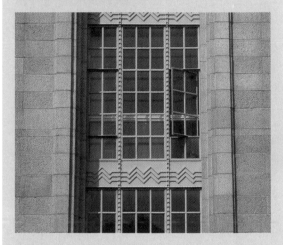

The design of Modern Movement windows represented a clean break with the past; often favouring horizontal lines and thin steel frames. Such windows are an integral part of the original design of an early or mid twentieth-century structure and replacing them in other materials and to different profiles almost always detracts from the character of the structure

Original and early window furniture and mechanisms can provide information about the history of the window. As fixtures of interest, they may be included in the protection of the building so that, even if they have been – or are about to be – supplanted they should be retained in situ

Balconettes and other external fixtures associated with windows were often more ornamental than practical, designed as part of the aesthetic of the structure or added later. Even where not in use they should be retained as part of the original design or as evidence of a subsequent fashionable alteration

CONSIDERATION OF PROPOSALS AFFECTING
WINDOWS

10.4.15 The visual impact of alterations to the windows of a
historic structure can be significant. Proposals to
remove, replace or otherwise alter historic windows
should be given close attention. Where repairs are
proposed, these should preferably be specified on a
window-by-window basis as the extent of repair can
vary widely depending on weathering and other
factors.

10.4.16 Repair and repainting of historic windows should be
carried out with due care for the joinery or
metalwork and any original or early glass and for
the appearance and character of the structure.
Where proposals are made to paint windows, care
should be taken to establish the original finish
before applying paint to unpainted joinery. Methods
and specification of repainting should be approved
by the planning authority before works commence.
It is rarely appropriate to remove paint from historic
timber windows by immersion (see 11.3.9 below) or
to remove paint from glazed lights using a heat
gun.

10.4.17 Replacement of sashes or entire windows should
only be permitted where the existing windows are
missing; are verifiably decayed beyond repair; or are
themselves inappropriate recent replacements.
Replacement windows should be of appropriate
material, design and detail and approved by the
planning authority prior to any work commencing.
The complete replacement of such elements in
historic buildings should rarely be permitted where
they are capable of repair.

10.4.18 Plastic and aluminium are inappropriate materials for
replacement windows in historic buildings (unless
these materials can be proved to have been used
originally).

10.4.19 It is of importance to the character and appearance
of a structure that fenestration patterns are
protected. Where replacement windows are
permitted, the materials, glazing divisions and
sectional profile of the new windows should be
appropriate to the date of the protected structure
or to the date when the opening was made. If the
latter, the design should be judged on its
contribution to the protected structure.

*While windows are vulnerable to the impact of the weather, it is
rare that a whole window is affected to the extent that complete
replacement is necessary. Repair by splicing and piecing is a
traditional method of prolonging the life of timber windows, and
many joiners still specialise in this work (this window is shown
after repair). The high quality of the timbers used historically
means that it makes economic sense to leave unaffected
elements in place, as they have proven their longevity, having
withstood centuries of use*

*While the recent sash windows on the upper floor of this house
seem reasonably accurate at first glance, the joiner or designer
did not base the detailing on the surviving original sashes on the
ground floor. The replacement windows are made to a thicker
profile and have horns which the original sashes do not. The
inclusion of horns is a common error made in fabricating new
sashes. In this case the original windows predate the use of horns,
which did not become standard until the second quarter of the
nineteenth century*

Where clues survive as to the correct detailing of a replacement window they should be followed in order to fabricate a historically-accurate new window. In the case illustrated here, evidence of the detailing of the original central sashes existed in the blind side lights but was ignored

From the middle of the nineteenth century a hierarchy of glazing within a single building became common: newly-available, but expensive, plate glass was used on the principal floor with smaller paned windows at the basement and upper floors. This arrangement was often original to the building and should be respected and plate glass sashes not mistakenly 'restored' as small-pane windows

10.4.20 Replacement windows should replicate the opening method of the original windows. Top- and bottom-hung or pivot windows are not suitable replacements for sliding sashes or side-hung casements. Their use will disrupt the visual integrity of a historic building and its setting and can be detrimental to the character of an ACA.

10.4.21 Where replacement of existing windows has become necessary, the opportunity may arise to consider the replacement of later, inappropriate or damaging alterations and allow for the installation of new windows whose design is more appropriate to the structure, or to the ACA. This is particularly relevant in unified terraces of buildings where inappropriate replacement windows have damaged the character of the entire group of buildings. However, such restoration should always be based upon firm evidence of the original design of the window using old photographs, drawings, or other reliable information, such as surviving original windows in the neighbouring buildings. Caution should be exercised as some past alterations may contribute to the cumulative historical interest of a building and should not be erased without due consideration of all the consequences. For example, improvements in glass-making technology led to a fashion in the latter part of the nineteenth century for replacing small-paned sashes with single panes of plate glass. These single-paned sash windows can now be seen as part of the historical record of the building and should only be permitted to be replaced after careful consideration by the planning authority.

10.4.22 The reopening of blocked windows may be appropriate in cases where this re-establishes the elevational design of the building. But an assessment needs to be made as to whether or not the blocked opening was part of the original design, such as a blind window, or part of alterations to the structure where the earlier opening may no longer relate to the present form of the building. Previously blocked openings should not be opened up where it would lead to the disturbance or destruction of later interior work of quality.

10.4.23 The erection of new external blinds and canopies should generally not be permitted where there is no evidence that they previously existed and when their effect on the appearance of the building and its setting may be considered damaging. The removal of redundant blind boxes should generally not be permitted where they contribute to the character of the structure or area.

10.5 **Glass and Glazing**

IDENTIFYING SPECIAL FEATURES FOR PROTECTION

10.5.1 All old surviving glass is important to the character and quality of a historic building. Historic plain glass types include blown cylinder glass, blown crown glass and blown or cast plate glass. Decorative uses of glass include stained glass, painted glass, coloured glass or old glass. Old glass may have early, etched inscriptions on it, adding to the importance of the glazing.

By its delicate nature, thinly blown historic glass is vulnerable to damage, making it remarkable that so much survives. The irregular surfaces of plain glass, naturally highly polished, contort reflections and add considerable character to the buildings and streets where historic glass is found

Crown and other plain glass

10.5.2 The irregularities and imperfections of handmade glass cannot be replicated with modern float glass and are essential to the quality of the historic window. Where crown, cylinder or early polished plate glass survives, its existence should be recorded. All original or early glass should be protected and retained.

Stained and painted glass, decorative zinc-framed or leaded glass

10.5.3 Individual pieces of stained, painted or coloured glass set in lead or zinc cames (used in H- or T-section strips respectively which hold the pieces of glass in place) are usually associated with church architecture. There are, however, many fine examples of stained, painted or coloured glass decorative panels in public buildings and in doors, fanlights and windows of houses, often within margin lights. The windows of many late Georgian churches and other buildings were glazed with leaded panels or cast-iron glazing bars containing clear glass quarries.

CONSIDERATION OF PROPOSALS AFFECTING GLAZING

Crown and other plain glass

10.5.4 Where old or interesting glass has been identified in a protected structure or in another building, such glass should be retained and protected during the building works. Where repairs are necessary to the window frames, the panes can be carefully removed and reset by a specialist. If a window is decayed beyond repair, the original glass can be removed with great care and set aside for re-use in repair work elsewhere within the same building. Small corner cracks should not be used as a reason to remove early panes of plain glass. Badly-damaged panes of significance, such as bullseye panes or those with inscriptions, can be plated with a thin glass layer and retained in place. The use of ultra-violet protective film on historic glass should be avoided particularly where the glass is thin.

10.5.5 Where the loss of historic glass in a prominent location would significantly affect the character of a protected structure or an ACA, the planning authority could make it a condition that damaged panes are replaced with new handmade panes.

Stained and painted glass, decorative zinc-framed or leaded glass

10.5.6 The repair and cleaning of artistically or historically important glazing, such as stained glass or painted glass panels, is the work of specialist conservators. Where it is proposed to carry out works to stained

Historically, the aim of glassmakers was to create perfect, uniform glass panes which, until recently, was not achievable with the methods available to them. Modern float glass is perfectly uniform but, as a result, without character. It is the very imperfections of handblown glass such as bubbles, undulations or tints, once seen as faults, that are now prized. In fact, historic glass is irreplaceable. Crown glass is no longer made as the skills to blow and spin thin crowns have been lost, while few makers still produce cylinder sheet glass

Stained glass comes in many forms, from finely-detailed floral patterns in a domestic building – as in this example – to illustrative panels by internationally important artists in public buildings

Most of the panes of this window, which will need maintenance as part of a larger project to repair the whole structure, are of cylinder sheet glass. Some are cracked while a few are missing. If timber repairs are necessary the glass should be carefully removed from the frames by one of several methods, securely stored and reglazed on completion, sealed with putty. Historic glass should always be adequately protected during general building works, even where no window repairs are proposed

or painted glass windows, the applicant should show that the proposed work is necessary and will involve the minimum intervention and replacement of historic material. Re-leading of panels should not be seen as routine and the buckling of leaded windows is not, in itself, a conclusive indication of a need to undertake re-leading. The repair of leaded-glass panels should preferably be carried out in situ. It is often acceptable to allow cracks in the glass to remain unrepaired and for small holes to be filled in situ. However, there may be cases where serious problems warrant the removal of the panel to an off-site workshop for repair. Before any works are carried out, the window should be recorded in situ with photographs, drawings or both. Alterations that involve the insertion of inappropriate modern panes into a window should not be permitted.

Modern forms of glazing

10.5.7 The use of modern wired glass, obscured glass, tinted glass or louvred glass panels or the insertion of extract fans, air-conditioning units and similar devices on prominent elevations should generally not be permitted.

10.6   External Protection

10.6.1 New external protection may be proposed to protect historic or interesting glass from breakage or from damage by the elements. Where this is the case, this protection should be provided in a way which is reversible and as unobtrusive as possible. The protection should not be made or fixed in a way that will damage the fabric or appearance of the structure or window. For example, the rusting of metal grilles or run-off from copper or iron fixings could cause damage to the fabric. The creation of unventilated cavities behind external secondary glazing panels can encourage excessive and damaging heat build-up or allow condensation to occur on the face of the historic glass. Where secondary glazing is proposed, the applicant should indicate how the original glasswork is to be ventilated.

Decorative panels of stained, painted or etched glass should be retained in situ until repairs are specified and carried out by experienced stained glass conservators, as unnecessary removal or poorly-detailed restoration could cause damage and possibly devalue the artistic work. If necessary, the panels should be protected (outside and inside, but with adequate ventilation), and all broken pieces stored carefully until professional help can be obtained

The insertion of new extract fans, louvres and the like should generally be confined to basements or minor elevations; however if the basement was designed as part of a principal elevation, as is the case in this structure, or is visible from the street or on the approach to the structure, then such additions should be avoided. The addition of items that would necessitate altering the frame or structural opening of a historic window should also be avoided, even on secondary elevations

10.6.2 The installation of secondary glazing to the exterior of windows can be visually obtrusive and proposals should be given careful consideration. The appearance and character of the building will be harmed by the use of plastic sheeting that can surface-craze or become opaque through exposure to the elements. This sheeting is also highly flammable and its use should not be permitted near valuable glass where the exterior is accessible to vandals. The appearance of the external protection will be enhanced by requiring it to be formed to fit the shape of the opening and any tracery while allowing for sufficient ventilation.

10.7 Improving the Thermal Efficiency of Historic Openings

Draught-proofing

10.7.1 Simple draught-proofing is usually the most acceptable method of improving the thermal efficiency of historic windows and doors. However, some caution should be exercised. Most draught-proofing systems have a shorter life-expectancy than the historic window or door frames themselves and so the installation of draught-proofing, which often requires routing out of sashes and frames, should not take place to the detriment of the existing joinery.

10.7.2 The installation of draught-stripping measures to openings should take account of the age, importance and suitability of the element for such work. The measures used should not compromise the condition of the fabric nor unacceptably alter the appearance of the element.

Double-glazing and secondary glazing

10.7.3 The installation of double-glazing to protected structures is problematic and should generally not be permitted where original or early windows exist. The installation of double-glazed units into existing openings, even where the existing window frames are not of any special interest, may not be visually acceptable and can rarely be achieved without making unacceptable changes to the profiles of the frames arising from the depth of the double-glazed units. It also makes the sashes much heavier and could strain the joints. The use of false spacer bars or bars applied to the interior or exterior is usually visually unacceptable. Additional problems may arise as many old buildings suffer from condensation problems following the installation of airtight windows.

This grille, possibly only intended as a temporary measure, is nevertheless damaging to the appearance of the window and the building as a whole and its fixings are starting to fail. If protection is indeed necessary – a question all custodians of stained glass should first ask themselves – the use of black coated stainless steel grilles would be preferable, shaped to fit each lancet and tracery light

In this case, the external secondary glazing is shaped to fit each light; however its design has two serious drawbacks: the adverse visual impact on the structure and, the potential to cause physical damage to the glasswork arising from the lack of ventilation of the cavity between the historic glass and the new protective layer. The micro-climate created between glass and outer glazing by the lack of ventilation can lead to the distortion of the lead matrix and damage to glass and paint from organic growth

10.7.4 Internal secondary glazing may be considered acceptable where the installation can be reversed without damage to elements of the historic fabric of the building, such as panelled shutters and the like. Secondary glazing can provide some thermal insulation and is usually a more effective means of providing sound insulation than double-glazing. A method should be designed to allow for the use of internal shutters where these exist. It should be borne in mind that there may be the possibility of unacceptable reflections from the secondary glazing when viewed externally. This may affect not only the character of a protected structure but also have an adverse effect on the character of an ACA.

Sealing measures generally

10.7.5 The fabric of older buildings was generally designed to allow for the absorption of moisture from the ground or from rainwater and its subsequent evaporation from the surface or through the natural ventilation of the interior of the building from open fireplaces or unsealed windows and doors. Measures to seal an older building can result in moisture being trapped within the building or within its fabric. This can lead to damage of the fabric and finishes of the building by condensation or by promoting fungal attack. For this reason, the proposed insertion of sealed units such as uPVC windows and doors into a historic building, even where the original elements have previously been lost, should be treated with great caution.

A draught-proofed window should not be visibly altered by the work, except on close inspection, as the patented strips inevitably make a small difference. It should be borne in mind that in most cases the brush or pile-edged parting bead is of white plastic, which limits the colours the sash window can be painted without making it unduly visible. The work should also be finished off well, retouching any disturbed paintwork, but the pile or brushes must not be over-painted as this could render them ineffective

Well-designed and fitted secondary glazing will provide a measure of both heat and sound insulation while allowing the historic window to remain intact. Two main aspects of the design should be carefully considered so as to limit both the aesthetic and physical impacts: the visual effect of the proposed glazing (this example is visually obtrusive from both the street and the interior of the building) and the means of fixing. Internal window shutters should not be disabled by the works and the glazing should be removable without damage to the historic fabric

Interiors

The interior of a protected structure is of primary importance to its character. Ideally, the special interest of the interior should be assessed when initially protecting the structure, but failing that, it should be evaluated when proposals are put forward to redevelop the structure. The importance of an interior is not confined to decorative features: the plan form or the structural system itself may be innovative, as in this early multi-storey, steel-framed store house

11.1 Introduction

11.1.1 The interior of any protected structure is of primary importance. Although the interiors of many protected structures are not accessible to the general public, they may nonetheless be essential to the character and special interest of that building and are therefore protected.

11.1.2 Protection extends to all features of quality and interest in the interior of a protected structure, not only to those features which are original. In making an assessment of the interior of a protected structure, a planning authority should obtain all necessary expert and specialist advice. This assessment should ideally be carried out on a room-by-room basis. Consideration should be given, in each room or space, to elements such as the floor, ceiling and walls and any interesting features or fittings present. An overall assessment of the interior and the interrelationship of different spaces should also be made.

11.1.3 Items to consider in the assessment of an interior include:

a) Does the structure retain its original plan-form?

b) If not, are there any alterations or additions of interest?

c) Have the proportions of the rooms or spaces been altered? Have they been damaged by alteration, improved or merely changed?

d) Are there any interesting, planned relationships between rooms or spaces, such as enfilades, processional routes, industrial processes and the like? Have these been altered or interrupted by changes or created out of previously existing spaces?

e) Is there a hierarchy to the various spaces? How do the principal spaces relate to the subsidiary ones; for example, dining rooms to kitchens or banking halls to offices?

f) Is the relationship of the spaces or the layout of rooms of interest because of the insight it gives into the workings of a bygone time; for example, the relationship of cells to a courtroom or a milling room to a store?

g) Are there elements of interest in the interior such as early iron and concrete floors, timber stud partitions, lath-and-plaster ceilings, exposed roof trusses?

h) Is there any joinery of quality such as internal doors, window shutters, skirting boards, dado rails, architraves, wall panelling?

i) Are there finishes of interest to flooring, walls or ceilings?

j) Are there any surviving original or good quality decorative schemes? These might include limewash, paint, wallpaper, wall-paintings, painted ceilings, tiling, gilding, and other finishes.

k) Are there any fixtures or features which are original to the building or of architectural or historical interest; for example fireplaces, counters or benching?

l) Is there surviving machinery connected with a building's present or former use, such as milling machinery, early lifts or dumb waiters?

11.1.4 Where features are considered to be worthy of protection, they should ideally be retained in situ. Even where elements or features are decayed or damaged, they should be repaired rather than replaced. Repairs and alterations should be carried out in a manner appropriate to the individual element or structure and preferably in a manner that is readily reversible.

11.2 Elements of the Interior

Plan-form

IDENTIFYING SPECIAL FEATURES FOR PROTECTION

11.2.1 The plan-form of a building is one of its most important characteristics. Where the original plan-form remains, or is readily discernible, it should be identified and respected. Later alterations of definite architectural merit should also be identified for protection.

CONSIDERATION OF PROPOSALS AFFECTING PLAN-FORM

11.2.2 Where alterations are essential for the continued viability of a building with an interior of value, attempts should be made to keep works to a minimum and preferably confined to areas of secondary importance. For example, where existing internal doorways are to become redundant, as a result of alterations to a structure, the doors should be retained in position and simply locked shut, rather than stripped out and the opening blocked up.

Whereas an important fixture of this interior was retained in the gallery of this former church; the original plastering, floor and other fixtures have all been lost. Even if an accurate reproduction of the missing features and decoration were to be undertaken, the result would largely be a new interior

The arrangement and inter-relationship of rooms and circulation spaces in an interior – here a top-lit long gallery in a large house – are key to how the building was designed to work and to be experienced. Proposals to change the plan form and alter or introduce new circulation routes should therefore be closely scrutinised

11.2.3 Wherever possible, the alterations should not change the interrelationships or the proportions of prominent spaces such as entrances, staircases or principal rooms. In a protected structure that retains its original spatial layout, proposals to subdivide the building into several smaller units or to open up a pair or series of rooms to create a larger space should be permitted only in exceptional circumstances after very careful scrutiny by the planning authority.

11.2.4 Where an earlier, unsatisfactory subdivision or opening up of rooms or spaces has taken place, in a manner which has distorted the original design, the opportunity could be taken to reinstate the earlier plan-form. Such inappropriate alterations could include the subdivision of principal rooms to form smaller rooms, lobbies or corridors, the addition of partitions which divide or obscure windows or obstruct designed circulation patterns.

11.2.5 Reinstatement work, such as the removal of later partitions or lobbies, should generally be undertaken where it can be readily achieved and does not involve the loss or damage of later alterations of quality.

Floors

11.2.6 All floor structures of interest, which could include structural members such as timber, iron or steel beams, trusses, joists and brackets and floor finishes or surfaces of interest, should be identified and respected, whether or not they are original. Finishes could include marble or stone paving, timber boarding or blocks, scagliola, tiles, cobbling, brick, rammed earth, lime ash, plaster, terrazzo, or early concrete.

11.2.7 Efforts should be made to retain these floor types and any others of interest. Associated architectural details such as cast-iron floor grilles should generally be conserved even where they have become redundant.

CONSIDERATION OF PROPOSALS AFFECTING FLOORS

11.2.8 Where historic flooring exists, due care should be taken when works are undertaken for the installation or repair of services or the installation of thermal or acoustic insulation or for fire-safety enhancement works. Many types of floor finish are easily damaged and difficult to re-lay and should not be disturbed without good reason. Where a floor of particular interest or merit exists, an alternative service route should be found in order to avoid the disturbance of the floor. For example, this may be the case where a previously undisturbed

The practice of the recent past of subdividing large rooms by forming boxed cubicles within the space has one advantage: it makes their removal less complicated and damaging than if the partitions extended up to the ceiling. However, the reversibility of this type of work may not always justify the insertion of new partitions into high-quality architectural interiors

Not just the visible finishes of a floor but also its structural elements may be of special interest. The painting of floors to imitate tiling is an unusual feature of some eighteenth-century houses; here the painted diamonds are shaped with pleasing eccentricity to fit into the available space

Taking up and relaying stone flags to accommodate underfloor heating and other services is delicate work which has the potential to cause irreparable damage if incorrectly or clumsily done. The use of skilled personnel is necessary to avoid cracking or damage to the arrises of the flags

floor is made of doweled floorboards, which would be irreparably damaged by lifting. Flooring such as terrazzo, scagliola and other composition materials are also extremely easy to damage and difficult to repair.

11.2.9   The cutting of old timber joists for new services should be avoided or kept to a minimum. It should be a requirement that any historical features, such as acoustic insulation or fire-proofing incorporated within the floor structure, should be preserved wherever possible. Where the need for improved fire protection demands the removal of such pugging, a full recording of the floor details should be undertaken before works commence.

11.2.10   Original floors and floor levels should be retained where they survive. In structures where the floor to ceiling heights are considered too low for modern habitation, consideration could be given to excavating the ground floor level or to raising the collars or ties of the roof in order to avoid raising wall heads. However, for an interior of significant quality or rarity, such proposals may not be acceptable.

Floor strengthening

11.2.11   Any works to strengthen the floors of an existing building can be very invasive. Major disturbance can be caused to floor surfaces, skirting, panelling, architraves, hearthstones, ceilings and cornices. All options should be considered to avoid irreversible damage or needless disturbance of important features.

11.2.12   There are no standard methods of strengthening the floors of old buildings. Where floor strengthening is proposed, the applicant should be able to show that there will be a minimum disturbance of good quality finishes and a minimum loss of historic fabric such as floor timbers. Other options should also be explored, such as restricting the location of heavy loads to basement areas or to areas of little architectural interest where the floors can be strengthened without damage to important features. Low-key methods of stiffening floors are often possible and practicable using traditional methods and materials such as scarfing on new timber, the use of flitch beams and other solutions.

11.2.13   Any substantial strengthening work should be carried out under the guidance of an appropriately qualified structural engineer with knowledge and experience of historic buildings. Methods and specification for the works should be approved by the planning authority before any works commence.

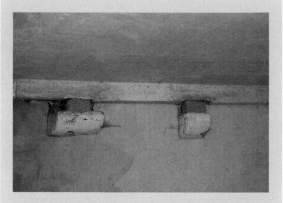

These sixteenth-century corbels continued to be used after an early alteration that raised the ceiling height. This change is of interest, adding to our knowledge of the evolution of the structure, but a similar proposal made today would require very careful scrutiny

Proposals to strengthen historic floor structures should take account of the potential impacts on the fabric of the building and any existing finishes that would be disturbed to accommodate it. In this case, the main beam supporting the floor above is a scarfed beam. The scarfing may be original to enable the beam span a wide space, but could also signify an old repair, in which case the reasons behind the earlier repair work should be investigated to rule out the possible overloading of the floor structure

Walls and partitions may be of interest due to archaic methods of construction, unusual materials or high quality of finish. Whether original or a well-crafted later intervention, as is this panelled bedroom corridor, internal walls and partitions can contribute to the special interest of the structure

Internal walls and partitions
IDENTIFYING SPECIAL FEATURES FOR PROTECTION

11.2.14 The walls and partitions in historic buildings may often be of interest in themselves and include examples of rare or interesting construction methods.

11.2.15 Earlier fireplaces, openings or decoration may be hidden behind later work. In protected structures where there are likely to be concealed features, the internal walls should be carefully investigated in advance of any alterations being carried out. However, where an earlier feature is known to be concealed by a later decorative scheme of interest, the later decoration should generally not be disturbed in order to reveal or investigate the earlier feature.

CONSIDERATION OF PROPOSALS

11.2.16 In addition to the loss of historic fabric, the removal of internal structural walls or chimney breasts also has the potential to jeopardise the structural stability of a building and any proposals should be given careful consideration.

11.2.17 Where new partitions are proposed, they should be installed in such a way that they can be removed at a later stage with little or no damage to the historic fabric. New partitions should not cut through decorative plasterwork, finishes or joinery but be scribed around them with extreme care and accuracy. The installation of new partition walls should generally be avoided in high-quality interiors.

11.2.18 The formation of new openings in existing walls or partitions should be minimised, or avoided altogether, in an interior of quality, as this inevitably leads to the destruction of existing fabric. Such damage can rarely be satisfactorily reversed. Some injudicious alterations may include the removal of plaster from brick-nog partitions, while the cutting of new openings in braced partitions may result in structural failure.

11.2.19 The addition of internal insulation or dry-lining to a protected structure should only be permitted where this would not adversely affect important internal features of interest such as cornices, wall panelling, skirtings, windowcases and doorcases or decorative finishes.

Ceilings
IDENTIFYING SPECIAL FEATURES FOR PROTECTION

11.2.20 Ceilings that have plaster decoration are important features in an interior. Even plain plaster that is old is also of interest, particularly if it was applied onto

Later finishes or features may cover earlier elements of interest such as this sixteenth-century doorway, partly covered by re-used original panelling and an eighteenth-century doorcase; it may be necessary simply to record the earlier feature while retaining the high-quality later work in place undisturbed

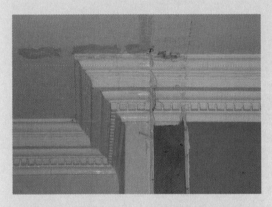

New partitions, where considered acceptable, should avoid disturbing historic fabric. They should be scribed around cornices, dado rails and skirtings to allow removal without damage. However, it is not generally recommended that important spaces within a protected structure be subdivided even if the subdivisions are reversible

Evidence may survive on a plastered vaulted ceiling or arch of the wicker centring used in forming the vault, seen in the hollows left by the wickerwork which was embedded in the plaster and left there when the centring was removed. In some rare examples, pieces of wickerwork also survive

timber laths. Decorative plasterwork may include highly decorated enrichments or relatively simple cornices. Ceilings may also be painted or incorporate painted panels.

11.2.21 Exposed roof or ceiling structures are of architectural interest and important to the character of an interior. These might include timber joists or trusses or iron beams. There may be associated details of interest to a ceiling such as iron or timber ventilation and heating grilles, lighting fixtures or chandelier winches.

CONSIDERATION OF PROPOSALS AFFECTING CEILINGS

11.2.22 It should be noted that where there is a proposal to alter or dismantle a historic decorative or plain plaster ceiling, the alternatives should first be considered. Irregularities in a ceiling surface do not necessarily indicate problems which require the ceiling to be demolished. An undulating ceiling surface may need to be appreciated as part of an old building. Proposals to replace or alter the supports of a historic ceiling should be carefully scrutinised.

11.2.23 Proposals to install new suspended ceilings should be carefully considered and care should be taken that they do not conceal original plasterwork or other features of quality and that their installation does not affect the proportions or character of an important room or the appearance of a building from the street. Whilst they may be considered acceptable in minor rooms, or in spaces without special interest, they should generally not be permitted where they conflict with the window head level and where this would affect the external appearance of a building. Where new suspended ceilings are permitted to be installed, the installation should be readily reversible without damage to the historic fabric of the building.

11.3 **Finishes**

Plasterwork

IDENTIFYING SPECIAL FEATURES FOR PROTECTION

11.3.1 Historic plasterwork should be identified and protected wherever possible. Not only decorative wall and ceiling plaster, but also plain, flat plasterwork are important parts of the internal fabric of a protected structure.

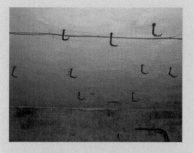

Lath and plaster ceilings or walls without embellishments may appear unimportant, but the craftsmanship in their fabrication and the resulting gently undulating surface can be part of the character of a historic interior. Functional fixtures such as meat hooks, ventilation grilles or exposed beams contribute to the character (although plastered beams should generally not be exposed)

Repairs to plastered ceilings should be appropriately specified to rectify any structural faults while avoiding unnecessary removal or reproduction of parts of the ceiling. Existing cracks and stains, while indicative of damage, should be monitored for ongoing problems before any invasive action is undertaken. Decorative ceiling plaster should be carefully repaired by an experienced conservation stuccadore, who may advise reinforcing the ceiling from above

This illustration, taken in the space above a previously-lowered ceiling, shows the drawback of carrying out such works; apart from the damage to the architectural character of the interior, the lowered ceiling has concealed problems caused by lack of maintenance to the fabric above it

CONSIDERATION OF PROPOSALS AFFECTING PLASTERWORK

11.3.2 Care should be taken when permitting works such as chasing-in of electrical wiring that the minimum possible disturbance is caused to important wall or ceiling plaster. Where the plasterwork is of particular importance or rarity, chasing-in should be avoided. Disturbance should not be permitted to decorative plasterwork such as cutting through or across mouldings or installing downlighters.

11.3.3 Where older, soft lime-based plasters are to be repaired, repairs should be carried out using a plaster that matches the existing material on a like-for-like basis while allowing it to be clear on close inspection which is the original material.

Joinery
IDENTIFYING SPECIAL FEATURES FOR PROTECTION

11.3.4 Elements of internal joinery often survive in large quantities in historic buildings. They can include doors, doorcases, windows, windowcases, skirtings, dado rails, panelling, staircases and fireplaces. The doorcases and windowcases can consist of architraves, plinth blocks, door leaves, panelled reveals and window shutters. Surviving door and window furniture such as hinges, locks, lockcases, door handles, shutter bars and the like should be preserved even when redundant.

CONSIDERATION OF PROPOSALS AFFECTING JOINERY

11.3.5 The planning authority should encourage the careful repair of the historic fabric with an emphasis on the conservation of as much as possible of the old material. Large-scale renewal of sections of joinery for the sake of convenience should be avoided. In repairing joinery, only the minimum amount of timber should be replaced using timber of a matching species and grain type. New pieces, where required, should be carefully jointed in. The profiles of decayed sections of moulded work should be copied exactly and spliced precisely into the existing work. The use of substitute materials such as glass-reinforced plastic to simulate carved joinery should not be permitted in interiors of architectural merit.

Decorative plasterwork is of prime importance in historic interiors. Not only is it aesthetically pleasing, it can also be used to indicate dates of construction or alteration. The best eighteenth-century Irish plasterwork has an international reputation, but the more modest examples found countrywide are of importance to the houses, churches, town halls, railway stations and other building types which they embellish

Plaster is generally a robust material, but continuous saturation can cause severe damage, both to the plasterwork and its timber supports, and provoke fungal attack in the latter. The fabric of the building will require drying out before an assessment can be made as to the extent to which replacement of plaster is necessary

The internal joinery of a protected structure, whether original or good-quality later additions, is often aesthetically pleasing in addition to being well-crafted from high quality timber with good metal fittings. Joinery elements, whether of painted softwood or elaborate polished mahogany, are key indicators of the date and social status of a historic structure and provide a physical record of the alterations made to it throughout its history

Timber is eminently capable of repair. Splicing, scarfing and other traditional methods of work that retain the maximum amount of sound material are still carried out effectively and unobtrusively by skilled conservation joiners

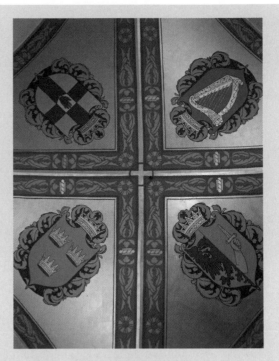

The intact survival of delicate internal finishes such as historic wallpaper or stencilling is unusual; however, in this illustration, an entire early twentieth-century heraldic scheme has survived in a vaulted entrance lobby and been retained despite a recent change of use

The installation of new locks, catches, hinges, door-closers and other items to high-quality joinery, such as this mahogany door, can be carried out with care but should not necessitate the removal of surviving historic fittings even where these have become redundant. The removal of inappropriate later fittings can cause as much damage as their installation: the consequent repair is a specialist task

The repainting or redecoration of walls, or parts of walls, which never had important decorative schemes will not affect the character of an interior but the opposite will be the case where there are details of interest, such as these historically-important mural panels

Decorative finishes
IDENTIFYING SPECIAL FEATURES FOR PROTECTION

11.3.6 Important early schemes of interior decoration should be identified and preserved wherever feasible. Decorative finishes of interest may include paint, wallpaper, anaglyptic papers, wall or ceiling-paintings, stencilling, decorative paint finishes, gilding, tiling and other forms of decoration. Where such decoration exists, and is clearly part of the character of the protected interior or is of historical interest, it should be retained and conserved.

CONSIDERATION OF PROPOSALS AFFECTING DECORATIVE FINISHES

11.3.7 No issue arises with the routine redecoration of rooms which have lost, or perhaps never had, important decorative schemes. However, where decorative schemes or details survive which are part of the character and special interest of the building these should generally not be over-painted or destroyed. Surviving decorative finishes need careful assessment and can be simply left as found, cleaned, restored or reproduced as appropriate.

11.3.8 Where there is reason to believe that earlier decoration of some quality survives below later layers, specialist advice should be taken as to whether to reveal it or how to conserve it. It could be a condition of a planning permission that any fragments of original or early decoration of merit, such as pieces of wallpaper, which come to light during renovation works, should be recorded and preserved where possible. Where there is extensive survival of a concealed decorative scheme of interest, specialist advice could be taken as to whether to reveal it or how to conserve it.

11.3.9 Where the stripping of paint is proposed, it should be remembered that this action would eradicate the evidence of the original or early decorative schemes where traces of these have survived. This will make it impossible thereafter to determine the original or previous colouring or paint types. Where there is likely to be early, interesting paintwork below the present surface, consideration should be given to leaving a small area of the wall, ceiling or joinery unstripped or undertaking a proper detailed paint analysis before any stripping takes place. The method of paint-stripping should be appropriate to the underlying material. In particular, account should be taken of the material's ability to withstand the stripping process. For example, old joinery should never be stripped by immersion as this will deform the timber and weaken the joints. Gesso ornament is not always identifiable when painted and is easily damaged by stripping off the overlying paint.

Fragments of handmade wallpaper are occasionally uncovered beneath later finishes; where this occurs it may be appropriate either to record and retain them in position or to allow for their careful removal and conservation. It may be possible – if sufficient evidence survives – to reproduce historic wallpaper, should the restoration of the original decorative scheme be of great importance to the interior. Consideration should be given to the fact that the change of use of a room could affect the conservation of a delicate wall finish such as wallpaper, whether from direct damage or from changed levels of relative humidity

Where existing paintwork is to be removed, and it is likely that evidence of an important decorative scheme survives, samples can be taken in advance to analyse the historic colours used as, once the paint is stripped, such evidence will be lost forever. The taking and analysing of paint samples is a specialised task. In the case illustrated, stripping has revealed an original joint in the dado rail (right hand of picture) showing the use of slightly differing sections, long hidden under layers of paintwork

Burning-off defective paint is not recommended where the joinery is in situ because of the potential danger of fire to the entire building fabric.

11.3.10 Where advice is sought from the planning authority, the opportunity could be taken to encourage a decorative scheme that is appropriate to the age and design of the building or room, as this will enhance the historic building.

Decorative items or works of art installed in an interior may be considered fixtures if they were intended to be an integral part of the design. In this case, the statue of Daniel O'Connell is a later addition, but is part of a group of statues positioned at key points around the rotunda adding to the special interest of the interior

11.4 Fixtures and Fittings

Interior fixtures and features

11.4.1 Protection includes all fixtures and features which form part of the interior of a protected structure. In some cases it may be difficult to establish whether or not a particular object or feature is a fixture. Although not defined in the Act, the term 'fixture' implies a degree of physical annexation together with indications that the annexation was carried out with the intention of making the object an integral part of the structure. In an interior, elements such as fireplaces, panelling or doorcases are fixtures which form part of the building. However, free-standing objects may be considered fixtures if they were placed in position as part of an overall architectural design. For example, in an interior such as a courtroom, fittings such as seating, screens, canopies, and the like, while they may or may not be physically fixed, were designed or made to fit a specific space to form part of the design.

11.4.2 Works of art, such as paintings or pieces of sculpture, placed as objects in their own right within a building, are unlikely to be considered as fixtures unless it can be proved that they were placed in particular locations as part of an overall architectural design. In such cases, the planning authority may need to take expert advice on assessing the contribution of the object to the character of the protected interior.

Staircases

IDENTIFYING SPECIAL FEATURES FOR PROTECTION

11.4.3   Staircases are often a major element of design within an interior. Iron or timber balustrades, handrails, decorative tread ends, moulded nosings and other stair details should be identified, respected and retained. Where the original service or back stairs in dwellings survive, these should also be retained.

CONSIDERATION OF PROPOSALS AFFECTING STAIRCASES

11.4.4   The removal or alteration of an original or fine staircase should only be permitted in exceptional circumstances. Generally, stone stairs should be retained in their original state and should not be painted, nor have sealant applied to them.

11.4.5   Where it is necessary for safety reasons to provide higher handrails or balustrades, it may be preferable to permit the addition of a new upper rail mounted above the handrail rather than allow the removal or remodelling of an important balustrade. Where this is not considered acceptable, for example on a landing, it may be necessary to consider measures to prevent people from approaching the low balustrade with an inner railing or similar barrier.

Stone staircases can suffer damage from the effects of expanding and corroding cramps and chipping of nosings. The repair of damage by indenting new stone is a traditional practice and still successfully used. However, expertise is necessary to assess the structural engineering issues relating to damaged or failing cantilevered stairs or to undo the effects of previous ill-considered repairs

Where it is necessary to raise the height of handrails for safety reasons, the new work should not be visually obtrusive or require invasive work to the original balustrade

The setting out of a staircase together with the fabrication of the carved and turned staircase elements was – and still is – highly skilled work. Elaborate staircases display the artistic taste of the owner and the abilities of the architect, joiner, carver, turner, metalworker or mason

Fireplaces

IDENTIFYING SPECIAL FEATURES FOR PROTECTION

11.4.6 Fireplaces or chimneypieces often formed the central element of design within a room. In addition to the timber, marble, stone, or cast-iron fire surrounds, care should be taken to identify and protect brass insets and grates, tiled cheeks, iron fire-baskets and hearthstones.

11.4.7 It has been the case that fine marble or stone fire surrounds are particularly vulnerable to unauthorised removal. This increases the importance of identifying and recording those which contribute to the character and special interest of a protected structure.

CONSIDERATION OF PROPOSALS AFFECTING FIREPLACES

11.4.8 The removal of fireplaces that are important to the character and special interest of the interior of a protected structure should not be permitted, even when the chimney has become redundant.

11.4.9 The design of a fireplace, particularly in Georgian and Victorian buildings, was often related to the function of the room in which it was located. For example, designs of dining room fireplaces often incorporated fruit and vine motifs and for that reason the moving of fireplaces from room to room within a protected structure should not generally be permitted. The painting of marble or stone fire surrounds should also not generally be permitted.

Fixed furniture and fittings

IDENTIFYING SPECIAL FEATURES FOR PROTECTION

11.4.10 Some building types such as banks, public houses and industrial buildings and dwellings may contain fixed furniture or fittings of quality which may form an important part of the architectural character of the interior of a protected structure. Such items may include counters, seating, screens, shelving, cupboards, light-fittings and machinery.

11.4.11 Items may be of interest for reasons other than their architectural quality. Rare items of machinery or service installations such as early lifts, industrial machinery, plumbing mechanisms, central heating systems etc. will be of considerable historical interest and of special relevance to the particular building. Specialist expertise may be necessary in order to identify the importance of some features.

The chimneypiece usually formed the focal point of a room and could range from simple timber or cast iron fireplaces to elaborate marble items. Although this chimneypiece appears plain, its partially-cleaned state should not disguise the fact that it retains its original elements, including carved slate facing and raised grate

Where a fireplace has become redundant, the chimneybreast should be left intact to allow it to continue to contribute to the character of the room. The intensification of uses within a structure and changes to other forms of heating, can lead to pressure to block up or remove chimneypieces. The adverse effects of such works on the building would not only include the loss of important architectural features but would also reduce the natural ventilation of the interior. Where possible, the re-opening of previously-blocked fireplaces should be encouraged together with the re-introduction of appropriate chimneypieces

Historic shop, pub and bank interiors are rare, as the periodic refitting of such premises is routine. Features such as shop counters, shelves and other fittings made specifically for the interior can be of architectural and social interest

Archaic machinery, mechanical fittings, heating and plumbing systems, of which the plated iron cistern illustrated here is a part, can be of considerable technical importance to a structure. Before items of interest are proposed for removal, it should be ascertained if they are of sufficient interest to be retained and, in some instances, even brought back into use. Often it may be possible for the items to be left in situ rather than allow them to be routinely stripped out

CONSIDERATION OF PROPOSALS

11.4.12 Where items of fixed furniture or fittings have been identified as important to the character or special interest of a protected structure, they should be retained in situ, even where they have become redundant. If, in particular circumstances, it is considered appropriate to remove these items, the planning authority should require that they be recorded before removal and necessary plans agreed for their future re-use or storage

11.5 The Installation of New Services

11.5.1 The introduction or alteration of services within the interior of a protected structure requires extremely careful consideration in advance. Where such proposals are made for an important interior the applicant should be able to show that detailed consideration has been given to the location and design of all proposed cabling, trunking, pipework, ductwork, air-handling units, boilers, radiators, grilles and all other new items to be installed. The location and design of the installation should be approved by the planning authority prior to any works commencing. Where the installation of new services and equipment has the potential to overload an existing structural system, the proposals should be reconsidered. In these circumstances, specialist advice may be needed.

11.5.2 Exposed runs of electrical trunking or pipework and ducting can be detrimental to the character and appearance of a good interior, as can poorly considered central-heating systems. However, the disruption to a protected interior and its finishes by attempts to conceal new services can also be harmful.

11.5.3 The installation of an intruder alarm system can have a significant impact on the fabric of a historic building. Great care is needed in selecting and locating the necessary devices and wiring. It may be acceptable for electrical wiring to be chased in, providing this does not involve unacceptable damage to important fabric or finishes. Where sensitive or rare finishes exist, surface mounting may be required and if so, it should be carefully planned in advance to avoid unacceptable visual disruption of the interior. Details of the proposed installation should be approved by the planning authority prior to any works commencing.

11.5.4 Alterations connected with service installations should be reversible and should not involve the loss or damage of features such as floor finishes, skirting, dados, panelling or doors.

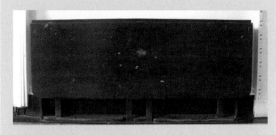

Some fixed furniture was designed to be capable of being folded away such as this Georgian butler's table making it easy to retain in situ following a change of use. Where fixed furniture of importance has been identified, its retention in situ should be the preferred option. The possible wear and tear that may be caused to such furniture should be borne in mind where a change of use is proposed

New service installations necessary to the present function of a room should be designed, located and fixed so as not to detract from the historic interior. Where a proposed change of use, or the intensification of a current use, requires enhanced levels of services, the effect on the historic interior should be assessed. In this case, the new use of a fine room required the installation of an obtrusive lighting rig which is not only visually inappropriate but which requires extensive fixings through the decorative plaster ceiling

The method of providing or upgrading the services in a high-quality interior should be considered from the earliest stages of design. The location of pipe or cable runs and fittings should be chosen to avoid conflict with historic plasterwork, joinery or decorative finishes. Consideration should also be given to locating water services away from important elements of the interior to avoid potential damage from burst or leaking pipes

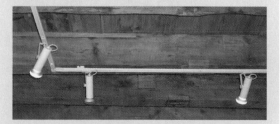

Depending on the character of the interior, it may sometimes be acceptable to provide new service installations in a distinctively modern manner. Surface mounting requires minimal contact with and disturbance of the historic fabric, therefore enabling relatively easy removal. However, consideration should be given to the potential effect of fixings on the fabric of the building

Shopfronts

Well-designed and constructed shopfronts, whether or not they are original to a protected structure, are generally of special interest, adding significantly to the attractiveness of shopping streets

12.1 Introduction

12.1.1 Carefully-designed and well-constructed shopfronts are important features of many buildings and streetscapes. There are now few shopfronts in Ireland remaining from the eighteenth century but many, mostly of timber construction, survive from the late nineteenth and early twentieth centuries. There are examples throughout the country of fine early twentieth-century shopfronts constructed in render and also a number of increasingly rare mid twentieth-century Art Deco or Modern Movement-style chrome, steel, marble and glass-panelled frontages.

12.1.2 Because of the prominent role which shopfronts play in businesses, they are frequently subject to pressures for alteration or replacement to meet changing needs. A balance will need to be struck between the commercial requirements of the owners and the protection of shopfronts of special importance within the context of architectural heritage.

12.1.3 The presence of well-crafted and historic shopfronts is an important part of the character of some ACAs. Every effort should be made to protect shopfronts that are of special interest. Expert knowledge and advice may be needed in order to identify such shopfronts and their associated features. In assessing the qualities of a shopfront, the following issues should be addressed:

a) Is the shopfront original to the building?

b) If not, how does the shopfront integrate with the rest of the building?

c) Does the shopfront complement the design of the upper floors of the building?

d) Does it obstruct openings at the upper levels of the building?

e) Does the shopfront stretch across two or more distinct buildings? If so, does it contribute to the character of the buildings or the ACA or detract from it?

f) What contribution does the shopfront make to the street?

g) Are the materials and proportions of the shopfront appropriate to the scale and fabric of the building and/or the street?

h) If not, is the shopfront nonetheless special in its own right and worthy of protection?

i) Is there good lettering or signage incorporated within the front? This could be on the fascia signboard, on other signboards, on the windows or on the façade and gable walls of the upper floors;

j) Are there any interesting details associated with the shopfront such as sill guards, retractable blinds, shutters, gates or tiling?

k) Are there any details likely to be concealed behind later work? These could include parts of an earlier shopfront or parts of the original building façade;

l) If there are concealed features, should they be re-exposed or is the later work of such merit that it should be left undisturbed?

m) Is the shopfront intact or are there small details missing or damaged? Would replacing these details enhance the appreciation of the design?

n) How is the shopfront now finished? Would its design and special character be enhanced by a more appropriate paint scheme?

o) Are there later added details, for example signage, lighting, cabling or advertising boards, which detract from the character of the shopfront and which could be easily removed or relocated?

IDENTIFYING SPECIAL FEATURES FOR PROTECTION

12.1.4 Features of shopfronts, which are likely to be of interest and which should be identified and protected, include pilasters or uprights, apron panels, stall risers or plinths below the display windows, any mullions or glazing bars to the display window, sill guards, fascia signboards, blinds and blind boxes, shutters and shutter boxes, cornices, cresting, consoles or brackets, doors, gates, decorative tiling to the floor of the entrance porch, and others. Where the frontage includes a display window of architectural merit at first or even second floor level, this should be protected as part of the composition.

12.1.5 Good lettering on fascias, signboards, windows or doors should be identified, as should interesting hanging signs or trade emblems, which are now increasingly rare.

12.1.6 While most of the features listed above are generally associated with traditional timber shopfronts, the importance and special interest of more recent types and designs of shopfronts and other commercial frontages should not be overlooked. Many of the materials used in twentieth-century shopfronts such as Vitrolite may no longer be manufactured and as such are irreplaceable.

The functional and decorative features common to many historic shopfronts including tiled stall risers (top), ornate brackets (middle) or original shutters (bottom) are all part of the special interest of a shopfront

Good lettering on sign boards, fascias or hanging signs advertising the shopholder or type of establishment may be of artistic interest, whether painted or gilt, in faïence, timber, cement, steel or neon. This watchmaker's sign is painted in gold paint on the reverse of a glass plate with acid-etched flourishes

While traditional timber shopfronts are often valued, there is also a legacy of Art Deco-style steel and Vitrolite fronts that should be equally treasured as they represent the modern spirit, new materials and design ethos of their time, illustrated in this elaborate example

CONSIDERATION OF PROPOSALS AFFECTING
SHOPFRONTS

12.1.7 Architecturally valuable shopfronts, whether original
to the building or of a later period, should not be
demolished or dismantled even if a change of use is
proposed which will make the shopfront redundant.
This may occur, for example, when a commercial
premises is to be converted to a dwelling. It could
be a requirement that the shopfront be retained in
place after the change of use. Proposals to remove a
good, but later, shopfront in order to build a new
ground floor façade purely on the basis of
speculation should generally not be considered
acceptable.

12.1.8 Where, within an ACA, there are proposals to
remove a shopfront that is obviously of little interest
or merit in order to restore a façade to its previous
appearance, either matching the rest of a terrace or
in accordance with the character of the area, this
should normally be acceptable.

12.1.9 All light-fittings, security alarms, cameras, cabling etc.
which are proposed to be fitted to or across a
historic shopfront, and cannot be located elsewhere,
should be required to be carefully located and fixed
in order to minimise their visual impact and to
avoid physical damage to the fabric.

12.2 **Repair of Shopfronts**

12.2.1 Where small amounts of detail are missing from a
shopfront that is part of a protected structure or is
within an ACA, matching replacements could be
fitted. However, any such replication should always
be based upon firm evidence of the original
design of the shopfront using old photographs
or drawings, or by replicating surviving details, for
example where one bracket is missing but others
remain. It should be clear on close inspection which
is the original material or detail and which the
replacement.

12.2.2 As with the repair of other external joinery items, as
much as possible of the original fabric should be
retained. The replacement of whole elements or
sections for the sake of cost or convenience should
not be permitted. Decayed sections should be
repaired by the splicing-in of new, matching pieces
of timber. The use of substitute materials such as
glass-reinforced plastic to simulate carved joinery
should not be permitted on shopfronts of special
interest.

*A good quality shopfront can be retained even following a
change of use, allowing it to continue to contribute to the
character of the structure and of the wider area*

*The essence of good repair work is to retain the maximum
amount of viable fabric that contributes to the character of the
shopfront, to carry out the work using proven methods of
repair and to fit appropriately detailed new elements where
necessary. This shopfront was carefully repaired with grant
assistance from the local authority*

12.3 Signage

12.3.1 New lettering and signage should be required to respect the character of the protected structure and its setting and, where relevant, the character of an ACA.

12.3.2 Where good lettering exists, but where it is imperative that new lettering be added, the new lettering could be mounted over the existing in a way which does not damage the earlier lettering and which allows for easy reversal at a later stage if required.

12.4 Awnings and Blinds

12.4.1 Proposals to install new awnings or blinds to the shopfront of a protected structure should be treated with caution. Some modern awnings require large blind boxes that can be difficult to integrate successfully with an existing shopfront without damaging its special character. Blind boxes should not be allowed to mask or cut through any detailing which contributes to the interest and quality of the façade or shopfront. Where this means that full protection of the window display cannot be achieved by means of an external blind, alternative protection such as internal filter blinds or glazing could be considered where these would not compromise the special character of the shopfront.

12.4.2 Where the fitting of a new awning or blind is considered acceptable, the design and materials should be appropriate to the character and quality of the building and its setting and, where relevant, to the character of an ACA.

12.5 Security Screens

12.5.1 External steel roller shutters are generally not suitable for use either on historic shopfronts or on the fronts of buildings within an ACA. Externally mounted shutters require large shutter boxes and side channels which are difficult to accommodate successfully on a historic façade without a substantial loss of architectural quality to both the building and its setting. The appearance of one or more closed shutters on a street can be damaging to the character of the street.

Where good lettering or signage exists but a premises has changed hands, it may be possible to add new signage while leaving the original lettering in place. For example, a new signboard can be mounted over the existing one without damaging the original lettering below or, as in this illustration, new signage can be placed elsewhere on the shopfront, leaving the old name in place

A new awning has been successfully fitted to this shopfront without the need for a visually obtrusive blind box

The entrance doors to this establishment have been fitted with roller shutters. Although the physical impact has been minimised, the closed shutters nonetheless have a large visual impact on the appearance of the structure and the streetscape. This impact can sometimes be overcome with the use of internal demountable grilles, a less visually obtrusive option of securing a historic shopfront, especially when painted a dark or neutral colour

12.5.2   Where there is an obvious need for enhanced security, the use of alternative methods of protection should be considered, including, where appropriate, the use of laminated glass, internal shutters mounted behind the shopfront display or external demountable grilles.

12.6   New Shopfronts

12.6.1   The design of a new shopfront for installation into a protected structure requires careful consideration and should not detract from the character of the rest of the building. This does not mean that the design of the new shopfront should be an imitation of past styles. A sympathetic well-designed modern intervention will usually be preferable to an ill-proportioned imitation of a traditional shopfront.

12.6.2   New shopfronts should generally not be permitted to extend into the floor above, thus concealing the first-floor windowsills and perhaps part of the openings, unless this was part of the original design of the building. Where a new shopfront is proposed as a replacement for an inappropriate one of little merit, the opportunity could be taken to ensure that elements of the new shopfront, such as the signboard and the display windows, are appropriately scaled in relation to the building as a whole.

12.6.3   Standard corporate frontages are rarely appropriate to historic buildings or streetscapes, nor are large plate glass frontages that require the partial demolition of a ground-floor façade. Large, illuminated fascia or projecting signs can potentially damage the character of a historic building or street and proposals to install these should be carefully scrutinised.

12.6.4   Where the shop or premises now occupies more than one original building, a new, single shopfront should not be allowed to straddle originally distinct elevations.

12.6.5   Commercial usage does not necessarily require the insertion of new shopfronts or display windows. Where the existing ground floor of a protected structure retains its original openings and intact wall fabric, the planning authority should not generally permit proposals to alter these original features to provide a shopfront or display windows.

Often new, so-called 'traditional-style' timber shopfronts have little in common in their proportioning and detailed design with the true traditional shopfront, sometimes using glass-reinforced plastic imitation brackets and plywood pilasters. A well-designed contemporary shopfront, such as this example, which reflects the design values of its own time while respecting its historic location, can be a more honest and pleasing solution

Some protected structures, in which every element of the façade is carefully orchestrated, cannot readily take the alterations required by a change of use without affecting the strong character of the original design. In this illustration, a successful transition has been made from a bank to a shop with discreet signage located inside the shop window

Curtilage and Attendant Grounds

CHAPTER 13

The formal layout of this small country house, with its outbuildings set on axis, is a good illustration of the physical, aesthetic and use-related connections existing between the principal and ancillary structures that help define the boundaries of the curtilage and the extent of the protected structure

13.1 Determining the Curtilage of a Protected Structure

13.1.1 By definition, a protected structure includes the land lying within the curtilage of the protected structure and other structures within that curtilage and their interiors. The notion of curtilage is not defined by legislation, but for the purposes of these guidelines it can be taken to be the parcel of land immediately associated with that structure and which is (or was) in use for the purposes of the structure. It should be noted that the meaning of 'curtilage' is influenced by other legal considerations besides protection of the architectural heritage and may be revised in accordance with emerging case law.

13.1.2 In many cases the curtilage of a protected structure will coincide with the land owned together with it but this is not necessarily so. For example, in the case of a town house, the main house, the area and railings in front of it, cellars below the footpath, the rear garden and mews house may be considered to fall within its curtilage even where the mews house is now in a separate ownership. The planning authority should ensure, in such cases, that all relevant owners and occupiers are notified of the protected status of their structures. In the case of a large country house, the stable buildings, coach-houses, walled gardens, lawns, ha-has and the like may all be considered to form part of the curtilage of the building unless they are located at a distance from the main building.

13.1.3 It should be noted that the definition of curtilage does not work in reverse – a stable building may be within the curtilage of the main house which it was built to serve but the main house cannot be described as being within the curtilage of the stable building. It should also be noted where a protected structure is an element of a structure, it may, or may not, have a curtilage depending on the degree to which is could in its own right be considered to be a structure. For example, a re-used doorway affixed to a later structure could not be said to have a curtilage.

13.1.4 The extent of the curtilage will need to be determined on a case-by-case basis and should ideally be identified by the planning authority prior to inclusion of the structure in the RPS, although this is not always necessary. Where the curtilage has not previously been identified, a planning authority should take the opportunity to identify its extent at the time of making a declaration in respect of the protected structure. Where parts of the curtilage are in different ownership, the planning authority should ensure that separate notification is issued to each owner and/or occupier.

13.1.5   In making a decision as to the extent of the curtilage of a protected structure and the other structures within the curtilage, the planning authority should consider:

a)   Is, or was, there a functional connection between the structures? For example, was the structure within the curtilage constructed to service the main building, such as a coach-house, stores and the like?

b)   Was there a historical relationship between the main structure and the structure(s) within the curtilage which may no longer be obvious? In many cases, the planning authority will need to consult historic maps and other documents to ascertain this;

c)   Are the structures in the same ownership? Were they previously in the same ownership, for example, at the time of construction of one or other of the structures?

13.2   Determining the Attendant Grounds of a Protected Structure

13.2.1   The attendant grounds of a structure are lands outside the curtilage of the structure but which are associated with the structure and are intrinsic to its function, setting and/or appreciation. In many cases, the attendant grounds will incorporate a designed landscape deliberately laid out to complement the design of the building or to assist in its function. For example, the attendant grounds to a mill building will include, where these survive, the mill-race, mill-pond, the tail-race, flumes, sluice-gates, and any related weirs and dams. Flax-mills may have had drying greens. The attendant grounds of a country house could include the entire demesne, or pleasure grounds, and any structures or features within it such as follies, plantations, earthworks, lakes and the like.

13.2.2   Where the curtilage of a protected structure has altered since the time of its construction, there may be important features of the original, or of a previous, curtilage which would not automatically be protected within the definition of the protected structure.

Changes in the ownership and subdivision of property can affect the extent of a curtilage. The structures illustrated here, including a dovecote, glasshouses and outbuildings have, for some time, no longer been associated with the principal house although originally within its curtilage. In order to be protected as items within the attendant grounds they must be specified in the RPS. Alternatively, they could be included in the RPS in their own right

13.2.3   A planning authority has the power to protect all features of importance which lie within the attendant grounds of a protected structure. However, such features must be specified in the RPS and the owners and occupiers notified in order for the features to be protected.

13.2.4   When identifying features for protection within the attendant grounds of a protected structure, it is important that the planning authority has knowledge of the historical development of the site and the interrelationship of the elements. This may require research into old maps, documents or drawings to determine the extent of any attendant grounds and to identify surviving features such as gate-lodges, designed vistas, avenues, gardens, earthworks, woodlands and other landscape features, boundary walls and any other structures associated with the protected structure. There may also be a need to consider the existence of any buried features such as the foundations of demolished ancillary buildings, filled-in mill-ponds, overgrown or grassed-over garden features and the like. An inspection of the site will be required to locate the existence of important features of the attendant grounds and assess their contribution to the character of the protected structure.

13.2.5   The planning authority should be clear about what land, structures or features it wants to protect and should use other legislative powers available to it to protect these rather than try to stretch the definition of curtilage beyond its true meaning. For example, where there is doubt as to whether or not distant features such as boundary walls, dovecotes, icehouses or gate-lodges are within the curtilage of a protected structure, the planning authority can ensure their protection by specifying them within the RPS as features for protection within the attendant grounds of the protected structure and notifying all owners and occupiers. Alternatively, the planning authority has the power to establish an ACA to include the land, structures or features it wishes to protect. The designation of an ACA could be used to protect a former country house demesne and the structures and features within it or a churchyard containing the church itself and a disparate group of fine monuments.

13.2.6 Where the present curtilage of the protected structure has not been established at the time of inclusion in the RPS, the planning authority should ensure that all important features are either:

a) specified as being in the attendant grounds of the protected structure or

b) are themselves entered in the RPS and

c) the owners and occupiers notified of the protection.

13.3 General Principles

13.3.1 Features within the curtilage and attendant grounds of a protected structure can make a significant contribution to the character of that structure. The designed landscape associated with a protected structure was often an intrinsic part of the original design concept and, as such, inseparable from the building. Where proposals are made for alterations to a designed landscape, ancillary buildings, structures or features within the curtilage or attendant grounds of a protected structure, a site inspection should be carried out by the planning authority in order properly to understand the potential effects of the proposed development.

13.3.2 When assessing the contribution of structures or features within the curtilage or attendant grounds to the character of a protected structure, and when considering any proposals to alter such features, the following should be considered:

a) What items of interest are there within the present curtilage of the structure?

b) Was this the original curtilage of the structure or are there likely to be other items of interest that are, or once were, associated with this structure and which now lie beyond its curtilage but within its attendant grounds?

c) Are there any other items of interest which, while not original, are later additions of merit?

d) Do any items within the curtilage or attendant grounds affect the character of the main structure and help to define its special interest?

e) Do any items within the curtilage or attendant

Where a demesne survives without its principal house but with many of its features intact – entrance gates and lodges, follies, bridges, service buildings and the like – these structures can be individually protected within the RPS. The demesne could also be designated as an ACA in order that these structures, and the designed landscape as a whole, may be considered as a group

grounds affect the character of other structures? For example, boundary walls, railings, gates and gardens can contribute to the character of other protected structures or to the character of an ACA;

f) How are the boundaries of the site enclosed or demarcated? Are there walls, railings, fences, ditches or ha-has, gates or gate piers?

g) Are there other buildings within the curtilage or attendant grounds? Were these other structures connected with the previous use or enjoyment of the protected structure? For example, with a country house there may be such structures as outbuildings, coach-houses, stables, icehouses, dovecotes, follies, gate-lodges and others;

h) Are there features of interest within the curtilage or attendant grounds connected with the use or enjoyment of the protected structure? For example, a mill may have associated features such as a mill-race, a mill-pond, a tail-race, sluice-gates, weirs, dams, and drying greens;

i) Are there designed landscape features within the curtilage or attendant grounds connected with the protected structure or its ancillary buildings? These may include ornamental planting, earth works, avenues, gardens, ponds, woodlands or other plantations;

j) Are there any items or structures within the curtilage which detract from the character of the protected structure? These might include, for example, later structures or planting which mar views of the structure or its relationship with other, more important, structures within the curtilage or attendant grounds. Does the opportunity exist to reverse any adverse impacts?

13.4   Features within the Curtilage of a Protected Structure or its Attendant Grounds

Boundary Features
IDENTIFYING SPECIAL FEATURES FOR PROTECTION

13.4.1   The features used to define the boundaries of a protected structure can often make an important contribution to the quality and character of the building and the surrounding streetscape or landscape. Such structures may include rubble, brick or rendered boundary walls, metal or timber railings on stone or brick-plinth walls, gate piers of iron, brick, ashlar or rubble and gates of iron or timber. There may be other ironwork details in addition to railings, such as gates, gate-posts and corner-posts, finials, bell-pulls, lamp-holders, lamp standards, overthrows, fencing, and the like.

13.4.2   The present curtilage of the protected structure may not be its original curtilage. Later structures may have been built within the original curtilage and the earlier site subdivided. In such cases, the planning authority should take care to identify, using old maps or other documentation, any surviving boundary walls and other details which originally pertained to the protected structure and now lie within its attendant grounds and which merit protection.

CONSIDERATION OF PROPOSALS AFFECTING
BOUNDARY FEATURES
Alterations to boundary features

13.4.3   Proposals to remove or alter boundary features could adversely affect the character of the protected structure and the designed landscape around it. Widening an entrance or altering flanking walls or railings will alter the scale and visual impact of the gate and gate piers. Relocating a gateway may destroy a carefully designed relationship between the entrance and the main building. Proposals to lower or raise the height of boundary walls should also be given careful consideration as such alterations can have a detrimental effect on the character of a protected structure and on the character of an ACA.

13.4.4   While some minor changes may be granted planning permission, the cumulative effect on the character of the street or area of a series of incremental changes may not be acceptable.

13.4.5   Many boundary features are in shared ownership with adjoining properties. Where this is likely to have implications for the adjoining owner or occupier, notification of the entry into the RPS

The style and materials of structures used to demarcate the boundaries of a protected structure, its curtilage and attendant grounds can add significantly to its character and that of the surrounding area. This rubble stone wall and fine stone gate piers line the approach to an important complex of stables and farm buildings

Boundary features such as gates were often designed and located to enhance the approach to a building, as seen with this example of an arched lamp bracket sited to light the gateway and path to the front door. Relocating or removing such features would not only make them liable to damage during the works but may also adversely alter the relationship between the structure and the features of its curtilage

Shared ownership of a protected structure most obviously occurs with boundary walls in urban locations; however historic items such as wall-mounted post-boxes, in separate ownership, can add interest to rural or urban boundary walls

should be issued to the joint owner/occupier of the feature in addition to the owner/occupier of the protected structure.

Repair of ironwork

13.4.6 Where the repair of historic ironwork associated with the curtilage is proposed, it should be made a condition of any planning permission that as much of the existing material as possible is retained rather than renewed. Additional material could be permitted where necessary to reinforce or to support the existing material. In situ repairs cause less damage to ironwork than dismantling and re-erecting. The embedding of the bases of iron railing balusters in concrete haunching should not be permitted. Not only is this aesthetically unacceptable, it is likely to encourage further fractures and deterioration of the ironwork.

13.4.7 Where paint-stripping of historic ironwork is proposed, and where there is likely to be evidence of original or interesting subsequent paint history, a small area of ironwork could be left unstripped or a proper paint analysis carried out before the work takes place. The method of paint-stripping should be appropriate to the type of ironwork.

13.4.8 Where recent inappropriate alterations have taken place, such as the replacement of part of the railings or an element such as a gate, the opportunity could be taken to restore or replicate the missing element. Any such restoration should be based upon firm evidence of the original element using old photographs, drawings, or other reliable information such as the features of identical adjoining buildings.

Basement Areas and Cellars
IDENTIFYING SPECIAL FEATURES FOR PROTECTION

13.4.9 A feature of many buildings with a basement is a basement area. This is commonly a yard located below street or ground level usually, but not always, accessed by stairs from above giving access to kitchens and other service areas of a house located in the basement. Basement areas have in the past been subject to extensive alteration as it was felt that, being only partly visible, such alterations did not impact on the quality of the overall building. As a result many have been changed beyond recognition and the resulting loss of historic fabric has greatly diminished, not only the character of the entire building, but also the quality of the streetscape.

Embedding the base of iron railings in concrete haunching can cause irreversible damage. While this set of railings had probably begun to deteriorate before the application of the concrete, it will now be impossible to successfully remove the concrete without damaging the delicate surviving ironwork

It is possible, using surviving details from other parts of a protected structure, or from suitable adjacent examples on other buildings, to accurately repair damaged ironwork and replace lost elements, as has been carried out in this project

The extension of a basement into the original area may have far-reaching impacts on the building. The need to provide natural light and ventilation to the extended basement accommodation, the loss of elements such as stairs and alterations to the façade, boundary walls and railings can result in a substantial change to the appearance of the structure at street level

13.4.10 Elements which are becoming increasingly rare and which should be identified for protection include the railings and plinths surrounding basement areas, wicket-gates, cisterns, ice-boxes, stone stairs, iron handrails and uprights, stone paving and drainage channels.

CONSIDERATION OF PROPOSALS AFFECTING BASEMENT AREAS

13.4.11 Many buildings with basements, particularly Georgian houses, also contain cellars that extend below the public pavement or occasionally the roadway. Where engineering works are proposed, these should be protected. Where coal holes with iron covers or interesting grilles and gratings exist, whether set into the pavement or the entrance landing, these should also be protected.

13.4.12 Proposals to allow separate use of the basement from the main building require careful consideration as this can lead to the development of the basement area separately from the main building, thus changing the entire character of the structure. It can also lead to pressure to replace the existing steep stone steps and iron handrails and to alter openings in the façade of the protected structure.

13.4.13 Proposals to infill a basement area below the entrance steps should not normally be permitted where this would damage the character of a protected structure. The erection of storage tanks within the basement area should not be encouraged.

13.4.14 Where previous inappropriate alterations have occurred causing damp problems in basement areas and cellars, consideration should be given to reopening original ventilation openings to cellars and basements, and other appropriate works. Such openings could include former window or door openings or flues and vents through existing walls.

Hard landscaping
IDENTIFYING SPECIAL FEATURES FOR PROTECTION

13.4.15 Elements of hard landscaping which are original or early make a significant contribution to the character of the building and its designed landscape and are important to the quality of an ACA. These may include elements such as stone paving, stone steps, cobbles or setts, tiling, gravelled or paved avenues, planting boxes, kerbs and the like. Their presence, form and detailing should be identified, protected and properly conserved.

This elaborate access gate to the basement area is fabricated of plate and cast iron to match the adjacent stone balustrade. Surviving high-quality eighteenth-century iron balustrading such as this is rare and significant

While coal holes are often considered part of the public domain, they may in fact be part of a protected structure whose cellars extend below the pavement, in this case one paved with fine flagstones. There are regional and local variations to the design and shape of coal hole covers, many impressed with their manufacturers' names

The wear caused by traffic over many generations across cobbles, setts, flagstones or brick paviours gives them a patina which often makes a significant contribution to the character of a protected structure or of an ACA

These recent stone bollards, of a plain and robust design, complement, in their solidity and materials, this important courthouse and discourage car-parking against the building and so reduce the potential for damage

Gardens are generally a combination of built features and planting. Regardless of its size, a garden can make an important contribution to the character and setting of a protected structure, whether a minute formal garden, as illustrated here, or one extending over a large area with several distinct compartments

CONSIDERATION OF PROPOSALS AFFECTING HARD LANDSCAPING

13.4.16 A proposal to remove, re-lay in a different way or resurface in a different material any element of hard landscaping within the curtilage of a protected structure or within its designed landscape may detract from its character and should be scrutinised with care by the planning authority.

13.4.17 Where there are worn or damaged stone steps or paving, these should preferably not be built up in cement screed or similar artificial compounds as this would alter their appearance. Where necessary, and if the surface poses a danger, the existing stone should be redressed by a skilled mason or indented with matching stone. It should be a condition of these works that the original stonework is conserved and protected.

13.4.18 The colour and texture of any new hard-landscape features and their effect on the protected structure should be carefully considered.

Gardens
IDENTIFYING SPECIAL FEATURES FOR PROTECTION

13.4.19 Some protected structures are set within their own enclosed gardens or pleasure grounds. Gardens can range from the smaller front or rear gardens of an urban dwelling to larger, more complex gardens surrounding a country house or institutional building containing many ancillary structures and walled gardens. Ancillary structures might be ornamental such as statuary, follies, grottoes, terraces, steps, sundials, fountains and many more. There may also be functional structures such as greenhouses, melon-pits or wells. Special attention should be paid to formally designed gardens, particularly where they lie within the curtilage of a protected structure. The existence and location of original or early elements of garden design such as built features, paths, and planting beds should be identified.

CONSIDERATION OF PROPOSALS
AFFECTING GARDENS

13.4.20 Gardens are generally a combination of built features and planting. Unlike works to structures, gardening does not require development consent.

13.4.21 Designed gardens associated with, and in the curtilage of, protected structures can be an integral part of the setting of the building. Such gardens can be seen as an extension to the house and, in some cases, planning permission will be necessary for major works such as significant landscaping or the removal or alteration of important design features. Careful consideration should be given to these proposals to ensure that they do not adversely affect the character of the protected structure or its curtilage.

Planted features

13.4.22 Within the curtilage and/or attendant grounds of a protected structure there may be planted features which are important to the character and special interest of the structure and which contribute to its setting. These could include tree-lined avenues, decorative tree-clumps, woodlands, species plants or plant collections.

Unlike the conservation of structures, the conservation of gardens involves cycles of renewal. Planted elements within a garden are not static and may require continual replanting while built features and long-lived plants, such as the trees and box hedging in this illustration, are likely to survive

13.4.23 Many planted features, although they may form part of a designed planting scheme forming the setting of a building, cannot be described as built features and may not be protected as part of the protected structure. Where planted features contribute to the setting of a protected structure or an ACA, they should be protected by means of tree preservation orders or by the designation of a landscape conservation area, as appropriate.

In order that the specimen trees and woodlands decorating the attendant grounds of a structure are protected, specific objectives should be included in the development plan. In this case the estate is designated an Area of High Amenity, with detailed policies including the preservation of all the existing woodlands, including individual trees, groups of trees and avenues

New development in the grounds of this important Gothic revival former convent is under construction between the structure and the nuns' graveyard and has altered their historical relationship

13.5   Development within the Curtilage of a Protected Structure

13.5.1   Proposals for new development within the curtilage of a protected structure should be carefully scrutinised by the planning authority, as inappropriate development will be detrimental to the character of the structure.

13.5.2   Where a formal relationship exists between a protected structure and its ancillary buildings or features, new construction which interrupts that relationship should rarely be permitted. There may be a designed vista between a building and a built or landscape feature within its gardens or a less formal relationship between a house and its outbuildings. Similarly, the relationship between the protected structure and the street should not be damaged. New works should not adversely impact on views of the principal elevations of the protected structure.

13.5.3   Where a large house or an institutional building has a garden which contributes to the character of the protected structure, subdivision of the garden, particularly by permanent subdividers, may be inappropriate.

13.5.4   Proposals are often made which combine works to a protected structure, often to allow a new use be made of it, with new development within its curtilage or attendant grounds. Proposals for the existing structure should normally be made and considered together with those for any new development. The new development can be phased in such a way to ensure that conservation works to the protected structure are satisfactorily carried out. In particular, where conservation works to the structure will be costly, a reasonable and considered approach should be taken to the phasing of the development which ensures both that the protected structure is successfully conserved and the works satisfactorily completed.

Floodlighting of Buildings

13.5.5   Proposals to floodlight a protected structure or a structure within an ACA will require careful consideration.

13.5.6   Issues to be considered which may affect the character of a protected structure or of an ACA will include the type and location of light fittings and any associated cabling or posts. The pattern, colouring and intensity of any proposed floodlighting scheme should be given consideration. An uncoordinated patchwork of different floodlighting schemes within a terrace or square may diminish the architectural coherence of the group of buildings.

13.5.7 In addition, consideration should be given to whether increased light and heat levels generated by the floodlighting would encourage organic growth on the surfaces of the structure.

13.6 Features within the Attendant Grounds of a Protected Structure

13.6.1 Designed landscapes which form the attendant grounds of a protected structure may form part of a unified design concept. The landscape and the structures can be complementary and interdependent. For example, a mill building was entirely dependent on the designed landscape surrounding it and could not have functioned without its mill-pond, mill-races and bridges. These features of the designed landscape are essential to the understanding of the building and vice versa.

13.6.2 The designed landscape associated with the protected structure can include other buildings or structures associated with the functioning of the main building such as stables, icehouses, dovecotes, walled gardens, greenhouses, gate-lodges or bridges. There may also be apparently natural man-made features within a designed landscape such as lakes, canals, mounds, woodland or parkland.

13.6.3 In order to identify special features of the designed landscape associated with a protected structure, it will be necessary to carry out a historical assessment of the site. Some of the most important features may not be obvious at the outset without adequate survey and research using old maps, drawings, aerial photographs (both old and new), documents and other historical material. When assessing a designed landscape it is important to identify the historical layers of intervention that may exist and to respect the integrity of the site. Landscapes were often continually adapted and altered in response to changing fashions or uses. As with buildings, it is important to recognise and respect the contribution of different periods of alteration.

13.6.4 Important or intact features should be identified and located where they survive. These may not always be readily visible. For example, early gardens or other features may have been simply grassed over and survive below the surface. These could easily be lost through uninformed alterations.

The floodlight here is positioned at a re-entrant angle, a sheltered location vulnerable to damp. Any increased levels of organic growth arising from the extra heat and light from floodlight fixtures should be monitored and if necessary the light fitting moved to a suitable distance from the historic fabric

Designed landscapes include industrial landscapes as well as pleasure grounds and can include a complex of inter-related structures and features integral to the industrial process. In some cases the identification of the features of an industrial landscape may require specialist advice

The attendant grounds of a protected structure can include structures designed and arranged solely for the purposes of pleasure; they are eye-catchers which adorn their setting and often contain rooms, as does this rustic arch, which allow for romantic contemplation of the artfully-arranged scenery. Follies are important elements of a designed landscape that should not be overlooked when identifying the features of the attendant grounds. The setting of follies and the views to and from them may be essential components of their special interest

The existence of structures and features within attendant grounds which have fallen down, been overgrown or dismantled may not always be obvious, as with this small Gothic Revival well; but many were marked on early editions of Ordnance Survey maps which should help to locate and identify any surviving remains

13.7 Development within the Attendant Grounds

13.7.1 It is essential to understand the character of a site before development proposals can be considered. Where attendant grounds of particular significance are proposed for development, a conservation plan could be prepared in advance of any planning application which would identify the significance of the site and locate areas within the designed landscape, if any, which could accept change and development and those areas which could not without damaging the architectural heritage of the place.

13.7.2 When dealing with applications for works within the attendant grounds of a protected structure, a visit to the site should be considered an essential part of the assessment. The planning authority should consider:

a) Would the development affect the character of the protected structure?

b) Would the proposed works affect the relationship of the protected structure to its surroundings and attendant grounds?

c) Would the protected structure remain the focus of its setting? For example, a new building erected between a structure and a feature within the attendant grounds will alter the character of both;

d) Do the proposed works require an alteration of the profile of the landscape, for example, the creation of a golf course? How would this affect the character of the protected structure and its attendant grounds?

e) Do the proposals respect important woodland and parkland? Do they conserve significant built features and landscape features?

f) Are there important views of or from the structure that could be damaged by the proposed development? Would important vistas be obstructed by new development?

g) Would distant views of important architectural or natural landmarks be blocked or changed? Would a significant skyline be altered?

h) Even where the proposed development is at a distance from the protected structure, could it still have an impact? This could include tall or bulky buildings interrupting views of or from the protected structure and other features of the designed landscape;

i) Where the new works would not be directly visible from the protected structure, would they be visible from the approaches to the structure or from other important sites or features within the attendant grounds? If so, would this be acceptable?

Developments proposed for demesnes should respect the established planting pattern where this is part of the designed landscape. Consideration should be given at an early stage in the design process to the conservation of important woodlands, individual trees, shelter belts and copses both during development and afterwards.

j) What effect would the scale, height, massing, alignment or materials of a proposed construction have on the protected structure and its attendant grounds?

Development within historic woodlands

13.7.3 Development proposals should have regard to the planted features of designed landscapes and efforts should be made to reinforce or to re-establish important structural planting such as avenues or clumps of trees, plantations, woodlands, hedging or shelter belts.

13.7.4 Proposals which attempt to 'conceal' housing or other developments within existing woodlands should be carefully scrutinised. Woodlands were an important feature of historic designed landscapes and were used as a design element to sculpt and enclose landscapes and vistas. They may contain paths, rides and drives. In addition to their aesthetic functions, woodlands played an important role in preserving game and wildlife. Many woodlands which are elements of a designed landscape may have been formed from older woodlands. The construction of new development within excisting woodlands can damage their character and integrity and have an adverse impact on the character of a wider designed landscape and the setting of protected structures.

Commercial Planting

13.7.5 Commercial planting and other agricultural uses can damage the character of the attendant grounds of a protected structure. In addition, they may conceal features of a designed landscape such as earthworks, decorative tree-clumps and other plantations. Carefully designed vistas and unfolding views may be compromised. Paths, rides and drives through deciduous woodland may be lost.

Golf courses

13.7.6 Proposals to redevelop the attendant grounds of a protected structure for use as a golf course should be treated with caution where this would adversely impact on the character of the structure. In some instances such proposals may require fundamental alterations to the ground profile. It may also bring about a requirement for the construction of clubhouses and ancillary buildings which may damage the character of the designed landscape and the setting of protected structures.

Car Parking

13.7.7 The loss of garden may seriously affect the setting and character of a protected structure or of an ACA. Careful consideration should be given to the location of the car park to avoid damage to the character of the structure or its attendant grounds. The demolition of garden walls and the combining of two or more areas of garden to provide car parking within an urban area should generally be avoided.

13.7.8 Where it is necessary to provide car parking, efforts should be made to minimise its impact by careful design and use of materials. The associated alteration of boundary features should not be permitted unless the changes are considered not to be damaging to the character of a protected structure or of an ACA and would not result in inappropriate cumulative changes.

13.8 Other Development Affecting the Setting of a Protected Structure or an Architectural Conservation Area

13.8.1 When dealing with applications for works outside the curtilage and attendant grounds of a protected structure or outside an ACA which have the potential to impact upon their character, similar consideration should be given as for proposed development within the attendant grounds. A visit to the site should be considered an essential part of the assessment.

13.8.2 New development both adjacent to, and at a distance from, a protected structure can affect its character and special interest and impact on it in a variety of ways. The proposed development may directly abut the protected structure, as with

The proposed construction of a golf course within a historic demesne requires careful scrutiny and consideration of all potential impacts. Alterations of the ground profile may be required, bunkers and greens can have a large visual impact on the character of the designed landscape and there may be a requirement for the construction of roadways, a clubhouse and other ancillary buildings within the demesne

The alteration of boundary walls and railings to facilitate off-street car-parking may sometimes seem minor; however the cumulative effect of a number of such incremental changes can have a disproportionately negative effect on the character of a group of protected structures and on the character of an ACA

buildings in a terrace. Alternatively, it may take the form of a new structure within the attendant grounds of the protected structure. A new development could also have an impact even when it is detached from the protected structure and outside the curtilage and attendant grounds but is visible in an important view of or from the protected structure.

13.8.3 The extent of the potential impact of proposals will depend on the location of the new works, the character and quality of the protected structure, its designed landscape and its setting, and the character and quality of the ACA. Large buildings, sometimes at a considerable distance, can alter views to or from the protected structure or ACA and thus affect their character. Proposals should not have an adverse effect on the special interest of the protected structure or the character of an ACA.

A protected structure may be more vulnerable to adverse impacts from new developments which, although located beyond the curtilage and attendant grounds, may nonetheless affect their character and setting. Important views to and from a protected structure and between it, and visible manmade landmarks such as spires or obelisks and sometimes natural landmarks such as mountains and lakes, should all be taken into account

13.9 Moving Protected Structures

13.9.1 There is a close relationship between a protected structure and its location which may have been established at the time of construction or which has grown up and adapted as the life of the building progressed. Moving a historic building separates it irrevocably from its setting. Dismantling a structure, no matter how carefully executed and well meaning, can result in damage to the fabric.

13.9.2 Proposals to move a protected structure, or features within the curtilage or attendant grounds of a protected structure, should only be permitted in exceptional circumstances. The planning authority should be satisfied that every alternative has been properly explored and that relocation is essential to safeguard the structure.

Non-habitable Protected Structures

Many structures make impressive ruins. In some cases restoration may be the preferred option where the ruin's character can be retained. Other ruinous structures may be more appropriate for consolidation as ruins where restoration would require loss of historic fabric and largely conjectural reconstruction. Care should be taken when considering the most appropriate approach concerning ruins which stand as landmarks of the past – religious, industrial, social or political icons

Non-habitable protected structures may pose different conservation problems to other structures because of the nature of their construction or use. Some frequently encountered types are dealt with in this section. Where proposed works under consideration concern the repair of structures, the appropriate methods are described elsewhere in these guidance notes.

14.1 Ruinous Buildings

14.1.1 There are many ruinous structures throughout the country including a variety of building types such as castles, houses, churches and cottages. Proposals concerning works to such structures are likely to fall into one of three types:

a) proposals to demolish the structure;

b) proposals to consolidate the ruin, or

c) proposals to restore the ruin and bring it back into use.

14.1.2 In the case of ruins which are recorded monuments in addition to being protected structures, it should be noted that there are separate additional procedures under the National Monuments Acts for notification to the statutory authority to be followed.

Demolition

14.1.3 There is a presumption in favour of the preservation of all protected structures and demolition may only be permitted in exceptional circumstances. Some structures may have been added to the Record of Protected Structures as ruins; other protected structures may, through major accident, have become ruinous.

14.1.4 A proposal to demolish a ruin, where the demolition would adversely affect the character of an adjacent protected structure or of an ACA should be carefully considered. For example, a ruin may be part of a streetscape or may be a folly building, or 'eye-catcher', designed to be viewed from a distance as part of a designed landscape or it may be a local landmark.

14.1.5 An applicant may be able to produce a convincing case for demolition following major accidental damage to the ruin, perhaps through storm or fire damage, which has destroyed its character and causes it to pose a danger to the public. But any such proposals should be carefully scrutinised by the planning authority and expert advice may be required with regard to structural stability. Where an application is made to demolish or dismantle (whether in whole or in part) a protected structure that is a ruin, based on reasons of structural instability, the onus should be on the applicant to prove that the proposals are valid and all relevant matters have been properly addressed. A record should also be kept of that structure if permission is granted for demolition or dismantlement.

Consolidation of ruinous buildings

14.1.6 There are cases where a structure of definite architectural, artistic or historical interest, such as a ruinous towerhouse, country mansion or church, cannot be restored and brought back into use without compromising its special interest or character. This will often be the case with structures which have stood for a considerable time as ruins. In order to prevent further deterioration of the protected structure, it may be proposed to consolidate the fabric as it stands and to preserve the structure as a ruin.

14.1.7 It should be a condition of permission for works to consolidate a ruinous structure that the methods used would not cause unacceptable damage to the character of the protected structure or an undue loss of historic fabric. The methods and detailed specification should be approved by the planning authority before any works commence. In some cases, even the removal of ivy or other vegetation from a ruinous building may have consequences for its structural stability and proposed methods of work should be carefully scrutinised.

14.1.8 Where a masonry wall has lost its facing or the core of a wall needs to be consolidated, proposals may be made to grout the rubble-core filling. The use of inappropriate materials such as strong cement-based grouts or poor work methods will damage the protected structure, often irreparably and, in extreme cases, may lead to the collapse of the structure. The applicant should be able to show that the proposed method of grouting will not endanger the structural stability of the wall.

In this instance, a ruined markethouse marks the centre of a planned village. Despite its ruined state it forms a local landmark which, if lost, would remove the focus of the historic townscape

Ivy has been removed from this mediaeval mural tower after a detailed record was made of the fabric to ensure that potential loss or damage to the stonework could accurately be remedied, reusing the historic fabric without resort to conjecture

Care should be taken to match repairs to the existing in terms of materials and workmanship. This mediaeval doorway was rebuilt using an inappropriate cement mortar. The stones above the point of the arch have been set in a random pattern and finished with wide joints quite unlike the surrounding stonework

14.1.9   Proposals may be made to take down and re-erect all or part of the walls of a ruinous structure where the walls are failing. Such proposals should generally only be permitted where it can be shown that the structure is in danger of collapse and no other option is available. It should be a condition of permission that the structure be fully recorded before dismantling is allowed to commence and be rebuilt using a maximum amount of the original material. In cases where there is good quality masonry, the stones should be individually numbered before being carefully dismantled to be re-erected in the same location.

14.1.10   In the consolidation of ruinous structures, attention needs to be paid to wall tops and openings as these areas are most vulnerable to water penetration and frost attack. However, works should not damage the fabric and appearance of the protected structure. The use of hard cement-based mortars may trap water against the surface of the wall or within the core of the wall and so promote decay. Where it is proposed to provide added protection to exposed parts of the ruin in the form of copings, flashings or mortar, these should not damage the fabric or appearance of the structure. Similar consideration should be given to proposed flashings which turn down over mouldings, cornices or the like and may unacceptably distort the proportions of the moulded work.

Restoration of ruins

14.1.11   Works involved in rebuilding or restoring a ruin have the potential to alter materially the character of a structure but are always preferable to demolition. Each case will have to be judged on its merits. It will rarely be possible to bring a building that has stood for a long time as a ruin back into use without the replacement of certain amounts of the original fabric. Proposals to restore a ruinous structure should not involve an unacceptable amount of alteration or loss of important historic fabric.

14.1.12   Where permission is granted, it should include conditions to repair and retain as much of the historic fabric as possible. The methods of rebuilding, and the materials used should not cause damage to surviving earlier work that contributes to the character of the protected structure. The applicant should be required to use expert advice in identifying original or early fabric. There may be traces of paint, plaster or render coatings to internal or external walls, which should be recorded and/or preserved.

Exposed wall heads are generally the most vulnerable parts of a ruined structure. The method proposed to cap exposed wall heads should not result in water being trapped inside the core of the wall and should be visually acceptable. In some cases, the ruinous structure may need to be monitored over a period of time before a decision can be made as to what work might be appropriate

Some ruins may require careful dismantling and re-erection of parts of walls that have become unstable. In this case, apart from the repair work required to the gable (containing pigeon nesting boxes), it is intended to re-roof the building. Where it is appropriate to re-roof a ruinous structure, the aim should be to retain the maximum amount of original fabric

14.1.13 The location of new floors and partitions, even where no remnants of the original remain, should not conflict with existing openings or other original fabric. Where ruinous buildings are to be restored or reconstructed, proper survey records and drawings should be included as part of the planning application, distinguishing existing fabric from proposed new work, to enable the planning authority to assess the potential impact of the interventions. In each case the planning authority will have to assess the appropriateness of the approach, be it in contrasting (modern) or replicating (historical) style. A decision will be needed as to whether or not such interventions ought to be physically distinguished from the old work or recorded by documentation. Modern materials, such as steel structural elements, may be used where they are not visually disturbing, would not damage the historic fabric, nor adversely affect the character and special interest of the protected structure.

14.1.14 Restoration may require alterations in order to allow the building to function properly. Such proposals may include the application of external render on stone-walled structures such as towerhouses. Where such proposals are made, the onus should be on the applicant to prove the appropriateness of the proposals. For example, there may be evidence that the building was originally rendered or, even where such evidence has not been found, it may be shown that the application of an appropriate external render is necessary adequately to weatherproof the building.

14.2 Bridges

IDENTIFICATION OF FEATURES FOR PROTECTION

14.2.1 There is a rich heritage of bridges throughout the country that requires careful consideration when any repair or alteration work is proposed. With the closure of some railway lines, many associated bridges and viaducts became redundant but nonetheless stand as important landmarks throughout the countryside and are of importance to the country's civil engineering heritage. On the other hand, proposals to upgrade other railway lines and roads may bring about proposals for changes to historic bridges.

14.2.2 Bridges which are protected structures may include road, rail and canal bridges, aqueducts, viaducts and footbridges. They may incorporate features of special interest including abutments, parapets, cut-waters, refuges, balustrades, string courses, railings, lamp standards, plaques and paving. Where such features exist they should be identified and conserved.

Bridges are primarily functional structures, however many of them are also aesthetically pleasing. On a finely detailed masonry-arched bridge, features of special interest may include abutments, parapets, cut-waters, string courses and paving

Ireland has a strong civil engineering heritage of railway bridges constructed of masonry, metal or a combination of both. Iron and steel bridges often contain decoratively finished elements, makers' stamps and other features that add to their special interest. Many masonry bridges incorporate datestones sometimes including details of their designers

14.2.3 Many early bridges are constructed of stone, either rubble stonework, ashlar or a combination of both. Iron and early steel bridges are less common and are usually associated with railway construction. Often a combination of iron and stone was used in the building of a bridge or viaduct. Early concrete bridges are relatively rare and should be carefully conserved. Timber bridges are also rare though timber components may be incorporated (in features such as handrails) in bridges built primarily of other materials.

CONSIDERATION OF PROPOSALS REGARDING BRIDGES

14.2.4 Proposals to reinforce, widen or infill sections of a bridge which is a protected structure, resulting in the concealment of any part of it, should be treated with caution. Where reinforcement is proven to be unavoidable, efforts should be made to ensure that the least possible structural and visual damage is caused to the bridge.

4.2.5   Proposals to reinforce, widen or infill sections of a protected bridge will require alterations to the character and quality of the structure. Where the impacts are likely to be substantial and would damage the character and integrity of the protected structure to an unacceptable extent, alternative solutions should be explored.

14.3   Harbours, Canals and Associated Features

IDENTIFICATION OF FEATURES FOR PROTECTION

14.3.1   The structures and features of interest associated with harbours and canals which should be protected could include quay walls, slipways, docks, dry docks, lifting bridges, locks, piers, jetties, breakwaters and associated buildings such as warehouses and boathouses.

14.3.2   Protection could also extend to features such as cranes, other machinery, bollards, lamp standards, chains, harbour lights, navigational structures or buoys and other items which may or may not be original to the construction of the harbour or canal but which contribute to the appreciation of the protected structure and should be retained.

CONSIDERATION OF PROPOSALS

14.3.3   Where it is necessary to infill a harbour, dock, canal or lock the works should as far as practicable be reversible; for example, the use of loose fill would allow for later reinstatement of the protected structure. Any other proposed works should have the minimum possible impact on the protected structure. Expert advice may be necessary to evaluate such proposals.

14.4   Street Furniture and Paving

IDENTIFICATION OF STREET FURNITURE OR PAVING FOR PROTECTION

14.4.1   An item of street furniture may be protected by being included in the RPS in its own right where it is special or rare; as part of the curtilage of a protected structure; or as part of an ACA. Such items could include lamp standards, seats and benches, bollards, railings, street signs, iron signposts, free-standing or wall-mounted post boxes, telephone kiosks, horse troughs, water-pumps, drinking fountains, jostle stones, milestones, paving, kerbstones, cobbles and setts, pavement lights, coal-hole covers, weighbridges, statues and other monuments.

The removal of parapet walls to provide cantilevered walkways should be carefully examined because of the potential impact on the fabric and appearance of important historic bridges. If bridges were altered in this manner in the past, the opportunity might be taken to restore parapets previously removed, where this can be accomplished and without resort to conjecture

The construction of safe harbours necessitated great engineering skills, which were matched by the stone-cutting and laying skills of the masons who quarried and cut the stones for massive harbour and quay walls and piers. Lighthouses, boathouses, lifting bridges and breakwaters are often integral parts of harbours and quays and add to their special interest

The machinery associated with canals, harbours and ports is often now redundant and liable to being removed or damaged. However many such items add to the special interest of a historic industrial area even where the site is no longer in industrial use

Many items of street furniture were fabricated locally in long-vanished small factories or workshops using locally-available materials, which gives them a social and historical interest in addition to creating regional design differences, as is evident in this Carlow granite fence

Damage caused to historic paving stones by repeated lifting can lead to breakage of individual stones. The replacement of areas of lost stone with concrete should be avoided as it significantly degrades the appearance of a historic pavement

Where new paving is required, the opportunity may arise to have a pavement designed especially to suit the character of the area. This paving outlines the site of excavated Viking housing and is interspersed with inset bronze plaques depicting finds made during archaeological excavations in the area

CONSIDERATION OF PROPOSALS

14.4.2 Proposals to remove or relocate items of street furniture or other features should not be granted permission without consideration of all the implications. Statues or monuments may close a vista. Other items of street furniture, such as jostle stones or weighbridges, may have close historical associations with an adjacent building.

14.4.3 Proposals to replace historic or rare items of street furniture such as telephone kiosks, post boxes or lamp standards should be resisted by the planning authority. Traditional paving elements are important to their locality and should generally be retained where found and not moved to alternative locations which are perceived as more prestigious or as having more character.

14.4.4 Historic street furniture and paving should be protected from accidental damage. Where planning permission is granted on a site adjacent to protected items of street furniture or paving, these elements should be sheltered from damage for the duration of the site works.

14.4.5 Regular or repeated lifting of historic paving for the installation and maintenance of public utilities is likely to cause damage and should only be carried out with due care and, if necessary, expertise. Where new utilities are to be installed, these should generally be located away from areas of historic paving whenever possible. If appropriate, the installation of bollards or other deterrents may be considered to prevent damage to important paving or street finishes.

14.4.6 Where it is proposed to pedestrianise a street in an ACA, or one that contributes to the character of a protected structure, it may be preferable that it should simply become a street without traffic rather than be converted into a new landscaped area which could adversely affect the character of protected structures or the character of an ACA. All original surfaces and finishes should be retained and protected. New paving materials should preferably be of natural materials, sourced locally and appropriate in scale and colour to the street.

14.4.7 New items of street furniture, which will impact on the character of a protected structure or of an ACA, should be appropriately and sensitively designed. The design of these objects need not imitate historical styles or detailing in order to be considered acceptable. The design and location of any proposed traffic-calming measures such as ramps, bollards or traffic islands should be carefully considered.

New street furnishings do not have to be 'traditional' in style or material to be considered appropriate. The use of modern designs and materials may provide a satisfying visual counterpoint to the historic setting

Whether small urban squares or airy expanses of open ground, parks add considerably to the character of an area and contribute much to the social life of the place. The features that are integral to the park or which have been added over time will usually be significant to its special interest, as will be important layouts or planting

14.5 Parks

14.5.1 Buildings or structures within a public park may be protected individually. A park may be an important element within an ACA.

14.5.2 Features of a park which should be identified and protected could include gates and gateways, pavilions, bandstands, shelters, greenhouses, statues, fountains, pools, bridges, terraces, steps, seating, and paving. Where these features are of quality and interest and are original or early additions to the park, permission should not usually be given for their removal or replacement. Where an original or an important layout or planting substantially remains, it should be conserved. Care should be taken not to allow the obliteration of evidence of historic landscaping when new works are being carried out.

14.6 Burial Grounds

14.6.1 A historic burial ground, or features within it, may be protected in its own right, as part of the curtilage or attendant grounds to a protected structure such as a church or mausoleum or as an ACA. Additionally, where a graveyard comes under the category of a protected site under the National Monuments Acts, the requirements of those Acts must also be complied with where any works are proposed.

14.6.2 There may be many features associated with the burial ground which should be respected and retained, including boundary walls, gateways, lych gates, mausolea, memorials, box tombs, architectural iron or stone burial enclosures, gravestones, steps and paving. There may be associated buildings or the ruins of such buildings, for example, gate-lodges or mortuary chapels, which should also be protected.

14.6.3 Where extensive works are proposed, a comprehensive survey of the burial ground and its features may need to be carried out in advance of any works commencing. In any case, the layout of the burial ground should be respected and existing pathways retained wherever possible. Proposals to 'tidy up' protected burial grounds that involve moving or reconstructing box tombs, gravestones or memorials, levelling the ground, or altering the boundary walls should not be generally permitted. The use of mechanical diggers within a historic burial ground should not be permitted where they could damage any features of interest above or below ground.

Many graveyards include important funerary monuments, such as this impressive eighteenth-century pyramidal mausoleum. They may also include gravestones with finely carved inscriptions, all of which have architectural as well as social and historical significance

While there is generally a respect in communities for burial grounds, the wish to maintain them should not lead to over-enthusiastic or misguided 'tidying-up' works or the uninformed reconstruction of damaged memorials. Where repairs are planned to damaged memorials, all fragments should be identified and reset using an appropriate mortar, and any poorly executed previous repairs rectified, if this can be achieved without further damage. Specialist advice will usually be required

14.6.4 Gravestones and memorials in old burial grounds are of immense historical, social and artistic interest and can be important sources of information to local historians and others. They should be treated with great respect, carefully maintained and re-erected where they have fallen. They should not be moved unnecessarily in order to facilitate activities such as grass cutting. The use of broken or dislocated headstones as paving should not be permitted. Where dislocated headstones or flat stones have been used historically as paving and where inscriptions or carvings survive, consideration should be given to preserving these either by removing them to a safe location or by re-routing paths to avoid future erosion by foot-traffic.

Enabling and
Temporary Works

CHAPTER 15

15.1 Enabling Works

15.1.1 Situations will arise where there are concealed elements within a building whose condition needs to be assessed in advance of proposals being formulated in order to inform those proposals. For example, there may be a likelihood that beam ends are rotted, fungal infestation is suspected or a case where sources of water penetration need to be identified. In such situations enabling works will be needed, such as the opening up of floors or ceilings, removal of panelling and the like, before detailed proposals can be made. It is important that these enabling works do not damage the character of the protected structure or any element which contributes to its special interest.

15.1.2 A planning authority may also require an applicant to carry out a schedule of investigative works where it considers the proposed redevelopment of a protected structure may be inappropriate. For example, where it is considered proposals may lead to an overloading of structural elements such as floors or staircases, enabling works may be required to ascertain the capacity of structural elements to accept increased loading, before detailed planning application proposals can be considered. It may also be considered necessary to ascertain the existence or location of concealed features.

15.2 Temporary Works

15.2.1 Temporary works may be necessary to preserve the fabric of a protected structure during development. Old buildings which are undergoing refurbishment or conservation works are particularly vulnerable to damage during the course of those works. Every care should be taken during works to a protected structure to ensure that the historic fabric is protected, particularly delicate features and high quality finishes. The methods and details of temporary works may need to be approved by the planning authority prior to the commencement of any works.

15.3 Potential Causes of Damage

15.3.1 Potential causes of damage should be considered by the planning authority when attaching conditions to a grant of planning permission in order to prevent or minimise damage to a protected structure as a result of building works. Even where the building owner has employed specialist consultants, the planning authority may consider the need for expert advice to satisfy itself

The importance of the original structural system and its capacity to accommodate a proposed development should be ascertained at an early stage in order to inform the design. This may require some limited opening-up works. Alternatively, some opening-up may be necessary ascertain the existence of suspected hidden fabric or features of importance, such as early structural timbers

Detailed consideration should be given at an early stage to the design of measures to protect structures and important features likely to be affected by a development, including those on adjacent sites. A protected structure should not be exposed to damage from construction works or from vehicle impacts and should not be used for purposes that might cause damage

that the matter of damage during the course of works has been properly addressed and to assess potential risk to the protected structure and those features which contribute to its special interest.

15.4 Structural failure

15.4.1 The planning authority could require that expert advice be sought by an applicant from suitably qualified architects or structural engineers to ensure that the structural stability of the building will not become endangered during building works. The quality and expertise of site personnel and the ongoing monitoring of site works could also be specified. Where a protected structure is particularly fragile or where significant temporary works are anticipated, the planning authority could require an applicant to submit designs for temporary works for approval in advance of the erection of any scaffolding or shoring.

15.4.2   Careful propping of elements of special interest within the building may be necessary before works commence. Valuable and irreplaceable objects, such as decorative plaster ceilings, should be propped if there is any risk to their stability. Propping itself can cause damage and should be designed and installed by properly trained and experienced personnel under the guidance of an architect or other building specialist who is aware of the value of the fabric. It should be established that no damage would be done by the movement or the concentration of loading from scaffolding, shoring or other temporary works on existing fabric or foundations.

15.5   Mechanical damage

15.5.1   Irreparable harm can be done to a historic structure by mechanical damage caused during the course of building works, particularly in the erection of scaffolding. Externally, sills, glazing, cornices, string courses, balconies, steps, paving and railings are particularly vulnerable to breakage, scratching and other damage. Inside a building, carved stonework and joinery, decorative plasterwork and decorative wall and floor finishes such as paint, wallpaper and tiling are all prone to accidental damage during general building works. Roofs, paving and flooring located below work in progress should be protected from items supported off them and from items dropping onto them from overhead.

15.5.2   A planning authority may require that all valuable ornamental work be provided with the necessary protective coverings before work commences. Where there are windows or doors with rare or interesting glass these should be protected, if necessary on both sides, to prevent breakage. Protection in situ should generally be preferred to removal. Historic glass should not be sacrificed to facilitate the erection of scaffold poles or ties through windows, doors or fanlights.

15.5.3   Scaffolding should be erected by trained scaffolders, guided by architects or other building specialists who are aware of the importance of the building fabric. Any part of a scaffold which touches, or is erected close to, historic fabric should be provided with protection to prevent damage and the ends of poles should be covered with plastic caps.

15.5.4   As with the potential problem of structural damage, the planning authority could require the employment of experienced site personnel, such as scaffolders, and proper site management in order to minimise the risk of accidental damage.

Structures may be in need of propping prior to, and during the course of, works which should be designed and installed to avoid causing damage to unstable fabric

The erection and dismantling of scaffolding in rooms or spaces with important surface decoration or finishes requires especial care. Scaffolders experienced in such work may be required in these circumstances

Glass is more vulnerable than most materials to damage during works, especially during the erection or dismantling of scaffolding. Historic glass should be protected at least to the exterior and, if necessary, also to the interior. Glazed windows should never be broken to facilitate scaffolding poles or ties, nor held open unless adequate protection is given to the glass and the sash is supported

Structures should be adequately protected from the effects of the weather where the temporary removal of windows, doors or roofs is necessary. The protective sheeting and any necessary supports should be attached securely and be fully reversible, without causing damage to window-frames, roof trusses or masonry

15.6 Fire

15.6.1 Refurbishment and maintenance works pose a risk of fire to a historic structure, and construction work to protected structures should be properly managed to minimise this risk. Clear safety instructions should be included in all contracts for works to protected structures. For example, 'hot' working procedures should generally be avoided in historic structures or, where unavoidable, should be carefully monitored. Examples of 'hot' working procedures could include works involving cutting, welding and burning-off of paint. Other threats may arise from the storage of flammable materials such as paints or solvents within the protected structure, the burning of debris and rubbish near the structure or the inadequate provision of fire-extinguishing equipment.

15.7 Weather

15.7.1 Works necessitating the temporary removal of all or part of the weatherproof envelope of a building, such as roofs, windows or doors, should also include the provision of a specified level of protection to the fabric from the weather. Temporary roofs should allow for the discharge of rainwater well away from the building to avoid flooding the interior or weakening the foundations.

15.8 Theft of Architectural Features and Vandalism

15.8.1 Building sites are particularly vulnerable to burglary, vandalism and arson. The presence of scaffolding on the exterior of a building may make the upper storeys accessible to burglars and vandals when a site is unattended.

15.8.2 The theft of architectural features and materials is widespread throughout the country. These features are at a particular risk when a protected structure is vacant or in the process of refurbishment. Vulnerable items include fireplaces, pieces of ironmongery, lead roof-cladding, carved stone features, panelling and the like. Where there are valuable interior or exterior features, these should be provided with protection before the contract work commences and adequate security should be provided to the structure during the course of the works. The protective casing to valuable features could be provided with alarms, security seals and/or viewing panels, and should be inspected regularly during the course of the works.

15.8.3 Where the structure is temporarily unoccupied for the duration of building works, the owner may be permitted to remove valuable features carefully from the building and move them to a safe and secure storage area for reinstallation at an early date. Owners of vulnerable items should be encouraged to make adequate records of them to help in their recovery in case of theft.

It is advisable that site supervisors or other senior personnel routinely check on all important protected items to make sure that alarms are not tampered with or the fixtures not surreptitiously loosened behind the protective boarding in preparation for theft

Historic joinery or other fixtures which have been temporarily removed from their locations should be stored carefully and safely within the structure and not left stacked on floors where they may be vulnerable to damage or theft prior to their re-incorporation within the building

Making Good Disaster Damage

CHAPTER 16

16.1   Disaster Plans

16.1.1   In the interest of protecting a historic structure, the development of a disaster plan can be useful, mitigating the endangerment of those parts of the structure which are saved from a fire, flood or other devastation. This could involve compiling an inventory of special architectural features and fixtures, a drawn record or photographs of the building or those parts of it considered as being of special interest. These records should be stored at a separate location, away from the protected structure. Priorities for saving objects or features in the event of disaster can then be made. The inventory could also serve as an archive in the event of a total loss.

16.2   Mitigating the Loss and Salvaging Materials

16.2.1   In order to mitigate damage to the protected structure and to minimise the loss of historic fabric, steps need to be taken speedily in the aftermath of a fire or other disaster. Firstly the stability of the remaining fabric should be assessed and the building made structurally stable before access is allowed for other purposes. Where necessary, the fabric of the building should be protected from further damage by weather or decay. This may require the erection of a temporary roof. Provision should be made to facilitate, in an appropriate manner, the drying-out of fabric and contents saturated as a result of fire-fighting measures. Careful consideration should be given to minimising the risk to remaining, and potentially salvageable, elements which could be further damaged through the drying-out process.

16.2.2   The building should be made secure against vandalism and all features of value, including architectural fragments and building materials, should be protected and salvaged. Records should be made of the remaining and damaged material and mapped locations of the salvaged debris. An owner or occupier may need to call on specialist expertise regarding methods of storing or conserving salvaged elements such as finishes, joinery or plasterwork.

16.3   Rebuilding After Total Loss

16.3.1   In most cases where a disaster such as a fire has caused total, or near total, loss of a historic building, the special interest which led to its inclusion in the RPS may be considered irredeemably lost and the building of a replica replacement will generally

As soon as it is safe to do so, the surviving fabric of a damaged structure should be inspected and measures taken to stabilise it, erecting a temporary roof if necessary and securing the site against unauthorised access

Where a protected structure has suffered devastating or irreparable damage to its special interest through a fire or other disaster, it may often serve little purpose to reconstruct or replicate it, except where a larger architectural design has been affected by the loss or the structure is an important local landmark; in such cases the reinstatement of the exterior or other elements of the structure may be considered

serve little purpose. In such cases, the building should be deleted from the RPS. However, if the building formed part of a larger architectural design such as a terrace, square or other group of buildings or was an important urban or rural landmark, then the reconstruction in replica of at least the exterior of the building may be considered necessary in order to protect the setting of other historic structures or the character of an ACA.

16.4 **Partial Loss**

16.4.1 The total loss of a building in a disaster is very rare. Partial loss of a structure is more common. This is also more problematic and will require a careful assessment of the remaining building fabric. A judgement will need to be formed by the planning authority as to what constituted the special interest of the structure and to what extent that special interest has been compromised by the damage. The effect of the damage on adjacent protected structures or on the character of an ACA should also be considered.

16.4.2 The assessment will need to consider the type and extent of the damage and the importance of the damaged portion to the quality of the whole. It may be difficult to identify the point at which the building is so damaged that full reinstatement is neither worthwhile nor desirable. Each case will have to be considered on its own merits, as standard procedures cannot be applied.

16.4.3 Where the damaged section of the building is part of an architectural composition, or one which is symmetrical or where the building forms part of a formal composition, then it may be considered essential to reinstate the damaged section fully, or at least externally, even where a substantial proportion of the historic fabric has been lost.

16.5 **Reinstatement of Interiors**

16.5.1 Where the interior of a protected structure is almost entirely lost but the external shell remains substantially intact, the requirement may be to repair or reinstate the exterior fabric but allow the interior to be rebuilt in a different manner. Much will depend on the quality of the interior before the disaster. Where a high-quality interior has been damaged and substantial fragments remain, the recreation of the interior incorporating those surviving fragments may be appropriate, providing this can be done without an undue amount of conjecture.

Many fires are successfully extinguished before major damage occurs, requiring a careful assessment of the remaining fabric to ascertain if its special interest has been compromised. An assessment of the extent of reinstatement appropriate following partial damage will require to be carried out on a case-by-case basis

The true extent of damage to important interiors may be disguised by smoke-blackening and blistered paint. Careful spot cleaning of the stained and blistered surfaces and examination of lath and plaster linings will be needed to establish whether or not decorative interior plasterwork or joinery is capable of repair

Alterations to Enhance Fire Safety

17.1 Introduction

17.1.1 Fire is one of the greatest threats to the fabric and contents of a protected structure. The object of fire safety legislation, quite rightly, concentrates on the saving of lives and prevention of injury to persons. However, in the case of a protected structure, additional consideration needs to be given to minimising damage to the historic fabric and contents in the event of fire. Many protected structures may be particularly vulnerable too because of their remoteness or lack of occupancy. Older buildings may be more vulnerable too because of traditional construction techniques which included the extensive use of timber in concealed spaces or because of unrecorded alterations, such as the installation of services, which created routes through the fabric for the spread of smoke and fire.

17.1.2 Compromise from all sides will often be needed to resolve conflicting requirements of fire safety and architectural conservation. Where possible, planning officials and fire officers should liaise during the course of a planning application, to ensure the best solution is found. This can be done by using the mechanisms available under Section 13 of the Fire Services Act 1981.

17.1.3 In the interests of good conservation, consultation between the applicant, the planning authority and the fire authority should take place, where possible, at a pre-planning stage. It is generally of advantage to all concerned to resolve any major issues at an early stage.

17.2 Applications for Works to Enhance Fire Safety

17.2.1 Where the planning authority considers that an application for works to a protected structure would require alterations to enhance fire safety that have the potential to adversely affect the character of the building, the planning authority should consult the fire authority. Where the fire officer advises that extensive or potentially unacceptable works may be required, the planning authority may then request that the applicant submit a fire risk analysis as further information in order to allow an assessment of the full impact of the proposed development on the structure. It may be advisable for the applicant to engage a specialist fire consultant in order to achieve a satisfactory level of fire safety with minimal intervention into the fabric of the structure.

17.2.2 Where an application for planning permission has been granted which does not address fire protection, an applicant should be advised that further planning permission will be required, where necessary alterations would materially affect the character of the protected structure.

17.2.3 It is impossible to prescribe a standard approach as each protected structure is unique and will require an individual assessment of its vulnerability. Fire-safety design solutions should impact as little as possible on the important elements and fabric of a protected structure. In principle, there should be minimal intervention into the existing fabric of the protected structure, and alterations which impact on important fabric should be readily reversible.

17.2.4 Occasionally works to enhance fire protection would necessitate a level of intervention which the planning authority considers unacceptable in terms of excessive loss or disruption of the historic fabric. In such cases, the developer should be encouraged to explore alternative fire-safety solutions, including alternative uses, which may have fewer implications for fire safety.

17.2.5 Where permission for works to enhance fire safety is refused, the planning authority should notify the fire authority of the decision.

17.3 Technical Guidance Document B of the Building Regulations

17.3.1 A flexible approach is required when considering the fire protection measures suitable for a historic building. It is recognised in Technical Guidance Document (TGD) B of the Building Regulations that, in the case of an existing building, there may be constraints that would not exist with a new building and that some variation of the provisions of TGD-B may be appropriate. The Department has also published a series of guides/codes of practice in relation to fire safety in existing buildings for the purposes of assisting building owners in meeting their statutory obligations under the Fire Services Act 1981.

17.3.2 Because of the importance of preserving the architectural character of a protected structure, imaginative compromises will often have to be made between active and passive fire protection measures. A number of possible compensatory measures are outlined in TGD-B of the Building Regulations for works to existing buildings. Where works would materially affect the character of the protected structure the onus should be on the applicant to show that alternative solutions to fire safety enhancement have been fully explored.

CHAPTER 17 ALTERATIONS TO ENHANCE FIRE SAFETY

17.4 Means of Escape in Case of Fire

17.4.1 The safe escape of occupants from a building in the event of fire is of primary importance. However, with a protected structure it may be neither practicable nor appropriate to comply with particular requirements of TGD-B of the Building Regulations. For this reason, compensating measures are allowed to be provided when dealing with an existing building. These measures include all or some of the following:

a) enhanced levels of life safety protection by automatic fire detection and alarm systems;

b) reduced travel distances;

c) enhanced smoke-control measures;

d) pressurisation of stairway enclosures;

e) protection to escape routes from places of special fire risk;

f) enhanced performance of fire doors;

g) additional structural fire-protection measures such as increased levels of compartmentation of the building.

There may be special requirements for providing means of escape for people with disabilities, which will also have to be considered.

Escape routes and exits

17.4.2 Escape routes should generally be internal where they can be accommodated without damaging good internal fabric or decoration. The use of external escape stairs should be avoided where possible because of their large and usually negative impact on the external appearance of the building. In addition, the requirement for windows or doors adjacent to an external escape stairs to have adequate fire resistance could involve the alteration of original joinery and the loss of historic glass. Where the installation of an external escape stairs is unavoidable, it should be carefully designed and efforts made to locate it inconspicuously. Escape stairs should not be permitted on principal elevations nor where they would impact on important views of the structure.

17.4.3 Requirements for adequate means of escape from a building may include proposals for the insertion of new doorways in external walls, the conversion of existing window openings into doors or the replacement of historic windows such as sash windows with other opening types. Such proposals should be carefully considered by the planning authority.

The use of external escape stairs should be avoided on important elevations or where they would be obtrusive in an important view of the structure

Proposals that require the conversion of original window openings into doors to facilitate escape will require very careful consideration and should avoid impacting on surviving early or original windows and on important elevations. There may also be a potential impact on nearby windows which may require re-glazing with fire resistant glass

17.4.4   For weatherproofing reasons, entrance doors traditionally open inwards and most internal doors open into rooms rather than outwards as may be required for escape purposes. Proposals to re-hang a historic door in order to reverse the opening direction may require unacceptable alterations to the doorframe or to the appearance of an important interior.

Lighting and signing of escape routes

17.4.5   The need for the lighting and signing of escape routes should be carefully considered so as to reduce the impact on the character of the interior while clearly defining the routes. In certain sensitive interiors, the applicant may be required to install specially designed fittings that suit the location while fulfilling fire-safety requirements.

Fire-protected lobbies and corridors

17.4.6   Where proposed alterations to provide enhanced fire protection would require the inclusion of protected lobbies, corridors or staircases into the interior of a protected structure, works may be necessary which would have a serious impact on the character of the building. This could include works to upgrade the fire resistance of historic walls, floors, ceilings, staircases or doorcases.

17.4.7   The insertion of a new fire-resistant lobby into an interior could damage the appearance of rooms and disrupt important decorative schemes. The applicant should be able to prove that alternative solutions and the provision of compensatory features have been explored. Where the insertion of a new lobby is permitted, its design should be appropriate and take account of the existing architecture of the interior. The reversibility of the new works should not be an excuse for poor or unsympathetic design.

Fire detection and alarm systems

17.4.8   A fire-detection and alarm system is an essential part of the fire-safety strategy for all buildings. The early detection of fire is of great benefit in reducing damage and danger to both life and property. Automatic detection systems can detect the presence of fire from smoke, heat or infra red/ultra violet radiation and other emissions. Some buildings may require a different form of detection system for different locations. The character of an important interior can be harmed by the inappropriate design or intrusive location of a detection system and its associated wiring, for example, smoke detectors mounted on a decorative ceiling.

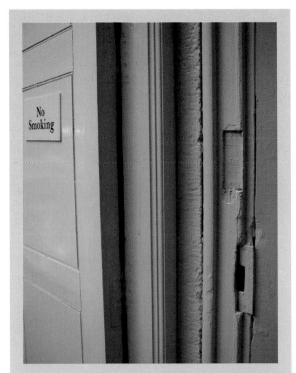

The reversal of a door to allow it to open in a different direction may require obtrusive alterations to a historic doorcase and may make the original hinges and locks redundant

The use of standard signage may not be appropriate in high-quality interiors. Alternative designs are available which minimise the visual impact while fulfilling fire-safety obligations

The design of a new protected lobby within a fine historic interior should take great care to avoid adverse visual and physical impacts; interrupting a symmetrical space or cutting across decorative plasterwork may not be acceptable regardless of whether the proposed works are reversible

17.4.9 Where a detection or alarm system is proposed for the interior of a protected structure, the installation should as far as practicable be carried out without damaging the fabric and appearance of the structure. The detection system chosen should be appropriate to the location in addition to satisfying fire safety legislation.

Fire suppression

17.4.10 Proposals may be made to install fire suppression systems, including hose reels or sprinklers. These systems together with their associated drainage can be difficult to conceal and their use in protected structures, particularly those with high-quality interior work, is often inappropriate. They may be considered acceptable in protected structures where they can be installed in concealed locations as part of major refurbishment works.

17.5 Internal Fire Spread (Linings)

17.5.1 Some protected structures may have internal finishes which are combustible such as timber panelling to walls or ceilings and which may constitute a fire risk. Alternative fire-safety solutions should be sought to the removal of important internal linings. Other inappropriate works could include proposals to cover over important internal linings or finishes with other linings in such a way as to damage the fabric or appearance of a protected interior.

17.6 Internal Fire Spread (Structure)

Load-bearing structural elements

17.6.1 Many protected structures will include load-bearing structural elements of combustible materials such as timber. Alternative fire-safety solutions to proposals which require the removal or replacement of combustible structural elements, where these are important to the special interest of the protected structure, should be developed. The encasement of timber, iron or steel structural elements to enhance fire safety may damage the appearance of a protected interior particularly where there are decorative elements such as scrolled brackets, cusped columns and the like.

Compartmentation

17.6.2 Compartmentation is a major part of passive fire protection but one which can cause difficulties when applied to a protected structure. In order to achieve the necessary subdivision of the building, works may be required to upgrade the fire

Recent advances have been made in the design of fire detection systems allowing for unobtrusive installations within fine interiors. Systems such as aspirating or air sampling systems (top) consist of a sampling unit, remotely located, and small diameter pipes requiring only minute holes in the ceiling fabric to allow air to be drawn and sampled. The impact on a decorative ceiling contrasts favourably with the large, usually white, plastic smoke detectors (middle) previously used in many historic interiors

Fire suppression systems have been developed for high quality interiors, using small, unobtrusive sprinkler heads and flexible pipework, which minimise the impact on the fabric of the building compared to traditional sprinkler systems. The decision to introduce a fire suppression system into a building must balance the benefits of early detection and suppression and the reduced amount of water used compared to traditional fire-fighting methods with the disadvantages of the risk of accidental discharge and the disruption caused to the building during installation

resistance of floors, ceilings, walls and doors in a historic interior.

Undivided roof spaces

17.6.3 Undivided roof spaces may exist not only between parts of a building but between different buildings in a terrace. It may be possible to deal with many of these concealed spaces by unobtrusively subdividing them.

Upgrading historic walls, floors and ceilings

17.6.4 The fire resistance of existing timber walls or floors may require to be upgraded. This can be achieved by the addition of fire-resisting layers above, beneath or between existing studs or floor joists. The voids between studs or joists can also be filled with flame-resisting materials. There are a number of proprietary methods which have been developed for upgrading the fire resistance of floors which may be appropriate. Upgrading works should not involve loss or damage to important plasterwork on walls and ceilings or of historic floors. The applicant should be advised to explore alternative methods of satisfying the requirements of enhancing fire safety.

Upgrading historic staircases

17.6.5 The removal or replacement of important staircases or parts of staircases should generally not be permitted. Alternative methods of meeting the requirements of fire-safety enhancement should be investigated by the applicant.

Upgrading historic doors

17.6.6 Historic doors and doorcases are particularly vulnerable to inappropriate changes in order to achieve a specific fire resistance. Panelled doors have an inherent weakness in terms of fire resistance because of rebated panels. Traditional door details often include voids behind architraves which also lessen the effectiveness of a doorset to perform in the event of a fire.

17.6.7 Where an authentic door or doorcase of acknowledged quality or interest remains, efforts should be made to retain it in situ rather than replace it with a replica fire-resistant door. While a historic doorcase may not appear to meet a recognised standard of fire resistance, it nonetheless offers some degree of protection which might be acceptable in particular circumstances. Modest upgrading may be possible by using seals and linings or the application of intumescent paint or paper. Proposals to replace existing timber or glazed panels with alternative materials may not always be acceptable. The same is true of proposals to dismantle a historic panelled door in order to insert fire-resistant layers within the construction.

There will generally be a visual and material impact on a building caused by encasing structural elements in fire-resisting materials. Alternative measures should be explored if these elements contain decorative detailing that would be disturbed or concealed by such work or if encased elements such as a timber floor, as shown here, or roof may become susceptible to fungal attack as a result of the treatment

Decorative plaster ceilings can be upgraded by adding fire-resisting layers between the joists, which should be carried out without loss or damage to the plasterwork, floorboards or structural timbers

Increasing the fire performance of panelled doors may require a combination of methods. It can be assisted by work such as applying intumescent strips to the door and frame edges. The composition and condition of the door and doorset and presence of surviving historic door furniture, such as box locks or wrought iron hinges, should be examined in order to find the most appropriate solutions

17.6.8   Where the historic door is located within a thick wall, it may be acceptable to incorporate an appropriate fire-resisting door within the same structural opening whilst leaving the original door in place.

17.6.9   As a last resort, where a door cannot be brought up to required standards without unacceptable alteration, it may be appropriate that it be recorded and tagged before being carefully dismantled and safely stored in the building for possible reinstatement at a later date and an appropriate replacement door fitted.

17.6.10   Added elements of ironmongery required for fire protection, such as door closers, hold-open devices and the like, should be visually acceptable for the location.

Concealed spaces

17.6.11   The presence of concealed voids or openings within the structure of an old building can make compartments ineffective. There may be interconnecting spaces behind panelling or wall linings or between floor or ceiling joists or there may be undivided roof spaces.

17.6.12   It may be possible to deal with many of these concealed spaces by unobtrusively subdividing them. Other situations will require a careful balance of other fire-protection measures in order to provide an acceptable solution.

17.7   External Fire Spread

Roof coverings

17.7.1   Some protected structures have combustible roof-coverings such as thatch or timber shingles and alterations may be required to improve the fire resistance of such roofs. However, consideration should be given to the fact that flame-retardant treatments for thatch must be renewed regularly to maintain effectiveness and the chemicals used may damage the material or encourage its decay.

17.7.2   The replacement of historic or decorative glass with wired or other fire-resistant glass in rooflights and skylights should not be permitted. It may be considered acceptable to allow for fire-resistant secondary glazing to be used but only where this would not adversely affect the appearance of the original glass.

Small and unobtrusive door closers and hold-open devices are available, which should be used if standard ironmongery specifications would be unacceptable due to the visual and physical impact on the interior and its elements

Where a door lining can accommodate a second door without requiring intrusive visual or physical alterations, the provision of an appropriately detailed fire-resisting door can be an acceptable method of upgrading the opening. In this example the new door is to the left in the photograph

Walls

17.7.3   The external walls of protected structures may be finished with combustible materials such as timber boarding, framing or shingles. Where these finishes form part of the special interest of the structure, proposals to enhance the fire resistance of such materials should not damage the fabric or appearance of these walls.

17.8   Access and Facilities for the Fire Service

Sources of water for fire-fighting

17.8.1   Where a protected structure is sited in a remote location away from a mains water supply, consideration needs to be given to the necessity for an adequate water supply for fire-fighting. Where an application is received for works to such a building, the planning authority could consider, as a condition of permission, the provision of water-storage tanks or otherwise adjacent to the protected structure. The appearance and siting of such water storage should not adversely affect the character of the protected structure or of an ACA. Consideration should be given to upgrading, or improving access to, existing water features located adjacent to the building such as ornamental lakes or fountains, which could serve as water sources. Alternatively, underground water-holding tanks could be provided where the construction of these would not disrupt important areas of hard landscaping or gardens.

Vehicle access

17.8.2 A range of compensating measures are considered appropriate under TGD-B where it is not possible to provide sufficient access for the fire service to existing buildings. These measures could include additional personnel access to the building for fire-fighting, additional internal fire mains and other facilities to assist fire-fighting. These requirements should be resolved in consultation with the fire authority.

17.9 Management

Fire prevention measures

17.9.1 In the case of fire damage to protected structures, prevention is obviously better than cure. No matter how well reinstatement works are carried out, lost historic fabric is gone forever and can only be replaced in replica. Under Section 18 (2) of the Fire Services Act 1981 it is the duty of the persons in control of a number of specified building types to take all reasonable measures to guard against the outbreak of fire on such premises. However, a planning authority may have little opportunity to input into the operational practices that are undertaken in the management of a protected structure. The owners and occupiers of these buildings should be encouraged to take certain steps in order to prevent their building becoming endangered by fire. Such steps might include the preparation of a regularly monitored fire-safety plan.

17.9.2 A fire risk assessment should be carried out for the protected structure. This would be most useful in advance of preparing a detailed planning application. The likelihood of fire can be reduced by the identification of risks and their elimination or by the management of those which cannot be eliminated. Common causes of fire in protected structures include electrical faults, building or renovation work, arson and accidental fire from hearths, smoking, kitchens and the like. Many of these causes can be eliminated or minimised by the adoption of certain operational procedures such as banning smoking in or around the building or adjacent to flammable material such as thatch, the use of 'hot work' procedures during refurbishment work and the storing of combustible materials within the building. Staff training, where appropriate, should include maintenance and testing techniques as well as preparation for emergencies. Lightning may be a possible danger, particularly to large isolated structures. Where appropriate, these structures should be protected with earthed lightning-conductors.

17.9.3 Some of these matters could be dealt with as conditions of planning permission for works to protected structures.

Lightning conductors may be a requirement on tall or otherwise vulnerable structures. The conductors should be channelled to earth unobtrusively; this example shows a discreetly coloured lightning conductor carefully concealed behind a downpipe

Improving Access

CHAPTER 18

18.1 Introduction

18.1.1 It is accepted that there should be easy access to all buildings for people with disabilities. The need to provide access is implied by the Employment Equality Act 1998 and the Equal Status Act 2000 and new requirements will be included in forthcoming disability legislation. In the case of a material alteration, regard must also be had to the need to make adequate provision for access as required by Part M of the Building Regulations 2000.

18.1.2 Careful consideration will be needed in the context of the architectural heritage, requiring innovative solutions and a degree of compromise from all sides. A fair balance will need to be struck between accessibility and the preservation of the special qualities of a protected structure and its setting or of an ACA. Improving access to a historic building will require a creative approach and flexibility on the part of owners, architects, planning authorities, building managers, users and others.

18.1.3 The goals of improving access to an existing building are those of independent access and of integrated access. That is, people should be able to move independently with ease and dignity into and around the building, use the building as intended and exit the building safely in case of emergency. Ideally the access routes for all users should be the same. Meeting these goals will present some of the most challenging issues faced in the alteration of historic buildings but, in some cases, adaptation may be essential to ensure the continued use and viability of a building.

18.1.4 Where it is proposed to improve access to a protected structure, the ability of the building and its setting to meet this requirement must be carefully assessed. If the application of universal design principles and measures to improve accessibility are likely to cause major problems and lead to unacceptable alterations of the character and fabric of the protected structure, the onus should be on the applicant to show that consideration has been given to exploring all possible options for enhancing the accessibility of the protected structure and its site. Applicants should actively seek innovative solutions and good designs which minimise intervention into the historic fabric.

18.1.5 The ideal solution would minimise the alteration of original or fine building fabric and avoid works which would have an adverse impact upon the character of the exterior or interior of the building,

Modern interventions can be acceptable where they use high-quality design and materials. Such work can address the needs of the users while respecting the architectural quality of the structure

whilst meeting the goals of improved access. The reversibility of proposals is an important conservation principle but should not be used to justify inappropriate interventions. Where barriers to access are found to exist, ways should be sought which avoid the obstacle rather than make alterations to it. For example, where a flight of stairs inhibits access to the upper floors of a building for some users, a lift installation could be considered. When intervention is unavoidable, permitted proposals should minimise the loss and alteration of the historic fabric and protect the architectural integrity and special interest of the protected structure. Unnecessary change should always be avoided.

18.1.6 It should be realised that there are some protected structures or groups of buildings within ACAs whose architectural qualities or rarity are such that they should not be compromised and it may have to be accepted here that full and easy access for all is not possible to achieve. For example, a Georgian terraced house which is separated from the street by a sunken area surrounded by stone plinths and iron railings and accessed by a flight of stone steps, may require excessive alteration and loss of historic fabric in order to provide access for wheelchairs. There may be an unacceptable loss of character or damage to the special interest not only of the individual building but also the terrace, street or square in which it is located. However, even in these cases, opportunities may nonetheless exist to improve access for the broader spectrum of disability. While it may not be possible to provide wheelchair access to a particular building or site, the provision of handrails or easily negotiable surfaces would still improve access for a larger number of people.

18.1.7   Where it is found not possible to make adequate provision for access and use of a building in accordance with the requirements of the Building Regulations, it will be necessary to receive a dispensation from, or relaxation of, this requirement from the Building Control Authority before commencement of the works.

18.2   Entering the Building

18.2.1   The conflict between improving access and the conservation of a historic structure is often most difficult to resolve at the entrance to the building. This is particularly so where there is a need to provide access to wheelchair users. Ideally, the principal entrance should be accessible to everyone, but compromise may be needed in sensitive cases.

18.2.2   Past styles of architecture have featured an impressive entrance approached by steps. Even humbler buildings had one or more steps up to the level of the ground floor for sound practical reasons such as preventing the ingress of water. There may exist several alternative means of improving the accessibility of an entrance.

External ramps, lifts and steps

18.2.3   Sometimes a well-designed and sensitively sited ramp may be the easiest way to achieve access for wheelchair users. Permanent, integrated ramps of a sympathetic design and materials should be encouraged. However, when dealing with buildings or ACAs of high architectural quality or rarity, the installation of an access ramp against the façade of the building may not be an acceptable solution, particularly where a ramp would destroy the balance of a symmetrical or harmonious façade or damage significant architectural features. Where this is the case, the planning authority should encourage the applicant to explore alternative or more innovative solutions.

The traditional Georgian terraced house with a basement area to the front can present problems with regard to improving access. Alterations to provide a ramp can result in the loss or disruption of historic fabric such as stone plinths, iron gates and railings and can compromise the natural ventilation and lighting of basement rooms.

Traditional buildings almost always include one or more steps at the entrance, which may be important to the composition of the entrance and make a contribution to the character of the structure in the way they have worn through use over several generations. In the example shown here, the narrow double-leaf door would also cause difficulties for some disabled users but is essential to the character of the entrance

18.2.4 Wheelchair platform lifts can be visually intrusive, although it may be possible to incorporate them sensitively within an existing porch or portico.

18.2.5 Proposals which require the demolition or partial removal of stone steps, balustrades, or other important features will not always be acceptable and should be carefully considered. However, in some cases, it may be appropriate to allow the alteration or partial removal of steps, iron railings or plinths to allow access to wheelchair platform lifts or ramps. Where this type of alteration is proposed, the planning authority should take into account the significance of the relevant building elevation and the quality of the elements proposed for alteration.

18.2.6 It should be borne in mind that while a ramp may be needed to facilitate wheelchair access, it should be supplied in addition to steps. Users with ambulatory disabilities may have difficulties in using ramps.

Re-grading the external ground level

18.2.7 Where the differences in level are small, it may be possible to re-grade the ground immediately in front of the entrance, provided this does not result in the unacceptable visual loss of parts of the building's plinth or base and does not involve the loss of important paving or other surfaces. Re-grading will not usually be an option in an urban context where entry is directly off a street.

Temporary facilities for wheelchair access

18.2.8 Occasionally the installation of a permanent ramped access may be considered inappropriate to the special character of the protected structure or of an ACA. In such cases, the provision of a temporary access ramp may be considered. In some particularly sensitive locations, the decision may be taken to allow the provision of a temporary ramp, constructed in compliance with current safety and health regulations, which is erected and dismantled by trained staff when required. The storage of such facilities should be given careful consideration. The ramp must be at hand when required, but should not obstruct access or cause unsightly clutter around the protected structure.

Access ramps against the façade of a building can conflict with or obscure important architectural features such as stone plinths. While a ramp may be physically separated from the masonry by a barrier to allow its removal without damage, the visual impact still needs to be resolved

A well-designed platform lift of a sympathetic design using high quality materials, and provided in addition to, and not as a replacement for, steps may be acceptable. However, alternative solutions may have to be explored where a symmetrical or harmonious composition would be unbalanced or damaged by the addition of a ramp

The option of re-grading the ground adjacent to an entrance could be considered where the difference in levels is small, where the raised level would not conceal architectural details, where there is no loss of historic pavement and of course where sufficient ground is available to create a gentle gradient

18.2.9   The use of temporary ramps is rarely preferable to an appropriately designed permanent access, as they are not compatible with independent access. But they may occasionally be a necessary expedient. Generally the design and location of such ramps should be chosen with equal care as a permanent installation and the temporary nature of the facility should not excuse inappropriate schemes. For access routes or part of routes that are subject to material alteration, reliance on temporary ramps will not normally satisfy the requirements of the Building Regulations.

Secondary entrances

18.2.10   Buildings such as narrow terraced houses and others will often not have the space necessary for an acceptable ramp to the principal entrance. It may be difficult to find an appropriate location for a wheelchair platform lift which would not involve undue loss or alteration of features such as railings, walls and steps.

18.2.11   In some cases, it may be possible, by means of careful design, to reorganise the internal spaces of some buildings so that access can be achieved through the adaptation of a secondary entrance. Ideally, where a second entry point is adapted to provide access for disabled users, it should also become the access point for all the building users. However this will cause difficulties where the new access route affects the appreciation of the building's plan form or a carefully designed succession of rooms.

18.2.12   In some cases, it will not be possible to improve access through the primary entrance without inappropriate levels of disturbance and damage to the historic fabric of the building or to the character of an ACA. In such cases it will have to be accepted that a separate entry point be provided.

Car parking

18.2.13   Ideally, dedicated car parking for visitors with disabilities should be provided at a location easily accessible to the entrance. This may have implications for the character and setting of a protected structure. On larger sites, car parking is often deliberately sited away from a protected structure in order to avoid impacting upon its immediate setting. In these cases, it may be necessary to permit separate dedicated parking nearer to the structure for users with disabilities. If this is not possible, suitable setting-down points for visitors may be an option.

A demountable ramp has the advantage of being readily reversible. In these examples no alteration of the existing historic fabric has been made. Even where a ramp is demountable, its design and location should be given equal consideration to a permanent installation

In some cases, it will not be possible to provide access for all users through the main entrance and the provision of a secondary entrance will be an acceptable compromise

Dedicated parking spaces adjacent to an entrance may be easily provided in some urban contexts where on-street parking is already provided. In other situations, the design or identification of suitable setting-down points may be necessary

There will be cases where the character of a building or area is so sensitive to change that it will not be possible to alter it to provide independent access. In such cases a managed solution should include a clearly-signed contact point and appropriately-trained staff to assist

Innovative solutions, combined with high quality design and materials, can avoid conflicting with existing features while adding to the richness of a historic interior

18.2.14 The surface treatment of the parking areas should be appropriate in texture and colour to the location and should not damage the setting of the protected structure.

18.3 Circulation within the Building and Egress

18.3.1 Circulation within a protected structure can cause problems for certain users, particularly vertical circulation between floors and changes of level within a floor. When considering applications for alterations to improve access to a protected structure it must be borne in mind that adequate provision must also be made for emergency egress.

Circulation between floors

18.3.2 The most effective means of providing for circulation between floors is a passenger lift. However, a lift, and machinery associated with it, can be unacceptably obtrusive in a historic interior. Proposals to install lifts in protected structures will need to be carefully considered on a case-by-case basis.

18.3.3 Care should be taken with such proposals to ensure that the installation of a lift shaft would not damage interior work of quality and that the associated machinery can be satisfactorily accommodated within a basement or within a roof space. In some cases, it may be more acceptable to locate a lift external to the existing structure but this may involve the alteration of existing openings or the formation of new ones. A lift which requires the remodelling of the roof profile of a protected structure should rarely be permitted. Hydraulic lifts could be considered as an alternative to conventional lifts where the location of lift gear above the roofline would be considered inappropriate.

18.3.4 Where the installation of a passenger lift is not possible, alternative means of providing vertical circulation, for example, wheelchair stair lifts or platform lifts, may be acceptable. In assessing the suitability of platform lifts, regard should be had to the acceptable maximum height of travel for such lifts.

18.3.5 The principal staircase of a protected structure, and often the secondary staircase too, are usually significant architectural spaces within the building. It will often be difficult or impossible to alter such principal staircases to fit mechanical devices such as wheelchair stair-lifts without adversely affecting the special qualities of the space and damaging the historic fabric. Where this is the case, it may be considered more appropriate to install a wheelchair stair-lift on a secondary staircase.

Changes of level

18.3.6 Changes of level may occur within a historic building. Minor changes can be overcome by the sensitive location and detailing of ramps, although careful consideration will be needed where ramps would conflict with important details such as plinths, skirtings, panelling and architraves. The minimum possible disturbance should take place to historic floors and any permitted works which impact on important fabric should be readily reversible. It must also be remembered that ramps can be unsuitable and potentially dangerous for a large number of people with ambulatory difficulties and so their use can be inappropriate.

18.3.7 Platform lifts can be used to overcome changes in level and may be preferable to a ramp where the difference in level is relatively large. However, the appearance of these devices can be obtrusive in sensitive interiors. Where a platform lift is to be installed, the installation should not involve the demolition or alteration of parts of important stairs or landings and the works should be readily reversible.

Emergency egress

18.3.8 It is important that the applicant adequately address the need for emergency egress for the disabled user. This may require alterations to the historic fabric of the building. Where there is access to upper floors of a protected structure for users with disabilities, there may be a requirement for the provision of refuge areas, alternative escape stairs, fireman's or evacuation lifts, and the like. Consideration must be given to how these will impact on the character and fabric of both the interior and exterior of the protected structure and, where relevant, the character of an ACA.

18.3.9 Where the impact of the requirements for emergency egress would require unacceptable alterations which would adversely affect the character of the protected structure, the planning authority should encourage the applicant to seek alternative, more appropriate solutions.

Stair lifts can be obtrusive when used in a historic context, even where the stair contains just a few steps. If the special interest of a staircase or flight of steps would be adversely affected by the visual and physical impact of such an installation, alternative solutions should be explored

18.4 Surface Finishes

18.4.1 The surface finishes of ramps and pathways are of great importance to people with mobility impairment and the finish chosen should satisfy safety requirements. The type of finish can also have a considerable impact on the protected structure and its setting. Where new surface treatments are to be installed, the texture and colour of materials should be appropriate to their location and to the requirements of all users.

18.4.2 Traditional finishes such as cobbling, setts and gravel can be unsuitable for wheelchair movement, the movement of children's pushchairs and ambulant people with varying levels of mobility. Where these surface finishes exist within the setting of a protected structure or in an ACA, efforts should be made to provide accessible routes through them with a minimum disruption to the historic landscaping. Accessible routes can be provided by replacing part of the existing surface with paved pathways of a complementary material, such as stone flags. Short routes across cobbling or setts can be made accessible by increasing the amount of mortar in the joints to prevent the trapping of wheels. This solution can have a large impact on the appearance of the hard landscaped surface and may not always be appropriate.

18.5 Requirements for Users with Cognitive and Sensory Disabilities

18.5.1 The full range of disability extends beyond mobility alone. Where proposals are made to provide improved access to and within protected structures, consideration will also need to be given to the requirements of users with varying degrees of visual, hearing and cognitive ability.

18.5.2 Such proposals may include the provision of tactile circulation routes, visually contrasting steps at top and bottom of flights of stairs, signage, enhanced lighting levels, tapping-rails, communication aids such as induction loops etc. Consideration will need to be given to the potential impact of such proposals on the fabric, character and appearance of the protected structure.

18.6 Introduction of New Elements

18.6.1 New elements associated with improving access to a protected structure will be required. These may include lifts, ramps, handrails and balustrades. These elements will often be highly visible and have the potential to impact on the special interest of the building. Where new elements are to be introduced, they should be designed to respect the character and materials of the existing fabric. The design does not need to imitate past styles to be considered acceptable, but should respect the quality of existing features. Designing new elements for incorporation within a historic building is a challenge. The planning authority should not seek to discourage contemporary and innovative designs, providing these are of sufficiently high quality and do not detract from the character of the historic fabric.

Traditional surfaces finishes can cause problems for those in wheelchairs or with walking difficulties but accessible routes can be provided through these areas using complementary materials

New elements which are provided to improve access to a protected structure should avoid being visually obtrusive, whether consciously modern or of a traditional design

Maintenance

CHAPTER 19

19.1   Regular and correct maintenance and repair are key to the conservation of protected structures and buildings within ACAs. Without them the structures, or elements of them, may deteriorate beyond recovery. Proper repair and maintenance slow the progress of decay without damaging the character and special interest of the structure but should generally be undertaken only after establishing the cause of deterioration. Aggressive or misguided works can lead to the permanent damage of the fabric of a building. In considering routine maintenance, care should be taken to require that such works always follow conservation principles and best practice. Repair and maintenance works should not generally include the replacement of elements, except where required to make good a shortfall or to replace individual broken items.

19.2   Maintenance works are generally the responsibility of the owner or occupier of the building and not of the planning authority. However, the authority can provide appropriate assistance in achieving these works in the form of aid (whether financial, materials, equipment or services) and of advice given formally through the declaration or informally in another context. The planning authority can take action, where a structure is becoming endangered through neglect, to specify works which it considers necessary to prevent the structure from deteriorating further. This can be done by issuing a notice under Section 59 of the 2000 Act or, if appropriate, a notice under Section 11 of the Derelict Sites Act 1990. However, it is preferable that intervention should take place at an early stage, before deterioration takes hold.

19.3   It is good building management practice for the owner or occupier of a protected structure to prepare a programme of on-going maintenance. It is also good practice to monitor regularly any critical aspects of a building envelope and structure, particularly if it is old or in fragile condition. If this is done regularly, deterioration can be arrested at an early stage, and tackled quickly and cheaply. It may be useful for an owner or occupier to prepare a maintenance manual containing the accrued experience of those previously charged with the care of the building.

19.4   Repairs should be carried out only after careful analysis of the problems that have led to deterioration so as to ensure that the repairs are appropriate and have a relatively long life. There is no point in spending money on a building, only to find out that the initial analysis did not pinpoint the essential problem and hence the steps taken to solve it are not relevant or durable. Repairs themselves can cause further damage, if based on an incorrect analysis of a problem.

These windows are pictured prior to a recent repair. While it was initially thought rails, sills or stiles would need replacement or splicing-in, on examination very little timber repair was required. The crown and cylinder sheet glass was retained in the repair and redecoration works. It is important to inspect all historic elements on an individual basis prior to specifying works, in order to ensure that only necessary repairs and replacement of parts are carried out

It is good management practice to regularly inspect a structure to ensure that rainwater continues to drain effectively. In this case a blockage in a new lead downpipe resulted in overspill onto the wall behind, which was not remedied in time to prevent efflorescence occurring on the face of the saturated brickwork

Appendices

Research Sources

Appendix A

**Department of the Environment, Heritage
and Local Government
National Inventory of Architectural Heritage**
Dún Scéine
Harcourt Lane
Dublin 2

telephone: 01 411 7100
email: niah@duchas.ie
website: www.buildingsofireland.ie

**Department of the Environment, Heritage
and Local Government
Archaeological Survey of Ireland**
6 Ely Place Upper
Dublin 2

telephone: 01 647 3000

Irish Architectural Archive
45 Merrion Square
Dublin 2

telephone: 01 663 3040
fax: 01 663 3041
e-mail: info@iarc.ie
website: www.iarc.ie

The National Archives
Bishop Street
Dublin 8

telephone: 01 407 2300
e-mail: mail@nationalarchives.ie
website: www.nationalarchives.ie

The National Library of Ireland
Kildare Street
Dublin 2

telephone: 01 603 0200
e-mail: info@nli.ie
website: www.nli.ie

Registry of Deeds
Henrietta Street
Dublin 1

telephone: 01 670 7500
website: www.landregistry.ie

Valuation Office Ireland
Irish Life Centre
Abbey Street Lower
Dublin 1

telephone: 01 817 1000
e-mail: info@valoff.ie
website: www.valoff.ie

**Industrial Heritage
Association of Ireland**
Tailors' Hall
Back Lane
Dublin 8

website: www.steam-museum.ie/ihai

Dublin City Archives
138-142 Pearse Street
Dublin 2

telephone: 01 674 4800
e-mail: cityarchives@dublincity.ie
website: www.dublincity.ie/dublin/archives2

Cork Archives Institute
Christ Church
South Main Street
Cork

telephone: 021 427 7809
e-mail: cai@indigo.ie
website: www.corkcorp.ie/facilities

Representative Church Body Library
Braemor Park
Churchtown
Dublin 14

telephone: 01 492 3979
e-mail: library@ireland.anglican.org

Architectural Heritage Impact Assessments

Appendix B

B1.0   Requirement for a Report

B1.1   The requirement for an architectural heritage impact assessment will generally come about for one of two reasons:

a) as part of a development application in order to provide sufficient information for the planning authority to make an informed decision on the potential impact on the architectural heritage, or

b) where permission has been granted for works to a protected structure or a proposed protected structure, to record the existing fixtures or features which contribute to its special interest and which would be lost or altered as a result of the works.

B2.0   Scope of the Assessment

B2.1   The detail and extent of the assessment should be appropriate to the nature and scale of the proposed works. The object of the assessment should be to describe how the proposals would affect the character of the protected structure or any part of it. This will normally require a description of the existing structure, a description of the works proposed and a description of how any potential adverse impact on the architectural heritage is to be mitigated.

B2.2   Where comprehensive or wide-ranging works are proposed, the entire protected structure and the land and features within its curtilage may require to be included in the assessment. However, where proposals are limited in scale or relate to a specific part or parts of the structure, it will generally be sufficient to include a brief description of the structure as a whole, to provide a context for the proposals, but to concentrate the detailed assessment on those parts of the structure which will be impacted upon. If the application relates to a new building within the curtilage of a protected structure or proposed protected structure, the assessment should concentrate on the relationship between the structure and its setting, and the merits of, and impacts on, existing structures and features in the curtilage.

B2.3   Ideally, there should be full access to the structure for the author of the assessment in order for him/her to have a full understanding of the potential for the works to impact on the building.

B3.0   Recording a Structure to be Altered or Demolished

B3.1   Where an assessment is intended as a permanent record of a structure, or part of a structure that is being altered or demolished, it may have to substitute for the structure itself and so must be capable of bearing on-going and repeated analysis, re-examination and reinterpretation. Specialist expertise may be necessary for the compilation of such architectural heritage impact assessments that describe and assess structural or other engineering matters or those relating to historic landscapes.

B4.0   Competency of Author(s)

B4.1   The author(s) of an architectural heritage impact assessment should be appropriately qualified or competent to undertake the assessment. Where the works to the protected structure are unlikely to have more than a minor impact on the character of the structure, it may be acceptable that the assessment be undertaken by a person, or persons, without specialised expertise. However, where the protected structure is of high quality or rarity, or where the impact on the architectural heritage may be substantial, the planning authority could make it a requirement that the assessment be carried out by those with relevant competence or expertise.

B5.0   Elements of the Assessment

B5.1   The content of the assessment will vary in individual cases depending on the relative significance of the structure for which the assessment is being prepared and the nature and extent of proposals under consideration. The information set out below can be used as a guide. Assessments should generally contain three distinct but interdependent elements:

a) a written account;
b) a set of well-presented drawings;
c) suitable photographs and/or other illustrations.

Written Account

B5.2   The written account of the building will usually comprise three parts:

a) core data;
b) short description of the building;
c) analysis.

Core Data

B5.3   The following core data on the building should generally included in every report:

a) purpose of the assessment. For example, where the assessment forms part of a planning application, this should be stated. Where the assessment is part of a response to a further information request from the planning authority, the planning reference and a copy of the further information request from the planning authority should be included with the assessment. Where the assessment is to fulfil the requirements of a condition of permission, the planning reference number should be given and a copy of grant of permission and relevant condition(s);

b) name and address of the structure, including any local reference by which the building is known, where this is necessary to identify it;

c) brief description of the typological aspects of the structure;

d) Ordnance Survey map reference for the structure;

e) National Grid reference, where necessary;

f) details of the form, or forms, of statutory protection which apply to the site, for example:
i. Record of Protected Structures, including reference number;[1]
ii. Architectural Conservation Area designation;[2]
iii. Recorded Monument, including RMP reference number;[3]
iv. Zone of Archaeological Potential;[4]
v. Registered Monument, including RMP reference number;[5]
vi. Preservation Order or Temporary Preservation Order;[6]

g) name of the individual (and their agency, if appropriate) who prepared the assessment, and his/her relevant qualifications or competency;

h) date of the assessment and of the inspection;

i) name of relevant planning authority;

j) details of any declaration issued regarding the structure;

k) National Inventory of Architectural Heritage registration number of the structure, where available[7].

Short Description of the Structure

B5.4   This should be a concise description of the structure as it exists, noting all its salient features, and describing its external and internal appearance and setting, form, present function, type or purpose, materials, architect and date (where ascertainable). For large sites, where there is more than one structure, separate descriptions of each should be made together with an account of their relationship to each other.

Analysis of the Existing Structure

B5.5   Following on from the basic data contained in the short description, the written assessment should contain all or part of the following information as relevant to the particular case.

B5.6   Where the development consists solely of new work, such as extensions or new build in the curtilage of a protected structure, items a) to c) can be briefly summarised:

a) a description of the structure, recording features of note or historical significance, architectural or engineering design, building materials, building techniques and craftsmanship. Where comprehensive works are proposed, it may be appropriate that this description be carried out on a floor-by-floor, room-by-room basis;

b) a description of the structure's overall development, noting evidence of successive building phases and supporting this analysis with annotated reference to stylistic elements, documentary sources or scientific dating methods, where appropriate. Reference should be made to original and present uses of the structure, or its parts;

c) a description of the current physical condition of both the fabric and the structure in order to establish the nature and extent of any apparent damage, including any indications of previous demolition or alteration to the structure;

d) a description of the relationship of the structure to its setting, noting the evolution and condition of the site, its impact on the landscape, ancillary structures (either current or removed) and their relationship to the principal structure in question. Where the proposal relates to new works this section should be comprehensive. However, it will not be relevant where internal works alone are proposed;

[1] Details available from the relevant planning authority or by consulting its current development plan

[2] Details available from the relevant planning authority or by consulting its current development plan

[3] Relevant RMP information should be available in the offices of the planning authority and local libraries

[4] Relevant RMP information should be available in the offices of the planning authority and local libraries

[5] The owner of the structure will have received written confirmation at the time of registration

[6] The owner of the structure will have received written confirmation at the time of the making of the order

[7] Available from published surveys or from the NIAH website

e)   information on persons or organisations associated with the construction, development or use of the building, including architects, engineers or builders, proprietors or other occupants, where known. Historically significant events with which the building was associated should also be included.

f)   certain structures may merit further investigation of record sources, such as Valuation Office records, deeds relating to the building in the Registry of Deeds, architectural drawings or other information in, for example, the Irish Architectural Archive, National Library of Ireland or the Archaeological Survey of Ireland, and historic census records.

Drawings

B5.7   Drawings of the structure, including site-plans, plans, sections and elevations, are generally necessary in order to locate the proposed works, the location and direction of the photographs included and to help in the assessment of the impact of the proposed development. Rooms or other spaces should be numbered and these numbers matched to written descriptions and illustrations where necessary to identify locations.

B5.8   Where alterations are proposed to only a small portion of the structure, it should not generally be necessary to include an exhaustive set of measured drawings for the entire protected structure. Indicative floor plans combined with photographs should be sufficient to support the assessment in such cases.

Maps

B5.9   Where the building or structure appears on early Ordnance Survey or other historic maps and its development, or earlier form, is relevant to the development proposals, it would be useful to include copies of the pertinent sections of the maps within the assessment and cross-referenced to other parts of the assessment as necessary.

Photographs

B5.10   A photographic survey of the relevant parts of the structure should be an integral part of the assessment. Where comprehensive works are proposed, the photographic coverage required for assessments could include floor-by-floor, room-by-room coverage of the internal appearance, and building elements, decorative features, details, fixtures or fittings, whether internal or external, noted as contributing to its character in the detailed written analysis.

B5.11   Where minor or small-scale works are proposed, photographs can be limited to those parts of the structure which will be impacted upon by the development. In such cases, it will nonetheless be useful to include enough general photographs of the structure to allow the context of the development to be appreciated by anyone reading the assessment.

B5.12   Colour-print film and digital images can be used for assessments to be submitted prior to a decision being made on the planning application. Scanned or digitally produced photographs should be printed legibly in the assessment to allow detailed examination. All copies submitted to the planning authority should be to the same standard, and not black-and-white photocopies. Captions should identify the purpose of the image and the location of the feature or space.

B5.13   Copies of relevant historic photographs, where available, could usefully be included with the assessment. All photographs should be clearly marked, identifying the location and the subject of the image, and when the photograph was taken and by whom (if known).

Anticipating Concealed Features

B5.14   Where the proposed works consist of alterations to an existing structure, concealed architectural features, such as chimneypieces, fireplaces, earlier openings, panelling, or decorative finishes, may come to light during the course of the works. Where there is any likelihood of this, the assessment should contain a schedule of reversible exploratory and enabling works and note whether or not it is anticipated that further future approvals will be necessary as a result.

B5.15 Where feasible, the assessment should indicate alternative design details or methods of work which would allow such features to remain in situ. Alternatively, the planning authority could attach an appropriate condition to the planning permission to ensure that these features will be retained or properly recorded as appropriate to their importance. Where removal is unavoidable, the assessment should suggest alternative locations within the structure for found features.

Impact Assessment

B5.16 The author(s) of assessments compiled to accompany a planning application should be fully appraised of the development proposal. The assessment should contain an evaluation of the quality and importance of the structure. In addition, it should contain a comprehensive assessment of the implications of the development for the character of the structure and the area in which it is located. This should highlight how the elements of this character (those which contribute to its special architectural, historical, archaeological, artistic, cultural, scientific, social and/or technical interest) would be materially altered by the development.

Recommendations and Conclusions

B5.17 Any recommendations and mitigation measures should be set out in accordance with the conclusions of the impact assessment, including an outline of proposed conservation works for agreement with the planning authority. Any scope of works statement or methodology included should be specifically written for the structure that is the subject of the assessment.

B5.18 It may not always be necessary or desirable to include conclusions or recommendations in the assessment. In some cases it will be sufficient for the assessment to describe and assess the structure, with clear and relevant illustrations cross-referenced to the text. Such assessments should describe in detail the existing architectural heritage, the impacts of the proposals, and the potential to mitigate any negative impacts in order to allow the planning authority to arrive at its own conclusions regarding the appropriateness of the proposed development.

Bibliography

Relevant legislation and statutory instruments
Planning and Development Act 2000
(in particular Part IV Architectural Heritage)

Planning and Development Regulations 2001

also
Architectural Heritage (National Inventory) and Historic Monuments (Miscellaneous Provisions) Act 1999

Building Control Act 1990

Building Regulations and Technical Guidance Documents 1997 - 2004

Derelict Sites Act 1990

Employment Equality Act 1998

Equal Status Act 2000

Fire Services Act 1981

Freedom of Information Acts 1997 - 2003

Heritage Act 1995

Local Government (Sanitary Services) Act 1964

Minister for the Environment and Local Government (Performance of Certain Functions) Act 2002

National Monuments Acts 1930 - 2004

Planning and Development (Amendment) Act 2002

Registration of Title Act 1964

Taxes Consolidation Act 1997
(in particular Section 482 – Relief for expenditure on significant buildings and gardens)

Wildlife Acts 1976 - 2000

Government publications
Archaeological Survey of Ireland, *Archaeological Inventories of Co. Carlow* (1993); *Co. Cavan* (1995); *Co. Cork 1. West* (1992); *Co. Cork 2. East and South* (1994); *Co. Cork 3. Mid* (1997); *Co. Cork 4. North* (2000); *Co. Galway 1. West* (1993); *Co. Galway 2. North* (1999); *Co. Laois* (1995); *Co. Leitrim* (2004); *Co. Louth* (1986); *Co. Louth (Full Survey)* (1991); *Co. Meath* (1987); *Co. Monaghan* (1986); *Co. Offaly* (1999); *Co. Tipperary 1. North* (2002); *Co. Waterford* (1999); *Co. Wexford* (1996); *Co. Wicklow* (1997)

Department of Arts, Culture and the Gaeltacht, *Strengthening the Protection of the Architectural Heritage* (Dublin: 1996)

Department of Arts, Heritage, Gaeltacht and the Islands, *Action on Architecture 2002 - 2005* (Dublin: 2002)

Department of Arts, Heritage, Gaeltacht and the Islands, *Framework and Principles for the Protection of the Archaeological Heritage* (Dublin: 1999)

Department of Arts, Heritage, Gaeltacht and the Islands *National Heritage Plan* (Dublin: 2002)

Department of the Environment, *Conservation Guidelines* (Dublin: 1996). Available in pdf format from **www.environ.ie**

Department of the Environment, *Sustainable Development – A Strategy for Ireland* (Dublin: 1997)

Department of the Environment and Local Government, *PL12 – A Guide to Architectural Heritage* (Dublin: 2002)

Department of the Environment, Heritage and Local Government, *National Inventory of Architectural Heritage Handbook* (unpublished May 2003)

National Inventory of Architectural Heritage, *Surveys of the Architectural Heritage of Co. Carlow* (2002); *Co. Clare* (2000); *Fingal Co.* (2002); *Co. Kerry* (2002); *Co. Kildare* (2002); *Co. Laois* (2002); *Co. Meath* (2002); *South Dublin Co.* (2002); *Co. Waterford* (2004); *Co. Wicklow* (2004); *Surveys of the Architectural Heritage of Athy* (2004); *Navan* (2004); *Tralee* (2004). See also **www.buildingsofireland.ie**

National Monuments and Historic Properties Service, Office of Public Works, *The Care and Conservation of Graveyards* (Dublin: 1995)

Council of Europe Conventions
Council of Europe, *European Charter of the Architectural Heritage* (Strasbourg: 1975)

Council of Europe, *Convention for the Protection of the Architectural Heritage of Europe* ('Granada Convention') (Strasbourg: 1983)

Council of Europe, *Convention on the Protection of the Archaeological Heritage of Europe* ('Valletta Convention') (Strasbourg: revised 1992)

Further information available from **www.coe.int**

Charters of the International Council on Monuments and Sites (ICOMOS)

ICOMOS, *International Charter for the Conservation and Restoration of Monuments and Sites ('Venice Charter')* (adopted at Venice: 1966)

ICOMOS, *Charter on the Preservation of Historic Gardens ('Florence Charter')* (adopted at Florence: 1982)

ICOMOS, *Charter on the Conservation of Historic Towns and Urban Areas ('Washington Charter')*, (adopted at Washington: 1987)

ICOMOS, *Guidelines for Education and Training in the Conservation of Monuments, Ensembles and Sites* (adopted at Colombo, Sri Lanka: 1993)

ICOMOS, *Charter for the Conservation of Places of Cultural Significance ('Burra Charter')* (adopted at Burra, Australia: 1979, revised 1999)

ICOMOS, *Charter on the Built Vernacular Heritage* (adopted at Mexico: 1999)

Further information available from
www.international.icomos.org

Irish: Architecture

Bence-Jones, Mark, *A Guide to Irish Country Houses* (London: Constable, 1996)

Bowe, Nicola Gordon, Caron, David and Wynne, Michael, *Gazetteer of Irish Stained Glass* (Dublin: Irish Academic Press, 1988)

Casey, Christine and Rowan, Alistair, *The Buildings of Ireland: North Leinster* (London: Penguin Books, 1993)

Clarke, Howard, ed., *Irish Cities* (Dublin: Mercier Press, 1995)

Cox, R. C., and Gould, M. H., *Civil Engineering Heritage: Ireland* (London: Thomas Telford Publications, 1998)

Cox, Ron and Gould, Michael, *Ireland's Bridges*, (Dublin: Wolfhound Press, 2003).

Craig, Maurice, *Classic Irish Houses of the Middle Size* (London: The Architectural Press, 1977)

Craig, Maurice, *The Architecture of Ireland from the earliest times to 1880* (London: B.T. Batsford Ltd, 1982)

Cruickshank, Dan, *A Guide to the Georgian Buildings of Britain and Ireland* (London: Weidenfeld & Nicolson, 1985)

Dunne, Mildred and Browner, Gerry (eds.), *The Courthouses of Ireland* (Kilkenny: The Heritage Council, 1999)

Galloway, Peter, *The Cathedrals of Ireland* (Belfast: Institute of Irish Studies, 1992)

Garner, W., *Architectural Heritage Guides* (Dublin: An Foras Forbartha). Including: *Cobh* (1979), *Bray* (1980), *Carlow* (1980), *Kinsale* (1980), *Tullamore* (1980), *Ennis* (1981), *Galway* (1985), *Drogheda* (1986). A number of county surveys were also published by An Foras Forbartha, which are out of print but may be available in public libraries

Glin, the Knight of, Griffin, David and Robinson, Nicholas, *Vanishing Country Houses of Ireland* (Dublin: The Irish Architectural Archive and the Irish Georgian Society, 1988)

Griffin, David J. and Lincoln, Simon, *Drawings from the Architectural Archive* (Dublin: Irish Architectural Archive, 1993)

Irish Architectural Archive, *The Architecture of Richard Morrison and William Vitrivius Morrison* (Dublin: Irish Architectural Archive, 1989)

Howley, James, *The Follies and Garden Buildings of Ireland* (New Haven: Yale University Press, 1993)

Irish Georgian Society, *Irish Architectural and Decorative Studies, the journal of the Irish Georgian Society* (Kinsale: Gandon Editions, 1998 -)

Kerrigan, Paul M., *Castles and Fortifications of Ireland 1485-1945* (Cork: Collins Press, 1995)

Lamb, Keith and Bowe, Patrick, *A History of Gardening in Ireland* (Dublin: National Botanic Gardens, 1995)

Lewis, Samuel, *A Topographical Dictionary of Ireland* (2 vols) (London: 1837)

Loeber, Rolf, *A Biographical Dictionary of Architects in Ireland 1600-1720* (London: John Murray, 1981)

McAfee, Pat, *Irish Stone Buildings* (Dublin: The O'Brien Press, 1998)

McAfee, Pat, *Irish Stone Walls* (Dublin: The O'Brien Press, 1997)

McCullough, Niall and Mulvin, Valerie, *A Lost Tradition: the nature of architecture in Ireland* (Dublin: Gandon Editions, 1987)

McDonald, Frank and Doyle, Peigín, *Ireland's Earthen Houses* (Dublin: A & A Farmar, 1997)

BIBLIOGRAPHY

MacLoughlin, Adrian, *Streets of Ireland* (Dublin: Swift Publications, 1981)

McParland, Edward, *Public Architecture in Ireland 1680 – 1760* (New Haven: Yale University Press, 2001)

Malins, Edward and Bowe, Patrick, *Irish Gardens and Demesnes from 1830* (London: Barrie & Jenkins, 1980)

Malins, Edward and Glin, the Knight of, *Lost Demesnes, Irish landscape gardening 1660 – 1845* (London: Barrie & Jenkins, 1976)

Morrison, Robin & Fitz-Simon, Christopher, *The Irish Village* (London: Thames & Hudson, 1986)

O'Dwyer, Frederick, *The Architecture of Deane and Woodward* (Cork: Cork University Press, 1997)

O'Keeffe, Peter and Simington, Tom, *Irish Stone Bridges* (Dublin: Irish Academic Press, 1991)

Roche, Nessa, *The Legacy of Light, a history of Irish windows* (Wicklow: Wordwell Ltd. 1999)

Rothery, Seán, *A Field Guide to the Buildings of Ireland* (Dublin: The Lilliput Press, 1997)

Rothery, Seán, *Ireland and the New Architecture* (Dublin: The Lilliput Press, 1991)

Rowan, Alistair, *The Buildings of Ireland: North-West Ulster* (London: Penguin Books, 1979)

Shaffrey, Maura and Patrick, *Buildings of Irish Towns* (Dublin: The O'Brien Press, 1983)

Shaffrey, Maura and Patrick, *Irish Countryside Buildings* (Dublin: The O'Brien Press, 1985)

Simms, Anngret and Andrews, J.H., eds., *Irish Country Towns* (Dublin: Mercier Press, 1994)

Simms, Anngret and Andrews, J.H., eds., *More Irish Country Towns* (Dublin: Mercier Press; 1995)

Williams, Jeremy, *A Companion Guide to Architecture in Ireland 1837 – 1921* (Dublin: Irish Academic Press, 1994)

Irish: General

Construction Industry Federation, *The Register of Heritage Contractors* (Dublin: 2001)

Dooley, Terence A. M., *Sources for the History of Landed Estates in Ireland* (Dublin: Irish Academic Press, 2000)

Helferty, Seamus and Refaussé, Ray, *A Directory of Irish Archives* (Dublin: Irish Academic Press, 1993)

Heritage Council, *Heritage Appraisal of Development Plans – A Methodology for Planning Authorities* (Kilkenny: 2000). For information on other Heritage Council publications see **www.heritagecouncil.ie/publications**

Irish Episcopal Commission for Liturgy, *The Place of Worship* (Dublin: Veritas Publications, 1994)

Irish Georgian Society, *Traditional Building and Conservation Skills: Register of Practitioners* (Dublin: 1998, revised 2000). Also available at **www.igs.ie**

Irish Professional Conservators and Restorers Association *Irish Conservation Directory*, (Dublin: 1998)

Nolan, William and Simms, Anngret, eds., *Irish Towns – A Guide to Sources* (Dublin: Geography Publications, 1998)

Royal Institute of the Architects of Ireland, *Guidelines for the Conservation of Buildings* (Dublin: RIAI, 2001)

Technical Guidance

Ashurst, John and Nicola, *Practical Building Conservation* (5 volumes) (Aldershot: Gower Technical Press, 1988 reprinted 1998)

Brereton, Christopher, *The Repair of Historic Buildings: advice on principles and methods* (London: English Heritage, 1991)

Bristow, Ian, *Architectural Colour in British Interiors 1615-1840* and *Interior House-Painting Colours and Technology 1615-1840* (New Haven: Yale University Press, 1996)

Cadw: Welsh Historic Monuments, *Overcoming the Barriers, providing physical access to historic buildings* (Cardiff: CADW, 2002). Further technical conservation advice available from **www.cadw.wales.gov.uk**

Cork Corporation, *Best Practice Guide, A practical approach to conservation based on experience in restoring one of Cork's mid-18th century terraces* (Cork: Cork Corporation, 1997)

Davey, Heath, Hodges, Ketchin and Milne, *The Care and Conservation of Georgian Houses* (Oxford: Butterworth Architecture, 1986, reprinted 1991)

English Heritage, *Framing Opinions Nos. 1-7* (London: English Heritage, 1991 -). A series of advisory leaflets on window and door conservation. Further information available from **www.english-heritage.org.uk**

Fawcett, Jane, *Historic Floors: their care and conservation* (Oxford: Butterworth-Heinemann, 1998)

Feilden, Bernard, *Conservation of Historic Buildings* (Oxford: Butterworth-Heinemannn, 1982, reprinted 1995)

Foster, Lisa, *Access to the Historic Environment – Meeting the Needs of Disabled People* (Shaftesbury: Donhead Publishing Ltd., 1996)

Historic Scotland, *Conservation Publications* (Edinburgh: TCRE Group/Sottish Conservation Bureau, 1992 -). Series of technical advice notes, study reports, guides and conference proceedings. Further information available from **www.historic-scotland.gov.uk**

Keohane Frank, ed., *Period Houses – A Conservation Guidance Manual* (Dublin: Dublin Civic Trust, 2001)

Lawrence, David, *The Care of Stained Glass* (Kilkenny: The Heritage Council, 2004)

Munn, Harry, *Joinery for Repair and Restoration Contracts* (Painscastle: Attic Books, 1983 reprinted 1989)

Nash, W.G., *Brickwork Repair and Restoration* (Painscastle: Attic Books, 1986 reprinted 1989)

Parissien, Steven, *The Georgian Group Book of the Georgian House* (London: Aurum Press Ltd., 1995 republished 1999)

Pavía, Sara and Bolton, Jason, *Stone, Brick and Mortar: historic use, decay and conservation of building materials in Ireland* (Wicklow: Wordwell Ltd., 2000)

Pearson, Gordon T., *Conservation of Clay and Chalk Buildings* (Shaftesbury: Donhead Publishing Ltd., 1992)

Powys, A. R., *Repair of Ancient Buildings* (London: SPAB, 1995, first published 1929)

Ridout, Brian, *Timber Decay in Buildings* (London: E & FN Spon, 2000)

Robson, Patrick, *Structural Repair of Traditional Buildings* (Shaftesbury: Donhead Publishing Ltd., 1999)

Sandwith, Hermione and Stainton, Sheila, *The National Trust Manual of Housekeeping* (London: Viking, 1991)

Society for the Protection of Ancient Buildings (SPAB); *Information Sheets and Technical Pamphlets* (London: SPAB, 1986 -). Further information available from **www.spab.org.uk**

Stagg, W.D., and Masters, R., *Decorative Plasterwork Repair and Restoration* (Painscastle: Attic Books, 1983 reprinted 1986)

U.S. Department of the Interior, *Preservation Briefs Nos. 1 - 42* (Washington, DC: Preservation Assistance Division, National Park Service). Further information available from **www2.cr.nps.gov/tps/briefs**

Other

British Standards Institution, *Guide to the Principles of the Conservation of Historic Buildings, BS 7913:1998* (London: 1998)

Kerr, James Semple, *The Conservation Plan* (Sydney: National Trust of Australia, 1982, revised 1996)

Thornes, Robin & Bold, John eds., *Documenting the Cultural Heritage* (Los Angeles: The Getty Information Institute, 1998)

Glossary of Architectural and Building Terms

Aggregate
Material such as sand or small stones used, when mixed with a binder and water, to form a mortar or concrete.

Anaglyptic paper
An embossed, decorative paper used on walls, dados and ceilings, particularly popular in the late Victorian period.

Anchor plate
A plate, usually of metal, fixed to the face of a wall and to which the ends of structural reinforcement, or tie bars, are bolted. Also known as a tie plate.

Apron
A panel below another significant feature, particularly the area of wall beneath a window.

Architrave
In Classical architecture, the lowest part of an entablature immediately above the columns. The term is also commonly used to describe a moulded surround to an opening, covering the joint between the door or window frame and the wall face.

Arris
A sharp edge at an external angle produced by the meeting of two surfaces.

Art Deco
A term used to describe a decorative style popular in the 1920s and 1930s, identified with the jazz age and characterised by strong geometric design.

Arts and Crafts
An architectural, artistic and social movement begun in England by William Morris in the mid-nineteenth century to revive the traditional skills of the mediaeval craftsman and to encourage the use of local materials.

Ashlar
Cut stone worked to even faces and right-angled edges and laid in a regular pattern with fine joints.

Balconette
A small iron balcony fixed to a window sill for either decorative reasons or to hold a window box or plant pots.

Bargeboard
Inclined board fixed at the gable end of a roof to cover and protect the ends of the roof timbers. Highly decorated in some styles of architecture.

Bell-cote
A small housing to hold a bell.

Blocking course
The course of masonry erected above a cornice to visually and structurally anchor it.

Brace
A timber or steel element set diagonally between two structural members to strengthen the joint or to reinforce a structural frame.

Bracket
An element designed to support, or to give the appearance of support to, a projecting weight. Some brackets are also called corbels and, in Classical architecture, consoles.

Cames
Grooved metal strips, usually of zinc or lead, holding glass pieces together in lattice or patterned glazing or in stained-glass windows.

Casement
A window frame hinged at one side to open like a door.

Cast iron
Also known as pig iron, this is a ferrous metal formed by pouring into moulds which allows it to be made into decorative panels. Cast iron is also used for structural elements but, while it performs well in compression, it is weak in tension.

Cement
A binding material mixed with aggregate and water to form a mortar or concrete. The term is usually taken to mean an artificial cement such as Portland cement.

Cheek
The vertical side of a dormer window.

Coade stone
A ceramic material manufactured by Mrs Eleanor Coade and her daughter in Lambeth between 1769 and c.1840. It was widely used in the late eighteenth and early nineteenth centuries in architectural ornament and has proved extremely durable.

Concrete
A strong quick-setting material made from cement, aggregate and water. Concrete can be cast in situ or in precast units. It can be used alone as mass concrete or cast around steel rods to increase its tensile strength, when it is known as reinforced concrete.

Console
A carved or moulded bracket used in Classical architecture.

Coping
A capping or covering to the top of a wall to prevent water entering the core of the wall.

Corbel
A projecting cantilevered block supporting elements over it such as a floor beam or truss.

Cornice
In Classical architecture, the highest projecting part of an entablature resting on the frieze. The term is also commonly used to describe any moulded decoration marking the junction between wall and ceiling.

Cottage orné
A picturesque, rustic house usually built to an asymmetric plan form and characterised by decorative timber features and elaborate thatched roofing. In Ireland, this building type usually dates to the first half of the nineteenth century.

Coving
A concave treatment of plaster at the junction between walls or ceilings.

Cramp
A metal strap or pin built into a wall to hold together elements such as adjacent blocks of stone.

Cresting
An ornamental finish, usually of iron, along the top of a screen, wall or the ridge of a roof. Sometimes known as ridge-combs when formed in terracotta.

Cupola
In Classical architecture, a small domed structure on top of a dome or a roof.

Curtilage
Although a word in common use and an important legal concept, curtilage has never been defined in law and so its meaning is open to interpretation (see Chapter 13 above).

Dado
The lower panelled portion of an internal wall, often surmounted by a moulded chair, or dado, rail. The dado rail was often used on its own, without the panelling below.

Damp-proof course
An impervious layer built into a wall a little above ground level to prevent rising damp or below window sills and above lintels to prevent water penetration of the interior of the building. Usually abbreviated to 'dpc'.

Demesne
That part of the historic estate associated with a country house which was reserved for the personal use and enjoyment of the owner.

Door leaf
The openable part of a door. It may be connected by side hinges to a frame or slide horizontally.

Dormer window
A vertical window in a sloping roof with a roof of its own.

Dovecote
A building housing pigeons or doves usually with small perching niches in the walls. Often a feature of country house estates.

Downlighter
A light fixture fixed to or recessed into the ceiling casting light predominantly downwards.

Downpipe
A vertical pipe which carries rainwater from the roof to a lower level or to the ground.

Dry rot
The common name for the fungus *Serpula lacrymans* which feeds on damp timber in poorly ventilated spaces causing the timber to lose strength and to develop characteristic cuboidal cracking.

Eaves
The lower edge of a sloping roof which overhangs the wallhead.

Electro-osmosis
A system to prevent rising damp within a wall, consisting of anodes inserted into a wall and linked by earthed wires along the base of the building. A small electric charge run through the system is intended to have the effect of repelling water molecules rising through the wall.

Enfilade
A suite of rooms, with aligned doors, opening off each other in sequence, thus creating a vista through the rooms when all doors are open.

Entablature
The upper part of a Classical order, supported by columns or pilasters and consisting of three horizontal bands: architrave, frieze and cornice.

Escutcheon
A cover plate to a keyhole.

Faïence
Glazed terracotta used as decorative cladding and usually fixed to the interior or exterior of a building in flat or moulded panels.

Fanlight
A semi-circular or semi-elliptical glazed area above a door. A similar rectangular feature is generally called an overlight but is often colloquially referred to as a fanlight

Fascia
A horizontal board. Usually given to the name-board above traditional shopfronts or to the flat vertical board that protects projecting ends of roof rafters at the eaves and to which the gutter can be fixed. Traditional eaves detailing in Ireland does not use fascia boards.

Fenestration
The arrangement of windows in a façade or other wall.

Finial
An ornamental capping to a pinnacle, spire, gable etc.

Fire mark
A plaque or plate issued by insurance companies and fixed to buildings to enable an insurance company to identify buildings insured by it. In Ireland fire marks usually date to the eighteenth and nineteenth centuries.

Fireskin
The protective outer layer formed during the firing process on the surface of bricks and terracotta units.

Flashing
A flat sheet of impervious material, usually lead, zinc or copper, covering the junction between materials or elements of a building to prevent water penetration.

Flitch beam
A timber beam with an inserted metal plate (flitch plate) to reinforce its structural strength.

Folly
A fanciful building erected in a designed landscape often with no specific purpose other than to form an eye-catcher.

French drain
A trench filled with gravel or other loose material to collect ground water and deflect it away from a building.

French window
A pair of glazed external doors usually leading onto a garden, terrace or balcony.

Frieze
The central portion of a Classical entablature located below the cornice and above the architrave. Can be plain or decorated.

Gable
The area of wall at the end of a pitched roof between the level of the eaves and the apex, usually triangular in shape.

Gallets
See 'pinnings'.

Gargoyle
A projecting water-spout designed to throw rainwater from a roof away from the wall. Often carved into grotesque heads of human or animal figures.

Gauged brickwork
Precisely-made brickwork laid with fine joints often of pure lime putty.

Gesso
A composition of gypsum and size which provides a smooth absorbent white surface. Used in the late eighteenth and early nineteenth centuries to add ornament to timberwork.

Graining
Also known as 'scumbling'. A decorative paint technique imitating the grain of timber.

Ha-Ha
A ditch with one vertical side and one sloping side used in landscape design as a means of containing livestock while maintaining an uninterrupted view.

Haunching
The building up of a mortar fillet around an element such as a pipe or the base of a column.

Hipped roof
A roof which slopes on all four sides, i.e. without gables.

Hopper head
A receptacle for collecting rainwater from gutters and channeling it into downpipes.

Icehouse
An underground or semi-underground chamber built to store ice or snow throughout the summer and to provide a cold store to keep food products fresh. Usually associated with a large country house estate.

Indenting

The process of replacing a damaged stone or part of a stone by inserting a piece of new matching stone.

Intumescent

A material used in strips or as a paint which expands on heating, such as in a fire, to seal gaps, prevent the spread of smoke and cut off the oxygen supply to the fire. Used to increase the fire resistance of doors or other elements of a building.

Ironmongery

The hardware associated with a door or window such as locks, hinges, handles and the like. Also known as door or window furniture.

Joists

Timber or steel horizontally spanning elements, usually in a parallel series, carrying floors or ceilings.

Jostle stones

Usually cylindrical stones set adjacent to the corners of buildings or gateways to protect from damage by the wheels of passing vehicles. Also known as 'wheel guards'.

Keystone

The central stone of an arch, sometimes prominently decorated.

Kneeler

The larger stone at the base of a gable which restrains the inclined coping stones above it and keeps them in place. Also known as a 'gable springer'.

Laths

Thin strips of wood, often chestnut or oak, forming a base for plaster.

Lime-ash

A floor-covering formed using the residue from the bottom of a lime kiln after firing, combining it with gypsum and water to produce a composite material which, when laid over a bedding material, formed a hard and durable flooring material usually for upper floors of a building.

Lime, hydraulic

Hydraulic limes contain a percentage of clay which produces a pozzolanic effect in mortars, that is, the mortars set chemically assisted by the presence of water. Hydraulic limes can be naturally occurring or can be artificially made.

Lime mortar

A mortar made from lime putty, aggregate and water that, on exposure to air, carbonises and hardens.

Lime, non-hydraulic

Non-hydraulic limes are pure, or almost pure, lime. Mortars made of non-hydraulic limes can only set through contact with air, a process known as carbonation.

Lime putty

A soft putty made from slaking quicklime in water. Used as a binder in most traditional mortars and renders prior to the invention of Portland cement.

Limewash

A form of thin lime putty used as a paint or protective coating. It differs from whitewash which is a mixture of chalk and water that does not carbonate.

Lintel

A horizontal beam, usually of timber, iron or stone, which spans across a structural opening.

Louvre

A series of horizontal sloping slats set in an opening which allow air and light to enter, but not rain.

Lych gate

A covered, usually timber, gateway with open sides at the entrance to a churchyard which traditionally provided a resting-place for a coffin.

Mason's mark

A symbol or initial cut into stonework by the mason executing the work. Usually associated with mediaeval masonry.

Mechanical damage

Damage caused by impact.

Mews

Stabling with living accommodation above. Usually built at the rear of large town houses.

Modern Movement

A functional undecorated style of architecture associated with the first half of the twentieth century.

Mortar

The mixture of a binder (such as lime or cement), aggregate and water to form a substance used to bind stones or bricks together in a masonry wall.

Mullion

An upright between the lights of a window.

Nail sickness

The widespread failure of the nails holding roof slates in place, usually due to rusting.

Newel
The large post at either end of a flight of stairs into which the handrail is fixed.

Nogging
The infilling between timber studs in a partition to strengthen and stiffen them.

Nosing
The projecting edge of the tread of a step.

Oriel window
A projecting or bay window to an upper floor.

Overlight
See 'fanlight'.

Parapet
The part of a wall that rises above a roof or terrace.

Pebble-dashing
A decorative finish to external walls in which pebbles are pushed into or thrown onto wet render and left exposed.

Pediment
In Classical architecture, a form of decorative treatment of a gable, often with sculpture to its tympanum. Although usually triangular, can also be arched or segmental. Also used above door and window openings.

Pilaster
A flat column-like projection from a wall with the profile of the orders of the Classical language of architecture and carrying an entablature.

Pinnings
Also known as 'gallets' or 'spalls'. Small pieces of stone or other material pressed into the mortar joints of a wall either as decoration or to reduce the amount of mortar required and thus reduce the danger of shrinkage.

Plaster
A surface covering for internal walls and ceilings. Traditionally made of lime, sand and water, sometimes reinforced with animal hair or straw, and applied wet.

Plinth
The projecting base of a wall or column.

Portico
A covered, open entrance in a Classical composition, with columns supporting the roof. It is often surmounted by a pediment.

Portland cement
An artificial cement invented by Joseph Aspdin in 1824 and so called because of its perceived resemblance to Portland stone. It sets rapidly and is very hard when set.

Pugging
A coarse material, usually sand or mortar, added between the joists of a timber floor or the studs of a timber partition to enhance sound insulation.

Quarry
In leaded-light glazing, a small square or diamond-shaped piece of glass.

Quarry sap
The moisture found in newly quarried stone which makes it easier to work.

Quoin
A dressed stone forming the corner of a building, often decorated or raised.

Rafter
A sloping timber roof beam running from eaves to ridge and supporting the roof-covering.

Reconstituted stone
A type of precast concrete which uses as aggregate a large percentage of stone particles.

Redressing
The cutting back of a material, usually stone, to a new surface.

Render
A mixture of a binder (such as lime or cement), an aggregate and water to form a coarse plaster which is applied to the external surfaces of walls (see also 'roughcast').

Repointing
The act of replacing mortar in the face joints of brickwork or stonework following either the erosion of the original mortar or its removal through raking out.

Reveals
The sides of an opening for a door or window, between the frame and the face of the wall. If cut at an angle, it may be called a splayed reveal.

Ridge
The apex of a pitched roof.

Ridge-combs
See 'cresting'.

Roughcast

A render covering for an external wall which is applied by throwing the mixture onto the wall. Also known as 'wet dash'.

Rubble masonry

Walls made of rough unworked stones, often field boulders, of irregular size and shape. The stones can be laid completely at random or brought to courses.

Rustication

In Classical architecture, the treatment of a wall surface with strong texture. In ashlar, rustication is often achieved by forming deep grooves in the joints or by working the surface of the stone.

Sash window

A sash is one of a pair of glazed frames which slide past each other within a frame. The sashes can slide either vertically or horizontally but vertically sliding sash windows are by far the more common in Ireland, and are usually counterbalanced using pulleys and weights.

Scagliola

A composition of gypsum or sulphate of lime made to imitate marble.

Scarfing

The uniting of two pieces of timber to form a continuous length without increasing the depth or width of the beam at the joint.

Secondary glazing

The addition of an extra pane of glass inside the existing glazing. It differs from double-glazing in that secondary glazing is often held within a separate frame and is installed for reasons of acoustic insulation rather than thermal insulation.

Sett

A rough-hewn cube of stone or timber used for paving.

Shake

A timber roof tile, usually of oak or cedar, split along the fissures radiating from the centre of a piece of timber.

Shelter coat

A sacrificial coating of limewash or thin render applied to a surface to protect it from deterioration.

Shingle

A timber roof tile, usually of oak or cedar, sawn or cleft along the grain of the timber. Also used as a wall cladding.

Sill guards

A metal obstacle, sometimes decoratively treated, fixed to a ground-floor windowsill to prevent its use as a seat or to protect it from accidental damage.

Size/Sizing

A liquid sealant for coating wood or plaster to prevent paint or varnish applied over it being too much absorbed into the substrate.

Solder

Any easily melted alloy used for joining metals.

Spalling

The breaking away of small chips or flakes of stone or concrete.

Spandrel

A triangular panel in the corner between a vertical and horizontal structural member.

Specification

A written description of work to be undertaken, including the materials to be used, the method of work and the finishing technique.

Splicing

The letting-in of a small piece to repair a damaged element of joinery.

Stall riser

In a shopfront, the panelled area below the sill of the display window.

String course

A moulding or projecting course continued horizontally across the wall of a building.

Strut

Part of a truss taking vertical loading.

Stucco

A plaster containing gypsum, lime and marble powder. Can be used externally to imitate ashlar or internally in ceiling or wall decoration.

Stud

A vertical timber member forming the frame of a partition.

Terracotta

Literally meaning 'burnt clay', the term is usually used to describe a more finely grained ceramic than brick or tile and is used for wall facings, chimney pots and the like.

Terrazzo
A hard flooring material containing marble chippings mixed with cement which is laid in situ, then ground and polished to a smooth finish.

Tie
A structural member which acts in tension.

Tracery
Ornamental intersecting timber or stone mullions and transoms in a window, panel or vault. Typical of the Gothic or Gothic-Revival styles.

Transom
A horizontal element of stone or timber between the lights of a window.

Tread end
The vertical surface to the side of a step in a staircase, sometimes decoratively finished with moulded or carved work.

Truss
A framed structure spanning between walls or columns and supporting a roof.

Tuck-pointing
A decorative form of pointing giving the effect of gauged brickwork. The joints are filled with a mortar matching the colour of the brickwork. A thin groove or tuck is then cut into the mortar and filled with white lime putty.

Tympanum
The area enclosed within a pediment, or the space between lintel and arch above, often carved or decorated.

Veranda
An open gallery or balcony on the outside of a building with a roof supported on light timber or iron posts.

Verge
The sloping edge of a pitched roof above the gable.

Voussoir
A wedge-shaped stone or brick forming part of an arch. The middle voussoir is called a keystone and is often carved and decorated.

Wall plate
A horizontal timber piece laid along the top of a wall to receive the ends of the rafters.

Wet rot
A generic term for fungi which feed on wet, or sodden, timber causing it to soften and lose strength.

Wheel-guards
See 'jostle stones'.

Wicket
A small door or gate set within a larger one to allow pedestrian access while avoiding the need to open the full door or gate.

Wrought iron
A ferrous metal smelted and then worked, or wrought, by hammering. Much used for elements such as railings and gates. It can also be used for structural members but while it performs well in tension, it is weak in compression.

Index